Lecture Notes in Computer Science 10172

Commenced Publication in 1973
Founding and Former Series Editors:
Gerhard Goos, Juris Hartmanis, and Jan van Leeuwen

More information about this series at http://www.springer.com/series/7407

Jens Knoop · Wolfgang Karl
Martin Schulz · Koji Inoue
Thilo Pionteck (Eds.)

Architecture of Computing Systems – ARCS 2017

30th International Conference
Vienna, Austria, April 3–6, 2017
Proceedings

 Springer

Editors
Jens Knoop
Vienna University of Technology
Vienna
Austria

Wolfgang Karl
Karlsruhe Institute of Technology
Karlsruhe
Germany

Martin Schulz
Lawrence Livermore National Laboratory
Livermore
USA

Koji Inoue
Kyushu University
Fukuoka
Japan

Thilo Pionteck
Otto von Guericke University Magdeburg
Magdeburg
Germany

ISSN 0302-9743   ISSN 1611-3349 (electronic)
Lecture Notes in Computer Science
ISBN 978-3-319-54998-9   ISBN 978-3-319-54999-6 (eBook)
DOI 10.1007/978-3-319-54999-6

Library of Congress Control Number: 2017933871

LNCS Sublibrary: SL1 – Theoretical Computer Science and General Issues

Printed on acid-free paper

This Springer imprint is published by Springer Nature
The registered company is Springer International Publishing AG
The registered company address is: Gewerbestrasse 11, 6330 Cham, Switzerland

Preface

The 30th International Conference on Computer Architecture (ARCS 2017) was hosted by the Complang Group at the Vienna University of Technology during April 3–6, 2017. It was organized by the special interest group on "Architecture of Computing Systems" of the GI (Gesellschaft für Informatik e. V.) and ITG (Informationstechnische Gesellschaft im VDE).

The ARCS conferences series has over 30 years of tradition in reporting leading-edge research in computer architecture and operating systems. It covers a wide spectrum of topics from embedded and real-time to large-scale parallel systems as well as from hardware design to software techniques required to exploit new hardware systems efficiently. It also covers various cross-cutting themes, such as autonomous optimization, power and energy awareness, and resilience, providing a comprehensive platform for systems research. Additionally, a new topic on post-Moore architectures was added for this year.

Each year the conference selects a special focus topic, which for 2017 was "Heterogeneous Node Architectures with Deep Memory Systems." This selection reflects current trends in node design in high-performance computing (HPC) environments, which increasingly feature deeper and more complex memory hierarchies, the integration of non-volatile storage, as well as the use of accelerators, such as GPUs, to satisfy the ever-rising demand for computational power.

The conference attracted 42 submissions from authors in 19 countries. Each paper was reviewed by a diverse and dedicated Program Committee, which submitted a total of 199 reviews. Most papers received five reviews and final decisions were made based on the reviews as well as online discussions. Following this process, the Program Committee ended up accepting 19 papers by authors from 11 countries. These papers were organized into seven sessions: Resilience (2 papers), Accelerators (3 papers), Performance (2 papers), Memory Systems (3 papers), Parallelism and Many-core (4 papers), Scheduling (2 papers), and Power/Energy (3 papers).

ARCS has a long tradition of hosting associated workshops, four of which were held in conjunction with the main conference this year: the 5th International Workshop on Self-Optimization in Autonomic and Organic Computing Systems (SAOS), the 13th Workshop on Dependability and Fault Tolerance (VERFE), the Second FORMUS³IC Workshop, and, for the first time in 2017, the Workshop on Computer Architectures in Space (CompSpace).

We would like to thank the many individuals who contributed to the success of the conference, in particular the members of the Program Committee as well as the additional external reviewers, for the time and effort they put into reviewing the submissions carefully and selecting a high-quality program. Many thanks also to all authors for submitting their work. The workshops were organized and coordinated by

Carsten Trinitis, the proceedings were compiled by Thilo Pionteck and Gerald Krell, and the website was maintained by Markus Hoffmann. Our gratitude goes to all of them as well as all other people who helped in the organization of ARCS 2017.

April 2017   Jens Knoop
                                                            Wolfgang Karl
                                                            Martin Schulz
                                                             Koji Inoue

Organization

General Co-chairs

Jens Knoop   Vienna University of Technology, Austria
Wolfgang Karl   Karlsruhe Institute of Technology, Germany

Program Co-chairs

Martin Schulz   Lawrence Livermore National Lab, USA
Koji Inoue   Kyushu University, Japan

Workshop and Tutorial Chair

Carsten Trinitis   Technical University of Munich, Germany

Publicity Chair

Miquel Pericàs   Chalmers University of Technology, Sweden

Publication Chair

Thilo Pionteck   Otto von Guericke University Magdeburg, Germany

Program Committee

Michael Beigl   Karlsruhe Institute of Technology, Germany
Mladen Berekovic   Technische Universität Braunschweig, Germany
Jürgen Brehm   Leibniz Universität Hannover, Germany
Uwe Brinkschulte   Goethe-Universität Frankfurt am Main, Germany
João M.P. Cardoso   Universidade do Porto, Portugal
Laura Carrington   San Diego Supercomputer Center/University of California, USA
Albert Cohen   Inria, France
Martin Daněk   daiteq s.r.o., Czech Republic
Ahmed El-Mahdy   Egypt-Japan University of Science and Technology, Egypt
Dietmar Fey   Friedrich-Alexander-Universität Erlangen-Nürnberg, Germany
William Fornaciari   Politecnico di Milano, Italy
Roberto Giorgi   University of Siena, Italy
Daniel Gracia Pérez   Thales Research and Technology, France
Jan Haase   Universität zu Lübeck, Germany

Additional Reviewers

Imran Ashraf
Andreas Becher
Christopher Blochwitz
Hendrik Borghorst
Markus Buschhoff
Chongxiao Cao
Florian Franzmann
Alexander Gabrecht
Jose Germano
João F.D. Guerreiro
Fabrice Guet
Jaco Hofmann
Joost Hoozemans
Timo Hönig
Boguslaw Jablkowski
Tobias Klaus
Gerald Krell
Steffen Köhler
Joerg Lenhardt
Paulo Martins
Dominik Meyer
Jörg Mische
Nizar Msadek
Julian Oppermann
Jutta Pirkl

Behnaz Pourmohseni
Thomas B. Preußer
Marco Procaccini
Oskar Pusz
Stefan Reif
Sven Rheindt
Johanna Rohde
Tajas Ruschke
Horst Schirmeier
Florian Schmaus
Alexander Schwarz
Syad Abbas Shah
Manu Shantharam
Romeo Shuka
Lukas Sommer
Akshay Srivatsa
Konstantinos Tovletoglou
Peter Ulbrich
Josef Weidendorfer
Sebastian Weis
Jakob Wenzel
Michael Witterauf
Wei Xie
Martin Zabel

Contents

Parallelism and Many-Core Systems

Scheduling

Power and Energy

Resilience

Effectiveness of Software-Based Hardening for Radiation-Induced Soft Errors in Real-Time Operating Systems

Thiago Santini[1]([✉]), Christoph Borchert[2], Christian Dietrich[3],
Horst Schirmeier[2], Martin Hoffmann[3], Olaf Spinczyk[2], Daniel Lohmann[3],
Flávio Rech Wagner[4], and Paolo Rech[4]

[1] University of Tübingen,Tübingen, Germany
thiago.santini@uni-tuebingen.de
[2] Technische Universität Dortmund, Dortmund, Germany
[3] Friedrich-Alexander-Universität Erlangen-Nürnberg, Erlangen-Nürnberg, Germany
[4] Federal University of Rio Grande do Sul, Porto Alegre, Brazil

Abstract. For decades, radiation-induced failures have been a known issue for aero-space systems, in which redundancy mechanisms are employed as a protection method. Due to the shrinking of structures and operating voltages, these failures are increasingly becoming an issue even for terrestrial applications. Unfortunately, redundancy increases costs, area usage, and power consumption, which can hinder its utilization in cost- and power-sensitive safety-critical applications, such as automotive. To overcome this limitation, multiple software-based approaches have been proposed, which assume the existence of an underlying error-free operating system. In this paper, we investigate the radiation reliability of two dependability-oriented real-time operating systems, namely, the popular eCos operating system hardened through aspect-oriented programming methods, and dOSEK, an embedded kernel designed from the ground up having reliability as a major concern. Both operating systems were evaluated through extensive neutron-beam testings on a 28 nm ARM-based state-of-the-art system-on-chip, and their fault tolerance mechanisms reached reductions in the overall cross-sections relative to their baselines up to 91% and 74%, respectively.

1 Introduction

Commercial-Off-The-Shelf (COTS) systems have become a valid alternative to specific radiation-hardened devices in safety-critical applications, like biomedical implantable devices, automotive control systems, and aircraft or satellite stabilizer and control circuitry. For instance, the spacecraft onboard computer in NASA's PhoneSat nano-satellite is built around COTS smartphones running the Android operating system [9]. The main reason for preferring a COTS device is that hardened devices are typically very expensive, as they require unique circuit design and lithography to meet the reliability requirements, and the produced volumes are very low. On the contrary, COTS components are low cost, flexible,

© Springer International Publishing AG 2017
J. Knoop et al. (Eds.): ARCS 2017, LNCS 10172, pp. 3–15, 2017.
DOI: 10.1007/978-3-319-54999-6_1

and provide fast time-to-market as well as low power consumption. Nonetheless, when reliability is a major concern, the use of general-purpose devices must be carefully evaluated. As technology scales down, CMOS devices are becoming more susceptible to soft errors induced by ionizing particles; in fact, nowadays radiation-induced failures are a concern not only in radiation-harsh environments, such as the space, but also in milder environments, such as at sea level. High-energy neutrons generated by the interaction of cosmic rays with the terrestrial atmosphere may in fact have enough energy to corrupt data stored in SRAM memories or to affect logic computations [2]. This is especially relevant in cost-sensitive domains, such as the automotive sector. Here, efficiency in terms of per-unit-prices is a key criterion, so full hardware redundancy can be prohibitively expensive. One of the proposed approaches to circumvent these limitations in a cost-effective and flexible way is through software-implemented fault tolerance, such as software-based redundant multi-threading [28] and process-level redundancy [25]. These approaches assume a fault-free underlying operating system. However, an operating system (OS) must keep several data structures containing critical data and pointers, such as device and file descriptors, memory information, and process list, which are very likely to lead to a device functional interruption if corrupted [8], thus making OSs particularly sensitive.

In this context, two approaches have been recently proposed in order to establish a reliable underlying operating system for real-time embedded computing: (1) a version of the popular eCos operating system hardened through aspect-oriented programming methods [4], and (2) dOSEK, an embedded kernel designed from the ground up with reliability as first-class design goal [12]. These approaches have been evaluated through ISA-level fault injection with the FAIL* [23] framework based on an IA-32 platform emulator and assuming a single-bit fault model over the entire fault space of the architectural view from the software's perspective (i.e., in the main memory as well as instruction pointer, general-purpose, stack, and flags registers). In this work, we expand on these evaluations through extensive neutron-beam testing on a 28 nm ARM-based state-of-the-art system-on-chip. Our main contributions are: (1) Cross-section data to help the device characterization. These data complement the information provided by sources that investigate the selected device's radiation sensitivity, such as its bit [15,19], cache memories [20], and general purpose operating systems [22] cross-sections. (2) A realistic evaluation of the radiation-reliability of the proposed OS mitigation approaches. Our experimental evaluation uses the ARM architecture, which is very common on the actual targets in the embedded domain. We provide expected Failure In Time (FIT) values in Sect. 4.3.

2 Background

2.1 eCos and Software-Implemented Fault Tolerance

For this study, we chose the off-the-shelf operating system *eCos* [16] as a typical representative for embedded real-time operating systems. eCos (embedded Configurable operating system), as the name suggests, offers configurability at compile time of various system components, such as file systems and networking, resulting in roughly one million lines of C/C++ code. To apply software-implemented fault-tolerance to such an enormous code base, we chose two *generic* error-detection and error-correction mechanisms with transparent compiler support – a manual implementation in C/C++ would be infeasible. **1 Generic Object Protection (GOP):** The principle of GOP [3,5] is to introduce redundancy into the program data structures to implement an error-correcting code. In this study, we use a Hamming code [10], since it can be efficiently implemented in software by bit-slicing [24]. The implementation processes 32 bits in parallel, which allows for correction of multi-bit errors, in particular, all burst errors up to 32 bits. At program run time, the Hamming code gets verified *before* an instance of a data structure (C++ *object*) is used. Then, *after* object usage and potential data modification, the Hamming code gets updated. The object-oriented software structure of the eCos kernel restricts data access to member functions of a data structure. Thus, it suffices to carry out checks *before* member-function calls and to update the Hamming code *after* the member function has returned. GOP is implemented by means of Aspect-Oriented Programming [14], which allows for a completely modular implementation separated from the eCos source code. The *AspectC++* [27] compiler automatically inserts the protection rules at compile time. **2 Stack Checksum:** The second fault-tolerance mechanism applied to eCos is a 32-bit checksum for stack memory. When the eCos kernel preempts a thread of control, or when a thread blocks while waiting for a semaphore, a checksum covering the thread's occupied stack memory is attached to the thread. When the thread is eventually resumed, the checksum gets verified. Thus, errors corrupting the stack memory while a thread is inactive are detected. Please note that extending this mechanism to error correction is straightforward by implementing a Hamming code similar to the GOP. Finally, the *Stack Checksum* mechanism is also implemented as a generic module in AspectC++, which instruments the eCos-kernel source code with minimal effort from the programmer.

2.2 dOSEK – A Soft-Error Resilient OS

As our second system, we chose *d*OSEK [12], a framework for generating dependable real-time kernels. The first-class design objective during the system development was resilience against soft-errors. In previous (exhaustive) fault-injection campaigns, the usage of *d*OSEKreduced the rate of undetected failures by multiple orders of magnitude.

*d*OSEKadheres to the OSEK-OS [18] specification, a standardized kernel Application Programing Interface (API) developed by the automotive industry. OSEK systems are specified declaratively: the number and configuration of threads, alarms, interrupts, resources, and events is known at compile time. *d*OSEK, following the tradition of OSEK system generators, exploits this static application knowledge to foster dependability. Furthermore, two basic design principles were also applied: removal of unnecessary indirections and integration of active dependability measures.

Like eCos, *d*OSEKprovides static configurability at compile time. We used three configuration sets of dependability measures in our test setup. **1 Baseline:** All system objects are allocated statically; pointer indirection is avoided wherever possible; the kernel is activated through a supervisor call, but executed only with user privileges; inside the kernel, function calls are avoided by massive inlining. **2 Encoded:** On top of the baseline, specialized data protection is applied: checksums for thread contexts, parity bits for saved stack pointers, and dual-modular redundancy (DMR) for counters. For the scheduler, ANB encoding was applied, an active measure that protects data flow as well as the control flow. **3 Asserts:** On top of the baseline, application-specific protection mechanisms were added. By system-wide static analysis, knowledge about the dynamic behavior of the application-kernel interaction was extracted and run-time assertions to check for compliance were injected.[1]

3   Experimental Methodology

In this work, we have opted to perform an evaluation of the proposed approaches through accelerated radiation testing. Radiation testing does not restrain faults to a single part of the chip, whereas fault injection can be performed only on a selection of user-accessible resources for those devices, like COTS, for which an Register Transfer Level (RTL) description is not usually available. Moreover, although simulators and emulators allow a more controlled fault injection, they are always an oversimplification of the physical reality and, thus, cannot replace radiation tests for Radiation Hardness Assurance (RHA) testing [11].

3.1   Device Under Test

The Device Under Test (DUT) is the Xilinx Zynq^{TM}-7000 AP System-on-Chip (SoC) implemented in a 28 nm CMOS technology. The DUT disposes of two ARM®Cortex^{TM}-A9 cores with a maximum frequency of 667 MHz. Each core has 32 KiB Level 1 4-way set-associative instruction and data caches, and they share a 512 KiB 8-way set-associative Level 2 cache [7]. During tests, only a single core (*CPU0*) was used. Parity checking was disabled for both cache levels to allow the assessment of the investigated approaches in the absence of hardware-based protection mechanisms. It is paramount to note that only the SoC chip was irradiated (i.e., the external DRAM chips were *not* irradiated). Both OSs were tested under heavy load, and the amount of threads and resources employed was selected as to fill up the cache memories in order to maximize attack surface.

---

[1] The Baseline and the Encoded variants are based on and discussed in more detail in [12], whereas the static application analysis and the system-state assertions are based on and detailed in [6].

3.2   eCos Configuration and Benchmarks

We used a port of eCos 3.0 for the aforementioned Zynq[2] hardware platform and selected a minimal configuration of eCos without unneeded device drivers. In addition, we ignored spurious device interrupts. To reduce corruption of program instructions, we disabled the instruction caching at the L2 cache (only allowing L2 data caching), and the L1 instruction cache was regularly invalidated before interrupt processing. For the evaluation of the OS under heavy load, we selected two benchmarks, both supporting a parameterizable number of threads, selected as to fill up the caches, from the kernel-test suite bundled with eCos itself: BIN_SEM2 (BS) implements a classical synchronization problem known as *Dining Philosophers*. We configured 400 threads (*philosophers*) that use 400 *forks* (i.e., Cyg_Binary_Semaphore objects) for mutual exclusion (*eating* with two forks). Once a philosopher acquires both neighboring forks, it checks by an assertion that neighboring philosophers are not in the *eating* state. After a pseudo-random delay, the philosopher releases both forks and tries again for 25,000 iterations. TIMESLICE (TS) verifies that the per-thread time-slice distribution works under preemption. We configured 800 low-priority threads that continuously increment a per-thread counter, and a single high-priority thread is scheduled at regular intervals to preempt the other threads. The benchmark finishes after a predetermined period of time, such that each low-priority thread should have received two time slices. Finally, an assertion tests whether all threads have run.

These benchmarks were evaluated with two eCos variants: a baseline variant with no protection mechanisms, and a variant hardened through the methods described in Sect. 2.1. BIN_SEM2 has a baseline run time of 1.98 s, whereas the hardened variant has a run time of 2.08 s (an overhead of 4.745%). TIMESLICE2 has a baseline run time of 1.6 s, whereas the hardened variant has a run time of 1.65 s (an overhead of 2.932%).

3.3   dOSEK Configuration and Benchmark

We ported the dOSEK system generator to the ARM platform used on the Zynq hardware while preserving dOSEK's basic design principles. To ease the comparison with the eCos benchmark, we did not use the MMU to provide spatial isolation between the OSEK threads. Privilege isolation was used to execute kernel and application in user mode; only kernel entry and thread dispatching were executed with supervisor privileges.

As benchmark, we generated an application compliant with the OSEK BCC1 conformance class, consisting of 250 threads organized in 125 pairs. The test case was designed to particularly fill up the cache, which is hit by the neutron beam, with OS state. Each thread pair has a lower-priority non-preemptable thread (*L-thread*) and a high-priority thread (*H-thread*). We configured 250 alarms connected to 250 OSEK counter objects; 125 counters are driven by a hardware

---

[2] https://github.com/antmicro/ecos-mars-zx3/.

timer and activate the L-thread. The other 125 counters are incremented by the L-threads and activate the associated H-thread on alarm expiration. The periods and phases for the alarms were shuffled once by a pseudo-random number generator. Besides the pair coupling, we also added (pseudo-randomly) cross-dependencies between pairs: a L-thread activates the H-thread of another pair; a H-thread chains its execution to another pair's L-thread; a L-thread waits actively for another H-thread to set a global variable. In total, 42 such cross dependencies were introduced.

During execution, each thread queries its associated alarm value, applies some calculation to it, and hashes the result and its thread *ID* onto a global CRC32 checksum. The hash update operation is protected by an OSEK non-preemptable critical section. After 1500 hash updates, the application asserts that the resulting hash equals to a golden value calculated at compilation time. Both, checksum storage and hash update counter are protected with triple-modular redundancy.

The exactly same application was evaluated with the three variants of *d*OSEK described in Sect. 2.2, namely, **Baseline**, **Encoded**, and **Asserts**. All variants exhibited a similar run time (≈ 3.42 s). Since the kernel run time is orders of magnitude smaller than the application run and idle time, the incurred run-time penalties of the additional protection measures can be considered negligible.

3.4 Experimental Setup

Radiation experiments were performed at Los Alamos National Laboratory (LANL) in the Los Alamos Neutron Science Center (LANSCE) Irradiation of Chips and Electronics House II, called ICE House II. The ICE House II beam line provides a white neutron source that emulates the energy spectrum of the atmospheric neutron flux. The available neutron flux was approximately 1×10^6 n/(cm^{2}s) for energies above 10MeV. The beam was focused on a spot with a diameter of two inches, which provided uniform irradiation of the SoC, without directly affecting nearby board power control circuitry and DRAM chips. It is worth noting that, even if the flux of neutrons at ICE House II is several orders of magnitude higher than the natural one at sea level (which is estimated to be about 13 n/(cm^{2}h) [13]), the test was tuned to make negligible the probability of having more than one neutron generating a failure in one single code execution (estimated through the method described in [21] to be no higher than 1.38×10^{-5} errors/execution). This allows the scaling of experimental data in the natural radioactive environment without introducing artificial behaviors.

To reduce the uncertainty of the experimental results, four DUTs were irradiated in parallel. The four boards with the same hardware revision were aligned with the beam, placed at 62, 64, 66.5, and 68.5 in. from the source, respectively. A flux de-rating factor was calculated for each board to take beam degradation due to the distance from the source into account. To minimize the statistical error and to avoid experimental results biased on the selected board and distance de-rating factor, the benchmarks were executed alternatively in all four devices. In total, the boards received a fluence of 9.87×10^{11} n/cm^2, thus receiving the radiation equivalent to 8.67×10^6 years of exposure in the natural environment at sea level. It is worth noticing that hardened variants received more beam time than baseline ones. Since these systems are intrinsically less prone to errors, they require longer testing times to achieve a statically significant amount of observed errors.

A test manager application was responsible for collecting and time-stamping incoming logs from the boards through UART connections. The test manager application also served as a watchdog, responsible for detecting otherwise irrecoverable failure situations and rebooting the boards through an Ethernet controlled switch. Whenever such situations happened, they were time-stamped and logged. Irrecoverable situations are considered when the board exceeds a time-out much larger than the application execution time without sending successful execution logs.

4   Experimental Results

We report our results as cross-sections. The cross-section σ is the most widely used metric to evaluate a device radiation sensitivity and is evaluated by dividing the amount of observed errors by the particle fluence (n/cm^2) received by the device. By definition, the cross-section, expressed in cm^2, is the device sensitive area – that is, the area that generates a failure if hit by an impinging particle [2]. Values are shown with relative intervals to account for the failure rate estimation error (95% CI) and neutron count uncertainty.

The outcome of each application run was classified as *benign* or *malign*. Benign executions are those in which the expected output was produced, or an error was detected before it could lead to a Silent Data Corruption (SDC) or Functional Interruption (FI). Malign executions are those in which a SDC was produced (e.g., one of the assertions described in Sects. 3.2 and 3.3 failed, garbage was found in the output) or a FI occurred (e.g., the board rebooted by itself, no correct output was produced before the test manager watchdog ran out). Each malign execution was accounted as a single error when calculating cross-sections and only if the preceding execution was benign. For the remainder of this paper, we will use the term *very rare* to refer to events that had less than three occurrences observed per benchmark; we consider their probability to be negligible and, since we cannot draw any additional statistically significant conclusion about these events, refrain from further discussing them. Events with zero occurrences are explicitly shown through a cross-section of *0*.

4.1   eCos

As shown in Fig. 1a, the hardening resulted in a reduction in the overall cross-section by a factor of at least 55% (upper $TS_{Hardened}$ relative to the lower $TS_{Baseline}$) up to 91% (lower $BS_{Hardened}$ relative to the upper $BS_{Baseline}$).

Table 1 details the possible outcomes for each benchmark run, and the overall cross-section is broken down into its contributors in Fig. 1b. The occurrences of *rst* and *scorr* were *very rare*. From the remaining (and major) cross-section contributors, it is clear that in all cases *tout* occurrences are fairly more probable than *fail* ones. In other words, a system hang (the system stops producing any output) was more common than an SDC. These *hangs* likely originate from illegal memory accesses and jumps; invalid data accesses can leave the system in a corrupt state, and deviant instruction accesses (e.g., stemming from corrupted return addresses in the stack) can lead to the execution of arbitrary code, both likely to stop the system from producing an output in a timely manner. Moreover, both the eCos kernel and the application run in supervisor mode [16], which can exacerbate this effect since invalid accesses from the application do not cause the OS to terminate the application.

The hardening had similar effects in both applications: *fail* became a *very rare* event, whereas *tout* occurrences were significantly reduced. Unfortunately, it is not possible to establish one-to-one relationships between the employed fault-tolerance mechanisms and the malign events reduction due to the Architectural Vulnerability Factor (AVF) [17]; in other words, there are errors that are corrected by the employed mechanisms that would not influence the system in an observable way. In fact, the cross-section for correction/detection events ($\approx 1.2 \times 10^{-8}$ for both hardened benchmarks) is much larger than those of malign events for the baseline versions. Nonetheless, we break down the relative activations for these mechanisms in Fig. 2. This figure suggests that stack data are the largest attack surface for the *BS* benchmark, in contrast to the *TS* benchmark, in which eCos class members data seem to present the largest attack surface. Furthermore, it is worth noting that the *d-trp* cross-section for both benchmarks ($BS_{Baseline} = 9.45 \times 10^{-10}$ and $TS_{Baseline} = 1.01 \times 10^{-9}$) were diminished with the employment of the hardening mechanisms ($BS_{Hardened} = 2.66 \times 10^{-10}$ and $TS_{Hardened} = 1.42 \times 10^{-10}$), showing a replacement of generic hardware traps by more specific detection mechanisms, which could be more easily corrected if possible and desired.

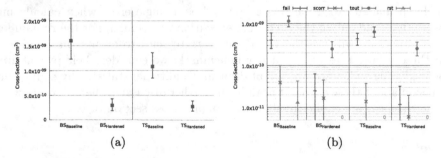

Fig. 1. Overall cross-sections for the BIN_SEM2 (BS) and TIMESLICE2 (TS) benchmarks (a) as well as their comprehensive cross-section list (b); note the *y-semilog* scale on (b).

Table 1. Possible outcomes for the eCos benchmarks

	Baseline	Hardened	Description
ok	✓	✓	Successful run
okcor	-	✓	GOP corrected
d-gop	-	Detect	GOP (uncorrectable)
d-stk	-	Detect	Wrong stack checksum
d-trp	Detect	Detect	Hardware trap
fail	SDC	SDC	Application assertion failed
scorr	SDC	SDC	Serial corrupted
rst	FI	FI	Board rebooted
tout	FI	FI	Timeout without output

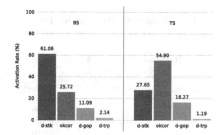

Fig. 2. Relative activations for the detection/correction mechanisms for the hardened benchmarks versions.

4.2 dOSEK

In Fig. 3a, the overall cross-section of the observed errors is shown for all three variants. The application-specific assertions reduce the cross-section by at least 0.93% (upper Asserts relative to lower Baseline) up to 64% (lower Asserts relative to upper Baseline); the kernel encoding by at least 28% up to 74%.

Each application run was classified into one of the categories from Table 2. *Fail, scorr, rst,* and *tout* are counted as errors and contribute to the overall cross-section, which is broken down in Fig. 3b. The results for *d*OSEK are similar to eCos: Occurrences of *scorr* were *very rare,* and *rst* events did not occur. A hanging system was more likely than a failing one, whereas Asserts and Encoded significantly reduced these *tout* events. The actual *fail* cross-section was reduced at least by 33% (Asserts) up to 92% (Encoded).

It is noteworthy that in both variants the detection was mainly driven by a single measure: the detection for the Assert variant ($\sigma = 8.57 \times 10^{-10}$) is dominated by the introduced assertions (76For the Encoded variant, detection ($\sigma = 1.36 \times 10^{-9}$) stems mainly from the ANB-encoded scheduler (68experiments.

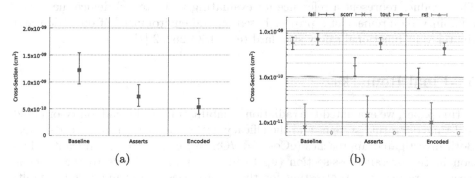

(a)   (b)

Fig. 3. Overall cross-sections for the three *d*OSEK variants (a) as well as their comprehensive cross-section list (b); note the *y-semilog* scale on (b).

Table 2. Possible outcomes for the *d*OSEKvariants.

	Baseline	Encoded	Asserts	Description
ok	✓	✓	✓	Successful run
d-xor	-	Detect	-	Thread context checksum
d-dmr	-	Detect	-	Counters DMR
d-anb	-	Detect	-	Scheduler ANB encoding
d-par	-	Detect	-	Saved stack pointer parity
d-sta	-	-	Detect	*d*OSEKassertion failed
d-log	Detect	Detect	Detect	Impossible control flow
d-trp	Detect	Detect	Detect	Hardware trap
d-unk	Detect	Detect	Detect	Spurious fault detection hook
fail	SDC	SDC	SDC	Application assertion failed
scorr	SDC	SDC	SDC	Serial corrupted
rst	FI	FI	FI	Board rebooted
tout	FI	FI	FI	Timeout without output

Table 3. FIT at sea level for energies higher than 10MeV (Flux $\approx$ 13n/(cm²h) [13]).

OS	Variant	FIT
eCos	Baseline/BIN_SEM2	26.65
	Hardened/BIN_SEM2	5.53
	Baseline/TIMESLICE2	17.68
	Hardened/TIMESLICE2	5.01
*d*OSEK	Baseline	20.02
	Asserts	12.40
	Encoded	8.98

4.3 FIT Figures

As mentioned in Subsect. 3.4, due to the characteristics of our neutron source and failure rate, it is possible to scale our experimental results to Earth's natural environment. Table 3 reports the worst-case FIT figures at sea level given the measured cross-sections, expressed as errors per billion hours of device operation. These values represent a reference for evaluating if the tested device meets the reliability requirement of a project based on the environment of operation and the relevant functional safety standard (e.g., ISO 26262 [1]).

5 Final Remarks

In this paper, we evaluated the radiation reliability of two dependability-oriented real-time operating systems and the efficacy of their fault-tolerance mechanisms. Both investigated approaches (eCos and *d*OSEK) exhibited a significant reduction in the overall cross-section (up to 91% and 74% relative to the baseline variants, respectively), attesting for the capabilities of the investigated fault-tolerance mechanisms for usage at an environment with similar neutron flux to the terrestrial one. In fact, the baseline versions would limit the Safety Integrity Level (SIL) of the Equipment Under Control (EUC) in *continuous operation* mode at sea level to IEC61508 SIL 3 – i.e., within $(10^{-7}, 10^{-8}]$ failures per hour [26]. In contrast, the *hardened* eCos variant and *d*OSEK*Encoded* variant would mitigate enough faults as to allow the EUC to attain SIL 4 (i.e., within $(10^{-8}, 10^{-9}]$ failures per hour), the highest SIL[3]. It is worth noticing that we cannot directly compare the results for eCos to those of *d*OSEK because the evaluation is highly dependent on the application. In retrospect, it would have been more advantageous to have used exactly the same application to evaluate both operating systems. Nonetheless, the evaluated applications are conceptually similar (in the sense that they stress-test the kernel scheduling, preemption, and timer functionalities), and the investigated approaches exhibited failure rates in the same order of magnitude. Furthermore, due to massive function inlining to avoid run time indirections, the code size of *d*OSEK is two orders of magnitude higher than that of eCos, and it is worth noticing that the protection mechanisms applied to harden eCos are generic and can be applied to other object-oriented C++ programs easily.

As future work, we plan to extend the FAIL* framework to evaluate the systems here evaluated through fault injection campaigns. The intention of this future work is threefold: (1) to corroborate FAIL* and the accelerated radiation tests, (2) to better comprehend the way in which these OSs fail and help developing further fault tolerance mechanisms, and (3) to provide an open framework to evaluate the reliability of ARM-based processors.

References

1. ISO/DIS 26262. Technical report (2011)
2. Baumann, R.: Soft errors in advanced computer systems. IEEE Design Test Comput. **22**(3), 258–266 (2005)
3. Borchert, C., Spinczyk, O.: Hardening an L4 microkernel against soft errors by aspect-oriented programming and whole-program analysis. In: Proceeding of the 8th Workshop on Programming Languages and Operating Systems. ACM (2015)
4. Borchert, C., et al.: Generative software-based memory error detection and correction for operating system data structures. In: 43rd Annual IEEE/IFIP International Conference on Dependable Systems and Networks (DSN), pp. 1–12. IEEE (2013)
5. Borchert, C., et al.: Generic soft-error detection and correction for concurrent data structures. IEEE Trans. Dependable Secure Comput. **PP**(99) (2015)
6. Dietrich, C., et al.: Cross-kernel control-flow-graph analysis for event-driven real-time systems. In: Proceeding of the Conference on Languages, Compilers and Tools for Embedded Systems (LCTES 2015). ACM, June 2015
7. Digilent: Zedboard data sheet overview (2014). http://www.xilinx.com/support/documentation/data_sheets/ds190-Zynq-7000-Overview.pdf

---

[3] It is important to notice that this is *based solely on the estimated failure rate figures and assuming all failures could lead to dangerous consequences*; no hazard and risk assessment was carried out, nor was the software tested for coverage; we do not claim the EUC to achieve these SILs.

8. Gu, W., et al.: Characterization of Linux kernel behavior under errors. In: International Conference on Dependable Systems and Networks (DSN). IEEE (2003)
9. Guillen Salas, A., et al.: PhoneSat in-flight experience results. In: Proceeding of the Small Satellites and Services Symposium, May 2014
10. Hamming, R.W.: Error detecting and error correcting codes. Bell Syst. Tech. J. **29**(2), 147–160 (1950)
11. Herrera-Alzu, I., Lopez-Vallejo, M.: System design framework and methodology for Xilinx Virtex FPGA configuration scrubbers. IEEE Trans. Nucl. Sci. **61**(1), 619–629 (2014)
12. Hoffmann, M., et al.: dOSEK: the design and implementation of a dependability-oriented static embedded kernel. In: Proceeding of the 21st Real-Time and Embedded Technology and Applications (RTAS 2015). pp. 259–270. IEEE, April 2015
13. JEDEC Solid State Technology Association: JESD89-3A: Test Method for Beam Accelerated Soft Error Rate. http://www.jedec.org/standards-documents/docs/jesd-89-3a
14. Kiczales, G., Lamping, J., Mendhekar, A., Maeda, C., Lopes, C., Loingtier, J.-M., Irwin, J.: Aspect-oriented programming. In: Akşit, M., Matsuoka, S. (eds.) ECOOP 1997. LNCS, vol. 1241, pp. 220–242. Springer, Heidelberg (1997). doi:10.1007/BFb0053381
15. Lesea, A., et al.: Soft error study of ARM SoC at 28 nanometers. In: Proceeding of the IEEE Workshop on Silicon Errors in Logic - System Effects 2014 (2014)
16. Massa, A.: Embedded Software Development with eCos. Prentice Hall Professional Technical Reference (2002)
17. Mukherjee, S.S., et al.: A systematic methodology to compute the architectural vulnerability factors for a high-performance microprocessor. In: Proceeding of the 36th Annual IEEE/ACM International Symposium on Microarchitecture. IEEE (2003)
18. OSEK/VDX Group: operating system specification 2.2.3. Technical report. http://portal.osek-vdx.org/files/pdf/specs/os223.pdf, Accessed 29 Sept 2014
19. Quinn, H., et al.: Single-event effects in low-cost, low-power microprocessors. In: Radiation Effects Data Workshop (REDW), pp. 1–9. IEEE, July 2014
20. Santini, T., et al.: Reducing embedded software radiation-induced failures through cache memories. In: 19th European Test Symposium (ETS), pp. 1–6. IEEE (2014)
21. Santini, T., et al.: Beyond cross-section: spatio-temporal reliability analysis. ACM Trans. Embed. Comput. Syst. **15**(1), 3:1–3:16 (2015)
22. Santini, T., et al.: Exploiting cache conflicts to reduce radiation sensitivity of operating systems on embedded systems. In: Proceeding of the International Conference on Compilers, Architecture and Synthesis for Embedded Systems, CASES, pp. 49–58. IEEE (2015)
23. Schirmeier, H., et al.: FAIL*: an open and versatile fault-injection framework for the assessment of software-implemented hardware fault tolerance. In: Proceeding of the 11th European Dependable Computing Conference, pp. 245–255. IEEE, September 2015
24. Shirvani, P.P., et al.: Software-implemented EDAC protection against SEUs. IEEE Trans. Reliab. **49**(3), 273–284 (2000)
25. Shye, A., et al.: PLR: a software approach to transient fault tolerance for multicore architectures. IEEE Trans. Dependable Secure Comput. (2009)
26. Smith, D.J., Simpson, K.G.: Safety Critical Systems Handbook: a straightforward guide to functional safety, IEC 61508 and related standards, including process IEC 61511 and machinery IEC 62061 and ISO 13849. Elsevier (2010)

27. Spinczyk, O., Lohmann, D.: The design and implementation of AspectC++. Knowl.-Based Syst. **20**(7), 636–651 (2007). Special Issue on Techniques to Produce Intelligent Secure Software
28. Wang, C., et al.: Compiler-managed software-based redundant multi-threading for transient fault detection. In: Proceeding of the International Symposium on Code Generation and Optimization, CGO 2007, pp. 244–258. IEEE (2007)

Fault-Tolerant Execution on COTS Multi-core Processors with Hardware Transactional Memory Support

Florian Haas[1](✉), Sebastian Weis[1], Theo Ungerer[1], Gilles Pokam[2], and Youfeng Wu[2]

[1] Department of Computer Science,
University of Augsburg, Augsburg, Germany
{haas,weis,ungerer}@informatik.uni-augsburg.de
[2] Intel Corporation, Santa Clara, USA
{gilles.a.pokam,youfeng.wu}@intel.com

Abstract. The demand for fault-tolerant execution on high performance computer systems increases due to higher fault rates resulting from smaller structure sizes. As an alternative to hardware-based lockstep solutions, software-based fault-tolerance mechanisms can increase the reliability of multi-core commercial-of-the-shelf (COTS) CPUs while being cheaper and more flexible. This paper proposes a software/ hardware hybrid approach, which targets Intel's current x86 multi-core platforms of the Core and Xeon family. We leverage hardware transactional memory (Intel TSX) to support implicit checkpoint creation and fast rollback. Redundant execution of processes and signature-based comparison of their computations provides error detection, and transactional wrapping enables error recovery. Existing applications are enhanced towards fault-tolerant redundant execution by post-link binary instrumentation. Hardware enhancements to further increase the applicability of the approach are proposed and evaluated with SPEC CPU 2006 benchmarks. The resulting performance overhead is 47% on average, assuming the existence of the proposed hardware support.

1 Introduction

Errors in computer systems can never be avoided completely and the field of application dictates the required counter-measures. With error detection, erroneous computations can be identified. However, re-execution is required, inducing down time for error correction and system restart. Dependable server systems are usually designed as *fail-stop systems*, i.e. erroneous execution is detected and the system is stopped or restarted. In contrary, *fail-operational systems* provide built-in error correction and thus can continue to operate correctly in case of errors. While current processors are already protected against faults on different memory levels with error correcting codes (ECC), transient faults can still occur within the data and control paths of the processor's pipelines. Processors often implement tightly coupled lockstep execution to detect transient faults, which

ⓒ Springer International Publishing AG 2017
J. Knoop et al. (Eds.): ARCS 2017, LNCS 10172, pp. 16–30, 2017.
DOI: 10.1007/978-3-319-54999-6_2

requires a complete duplication of the hardware resources and cycle-by-cycle synchronization. However, the integration of hardware-based lockstep mechanisms in up-to-date COTS multi-core processors is complex and would require deep changes to the microarchitecture, since COTS processors also implement various power management and performance optimization mechanisms, which complicate synchronization at a cycle-by-cycle granularity [1]. Furthermore, current dual-modular redundant (DMR) lockstep processors only detect faults and therefore only support fail-stop execution. Triple-modular redundancy (TMR) is required to provide fault tolerance through forward-error correction. While hardware fault-tolerance mechanisms require complex and costly modifications to the microarchitecture of state-of-the-art COTS processors, pure software-based fault tolerance techniques, which duplicate instructions or processes to detect faults, e.g. [13,14], usually have a high performance impact, require specific compilers, and support limited recovery capabilities.

Hardware Transactional Memory (HTM) was first proposed for concurrency control [7] and is able to increase the parallelism and ease the programmability of parallel applications. Intel introduced the *Transactional Synchronization Extensions* (TSX) as part of the Haswell instruction set architecture [5]. The rollback mechanism of TSX, where all modified data from within a transaction is restorable, can be utilized for fault tolerance. A rollback to the implicitly created checkpoint helps to recover from detected errors. In this paper, we propose a software/hardware hybrid fault-tolerance mechanism to lift check-point restart systems from fail-stop to fail-operational by fast and fine-grained checkpoint generation and restart using Intel TSX. We leverage the recovery capabilities of TSX to support fault-tolerant execution of arbitrary, single-threaded applications. Our approach combines redundant execution of processes to detect differences in their executions, and backward error recovery by restarting transactions in the case of detected errors. Modifications of the existing hardware to facilitate error detection can increase the performance of our approach. We therefore evaluated the benefits to be expected by hardware support for signature generation and exchange. Our approach is based on binary instrumentation to achieve fault-tolerant execution. Post-link binary instrumentation allows the fault-tolerant execution of existing and already compiled programs on POSIX-compatible platforms.

We proposed the idea of leveraging Intel TSX for recoverability on existing hardware in [3,4]. A software-based implementation was presented to show the general applicability of Intel TSX for checkpointing in redundant processes. In this first approach, source code modifications were required and no full coverage of the instrumented application was achieved. This paper makes the following new contributions: (1) We present a software/ hardware hybrid fault-tolerance approach, which uses redundant process execution and post-link binary instrumentation to detect faults, and exploits the rollback-capabilities of Intel TSX to support efficient and low-overhead checkpointing and error recovery. (2) We propose hardware enhancements, which can significantly speed up our fault-tolerance mechanism. (3) We present a detailed evaluation of our approach for SPEC2006 integer and floating point benchmarks and show a performance overhead of 47% on average, assuming the existence of the proposed hardware support.

The rest of this paper is organized as follows. Section 2 provides a short overview of related work. The concept of our approach to detect errors through redundant execution and the recovery mechanism are described in Sect. 3. Possible hardware modifications and enhancements are discussed in Sect. 4. A detailed evaluation is presented in Sect. 5. Limitations and future work are discussed in Sect. 6. The paper is concluded in Sect. 7.

2   Related Work

Various methods for fault-tolerant execution on different types of processors exist. The most well-known method is lock-stepping [11], where two cores are coupled tightly. Comparison of the equality of both cores' computations happens on cycle or instruction level. Loosely coupled lockstep architectures support SMT [12] and multi-core processors [9]. However, to support error detection and recovery in such systems, complex changes are required to the pipeline and the memory hierarchy. This renders the applicability of such approaches on current high-performance COTS processors difficult and costly. As an alternative to hardware-based approaches, different software-only fault-tolerance mechanisms exist. They need to modify the program, either after compilation by binary instrumentation, or during compilation. A well-known compiler-based approach is SWIFT [13], where instructions are duplicated within the same process and a comparison of both results ensures correct execution of single-threaded applications. Unlike our approach, SWIFT cannot guarantee error isolation among dual executed streams, since memory protection works only between individual processes. A technique that uses process level redundancy was introduced with PLR [14] where a whole single-threaded process is duplicated. On system call granularity, both processes are compared. However, these software-based approaches cannot recover from detected errors, or impose high cost on checkpoint creation and recovery.

Transactional memory originated in high performance computing to allow optimistic synchronization. As the first commercial hardware implementations became available, the application of hardware transactional memory in embedded systems was suggested [2]. Beside the possibility of increased performance by optimistic synchronization in COTS-based dependable systems, the authors encourage the use of implicit checkpointing and rollback mechanism for fast and easy recovery in case of detected errors. Yalcin et al. [15] implemented a custom hardware transactional memory to support fault-tolerant execution of multi-threaded applications. The extendability of this transactional memory system allows execution of redundant transactions in parallel and comparison of signatures in hardware. In contrary to custom hardware implementations of transactional memory with focus on fault tolerance, our paper is based on Intel TSX, an existing, performance-oriented hardware transactional memory. As an alternative to full redundant execution, instruction level redundancy [8] allows error detection without process duplication. Instead, instructions are replicated to repeat the computation on different registers. Before writing to memory and at basic block boundaries, the data is compared to detect errors. This approach instruments applications during compilation, and also uses TSX transactions for checkpointing and rollback.

This paper presents a comprehensive evaluation of the performance overhead of redundant process execution on the Intel Haswell architecture. Furthermore, we propose hardware enhancements to increase the performance of our approach. The instrumentation mechanisms provide an increased code coverage with less performance overhead than other approaches. Combining the flexibility of software-based redundant execution with existing hardware transactional memory allows efficient checkpointing and rollback for specific applications, or selected critical parts of applications, for fault-tolerant execution.

3   Error Detection

We target a fault model where transient errors in the cores can be tolerated, and permanent errors can be detected. Transient faults (also known as single event upsets) induced for example by environmental radiation, electromagnetic interferences, or voltage fluctuations [11], occur sporadically and can lead to the so-called soft errors. We assume that all memory is protected with ECC, but errors may still appear in the CPU itself. The main objective of our approach is to ensure correct execution even when soft errors occur. For this, fail-operational execution requires error detection, error recovery, and error containment. We use the error containment and recovery capability of Intel TSX to provide fail-operational execution. Our approach consists of an enhanced binary instrumentation tool and a dynamic library, which provides the required functionality for redundant execution, comparison and rollback. No modifications to the source code of the application are required. The instrumentation enhances the application's binary with signature generation instructions to provide error detection. The remaining functionality for process management, signature comparison, and error recovery is implemented in a library to keep the required instrumentation of the original binary minimal.

3.1   Redundant Execution

The main principle of our approach is to redundantly execute user processes. The loosely coupled redundant execution allows error detection by repeatedly comparing both processes through signatures of blocks based on function boundaries. With the encapsulation of these blocks in transactions, error recovery is implemented. Our approach is based on process level redundancy, which results in two mostly identical processes with the same virtual address space. The advantage of process redundancy in contrary to redundant threads is that the virtual memory management of the operating system guarantees physical memory isolation and thus prevents error propagation from a process to its duplicate. Also, since virtual addresses are equal in both processes, no modifications of memory addresses are required. Existing programs are enhanced with error detection and recovery capabilities by modifying the program's binary with help of the instrumentation tool PEBIL [10]. Some of the required functionality is implemented in a library, which reduces the amount of code to instrument directly. To setup redundant execution, the binary instrumentation tool inserts a call to the library's setup function at the very beginning of the program, which usually is before calling **main**. Another call to end redundant execution is inserted into the exit code. The output of the instrumentation is a new binary ready for fault-tolerant execution on a common Intel CPU with support for TSX.

To enable redundant execution, the application's process is duplicated in the library's setup code by invoking a **fork** system call. The program then executes a *leading* and a *trailing* process. Both processes execute the same program code and also have identical virtual address spaces, which are physically separated by the memory management unit. Since the instrumentation is done on the binary and the process duplication takes place at run-time, the executed code of both processes is almost identical. As a consequence, the instrumentation requires no awareness of the actual process that executes the instrumented code. The distinction of the processes happens only in the library functions by means of the value of a global variable. Comparison of both processes is done on the level of function-based blocks, or also called *dependable blocks*. For an efficient comparison, we create signatures of these dependable blocks, which are exchanged between both processes. Figure 1 shows a schematic of the redundant execution and block-based comparison. A process is duplicated at its entry point before calling **main**. All code within the program is executed redundantly (step 1). Binary instrumentation divides this code into blocks, which are aligned at function boundaries (step 2). Signatures of these blocks are calculated in each

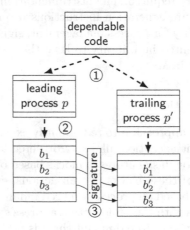

Fig. 1. Instrumentation on function-based dependable blocks b_n and redundant execution in processes p and p'.

process and transferred from the leading process to the trailing process (step 3). There, signatures are compared to detect errors. We use a FIFO queue in shared memory between both processes for signature exchange, which implicitly enforces the correct ordering between the leading and the trailing process.

3.2   Signature Generation

To compare both executions of redundant blocks, we implemented a signature-based approach to integrate all modified data within a block. For signature creation we selected 32 bit CRC, which is available as the crc32 instruction in the Haswell ISA. This allows a fast calculation with guaranteed detection of single bit flips. To create a signature, all registers of a dependable block are examined by the instrumentation tool and instructions are inserted for all used or defined registers to calculate a signature of the register content. If the same register is written multiple times inside a single block, it is sufficient to include the last value of the register in the signature. This is due to the fact that erroneous intermediate values either are propagated to other registers that are also added to the signature or the erroneous value is transitive over multiple operations (for example additions with same source and destination). Any register that is redefined inside the block would need to have the last value before the redefinition to be accumulated into the signature. A special case involves the memory write operations, since afterwards, their used registers are free to be newly assigned. In this case, data and addresses of the memory operation could be lost at the end of the block. As a consequence, memory write operations are immediately followed by their signature accumulation instructions. Further, floating-point operations are supported, and their used registers are also added to the signature. Since these instructions work on floating-point registers, an additional step is required, where we copy chunks of 64 bits into a general purpose register before calculating the CRC signature. Figure 2 shows an example instrumentation with two memory instructions and three ALU instructions. Register R15 is used to accumulate the CRC signature, while register R14 holds the signature of the other process for comparison. If these registers are already in use by the program code of the current block, two other free registers are used. A block is split in case no

```
                                    mov    (%rax),  %rbx
                                    add    $0x01,   %rbx
    mov    (%rax),  %rbx            add    $0x02,   %rbx
    add    $0x01,   %rbx            mov    %rbx,    (%rax)
    add    $0x02,   %rbx   ──→      crc32  %rbx,    %r15
    mov    %rbx,    (%rax)          mov    $0x03,   %rbx
    mov    $0x03,   %rbx            crc32  %rax,    %r15
                                    crc32  %rbx,    %r15
```

Fig. 2. Instrumentation of five instructions: used registers are accumulated by the hashing function crc32 at the end of the block. Memory write operations require an immediate signature accumulation (see 5th line in code listing on the right).

free registers can be found for storing the signatures. Splitting is repeated until at least two free registers are available.

3.3   Signature Exchange

Error detection requires the comparison of the redundant processes' signatures. Unfortunately, exchanging the signature within a transaction always results in an abort due to conflicting accesses. To overcome this, the signatures must be exchanged before the transaction is started in the trailing process. As a consequence, the process without transactions has to execute its block completely before the corresponding block of the transaction-enhanced process can be executed. In between, the signature is exchanged through a FIFO queue implemented in shared memory. The process that writes its signature to the queue is named *leader*, since its execution is at least one block ahead. The other process is named *trailer*. The trailer reads the leader's signature from the FIFO queue, stores it in a reserved register, and executes its block transactionally (see Fig. 3). Then the transaction is started, the block's code is executed and the signature is calculated. Before committing the transaction, both signatures are compared. In case of a mismatch, the transaction will be aborted. The use of a FIFO queue instead of a simple signature exchange buffer is beneficial for performance. The trailing process is slower, due to additional instructions for transactions and signature comparison. The FIFO queue now allows the leader to run ahead a fixed number of blocks, which is determined by the size of the queue. If writes from

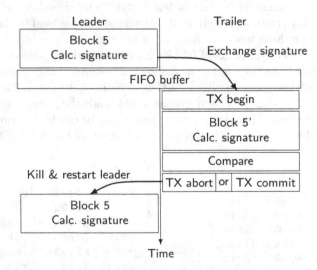

Fig. 3. Detailed view on the interlaced execution of both redundant processes. The calculated signature is exchanged through a FIFO buffer and compared with the local signature of the trailing process. Mismatches lead to transaction rollback of the trailing process and restart of the leading process.

the leader process and reads from the trailer process are separated, cache line collisions vanish.

3.4   Error Recovery and Containment

Error detection takes place at the end of the transactional block in the trailing process. Before committing the transaction, the locally calculated signature and the leading process' signature are compared. In case of a detected error, the transaction is explicitly aborted. Afterwards, the trailing process starts over at the beginning of the block, which previously was hit by the transient error. However, the leading process is at least one block ahead and not able to roll back to a point before the execution of the erroneous block. To overcome this, the leading process is killed by means of the operating system and a `fork` creates a new leading process. Also, the FIFO queue is cleared, since the signatures, which have already been produced, are probably faulty. The program execution then continues at the beginning of the previously faulty block. Figure 3 shows the transaction abort after signature comparison, with termination and restart of the leading process, which then executes the same block again. After rollback and forking the new process, the execution is guaranteed to be error-free, since the transaction rolled back and the leading process is replaced by a copy of the correct process. Memory protection between both processes avoids error migration from one process to the other. All data that is written to memory by the trailing process within a block becomes visible only if both signatures are equal, since the signatures are compared inside of the transaction.

Transactions may not only abort explicitly due to detected errors. Over-flowing cache, unfriendly instructions, or other external influences can cause a transaction to abort. If a transaction aborts, the abort handler checks the status and only if an explicit abort was forced due to a detected error, the error handler is called. Otherwise, the transaction is simply restarted.

4   Hardware Enhancements

The unmodifiable Haswell micro architecture impedes hardware enhancements, which can further improve our approach. Thus we investigated the potential impact of the following hardware-based enhancements.

4.1   Signature Generation

Since the most relevant bottleneck is the signature generation, our approach benefits from hardware signature generation. A possible hardware extension may calculate the signature implicitly, by issuing an accumulation on every read from a register and on every write to a register or to memory. The accumulation can happen in a dedicated register, which can be reset and read by the software. The instrumentation tool is then only required to reset the signature register at the beginning of a block. The comparison at the end of the block reads from this signature register instead of the reserved general purpose register.

4.2 Hardware Queue

Further improvement is possible by supporting signature exchange in hardware. This requires a mechanism to send data uni-directionally between individual cores, additionally with buffering to form a FIFO queue. It is sufficient to connect pairs of cores, a queue between every single core is not required. The assignment of processes to cores is handled by the software library.

4.3 Transactional Memory

Enhancements to TSX can also increase the performance and the versatility of our approach. Transactions should not abort in the error-free case, since conflicts do not occur. However, transactions are limited in their size, which depends on the cache, and are sensitive to interrupts and other system-related events. Also various instructions are not allowed to be executed inside of a transaction. Robust transactions surviving such events would allow a guaranteed transactional execution, resulting in a better coverage and less overhead for instrumented programs. Escape actions allow to read or write data in or out of a transaction without triggering a conflict. This enables parallel transactional execution of both redundant processes. In this case, signatures can be exchanged during the commit phase, and the transaction will only be allowed to commit if the signatures match. Otherwise, both transactions are rolled back and restarted.

5 Evaluation

The implementation of the concept described in the previous sections was evaluated by enhancing real-world programs. Execution of these programs is possible on existing hardware that supports the TSX instructions. In our setup, we used an Intel Xeon E5-2697 v4 "Broadwell-EP" with Turbo-Boost disabled. Further, hyper-threading was disabled to avoid transaction capacity problems due to shared L1 caches. A subset of the SPEC CPU 2006 benchmark suite [6] was used to compare the execution times of software with fault-tolerance disabled and enabled. Due to the restrictions of TSX on the length of transactions, and instructions that are not allowed in transactions, some benchmarks must have been elided from the evaluation. In this section, we break down the run time overhead and discuss its main sources. The effect of the possible hardware improvements proposed in Sect. 4 on the performance is shown afterwards.

5.1 Performance Overhead

On the Xeon E5 v4, the redundant execution on two cores takes more than twice the time for some benchmarks (see Fig. 5). To determine the sources of the overhead, individual parts of the instrumentation have been disabled. Results are shown in Fig. 4 and described in the following paragraphs.

Transactional Overhead. One source of overhead is the transaction instructions, which wrap the dependable blocks in the trailing process. Since TSX does not guarantee a non-conflicting transaction to commit eventually, aborts due to other reasons may occur. These reasons are for example cache overflows, exceptions, and interrupts. Such aborts are transparent to the instrumented program, since the affected transaction is executed again. The chances to commit successfully are high for the second try of a transaction, depending on the abort reason. The resulting overhead of aborted and restarted transactions consists of the time needed to rollback the transaction plus the time needed to re-execute the code inside of this transaction. Cache overflows and exceptions may lead to never-committing transactions. In this case, the affected block is executed non-transactional by setting a flag for a conditional jump placed before the transaction start and end instructions. Within Fig. 4, the fraction of the performance overhead related to transactional memory instructions is shown in the black bars at the bottom ("Transaction"). Table 1 lists the executed transactions per benchmark, together with the average percentage of transaction aborts. Aborts due to cache overflow relative to the total number of transaction aborts and the number of non-transactionally executed blocks relative to the overall number of transactions are shown in the middle of Table 1.

Signature Generation. Signatures are calculated at the end of every block, except for memory write instructions. For these, the signature is accumulated directly after the write instruction. The overhead of signature generation depends on the size of the blocks and on the number of blocks. Larger blocks decrease the overall overhead of signature generation, since less signature calculations are required. The percentage of overhead due to signature generation is shown in the bars labeled "Signature" in Fig. 4.

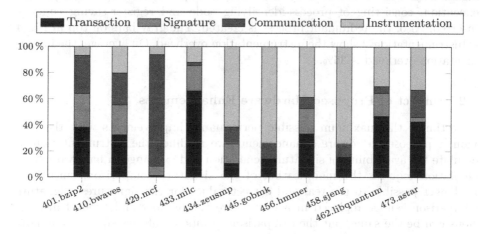

Fig. 4. Performance overhead arising from transaction instructions, signature generation and exchange, and binary instrumentation.

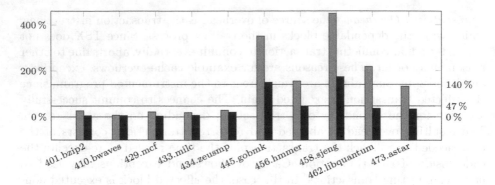

Fig. 5. Relative execution time overhead on an Intel Xeon E5 v4 (gray bars). Average performance overhead is 140%. With emulation of hardware support for signature creation and exchange (black bars), average overhead is reduced to 47%.

Core-to-Core Communication. The performance of the communication between redundant processes is crucial, since signature reception is on the critical path of the trailing process. The FIFO queue decouples writing to and reading from the signature exchange buffer. Transmitting signatures from one core to another is still costly, since reading a cache line full of signatures always entails a cache miss. The execution time overhead related to signature exchange is shown in Fig. 4, labeled "Communication".

Instrumentation Overhead. Additionally, we evaluated the performance overhead induced by the duplicated execution itself. In the instrumentation phase, signature generation, exchange, and comparison, as well as the transaction instructions were omitted. Only code that is required for duplicated process execution, consisting of process-identifying code and register-saving code, is inserted. Also, the redundant process is created. The gray bars on top in Fig. 4 ("Instrumentation") show the instrumentation overhead. On average, the instrumentation overhead is 36%.

5.2   Impact of Proposed Hardware Enhancements

To estimate the maximum possible performance improvements with the previously proposed hardware enhancements, we modified the instrumentation to emulate the availability of signature generation and exchange in hardware. This emulation requires the modification of the signature comparison, since it is no longer possible to use real and correct values for the signatures. Signature comparison can be replaced in a way where the number and type of instructions can be the same, but the comparison results are always equal. By removing the crc32 instructions in the instrumentation, we get an emulation of the hardware-integrated signature creation and a timing behavior close to what can be expected. To estimate the maximum performance improvement in case of a hardware-assisted core-to-core communication, we modified the instrumentation to assume zero cost for writing and reading signatures. Calls to the appropriate functions are replaced with nop, and the signature comparison was disabled as described above. This is required to execute the program, otherwise the error detection would always roll back due to mismatching signatures. The emulation of hardware support for signature generation and exchange leads to significantly improved performance. The relative performance overhead of our approach decreases to 47% on average and below 10% for some benchmarks (see Fig. 5 and the rightmost column in Table 1).

Table 1. Performance of instrumented benchmarks. The number of transactionally executed blocks is listed with the relative amount of aborted transactions. Cache-related aborts are relative to aborted transactions and the number of non-transactionally executed blocks is relative to the total number of blocks. The execution time is relative to the execution time of the original benchmark. In the rightmost column, the relative execution time of instrumented benchmarks with emulation of hardware support is listed.

Benchmark	# blocks	Aborts	Cache	no TX	rel. ex. time	HW opt.
401.bzip2	10.9 M	0.64%	78.7%	0.25%	1.26	1.05
410.bwaves	3.6 M	3.52 %	22.6%	0.33%	1.07	1.05
429.mcf	2.6 M	8.91%	95.6%	4.30%	1.21	1.03
433.milc	9.6 M	19.13%	5.8%	2.19%	1.19	1.07
434.zeusmp	27.7 M	0.15%	83.3%	0.03%	1.28	1.20
445.gobmk	653.6 M	0.03%	59.5%	0.01%	4.50	2.49
456.hmmer	47.8 M	0.22%	83.6%	0.09%	2.55	1.45
458.sjeng	265.6 M	0.06%	10.1%	0.00%	5.49	2.73
462.libquantum	0.7 M	2.48%	99.6%	1.24%	3.18	1.36
473.astar	127.3 M	2.27%	99.0%	1.03%	2.32	1.34

6   Limitations and Future Work

The efficient implementation of transactional memory in Intel TSX allows fast checkpoint creation and rollback. Since it is a fixed hardware implementation, some limitations appear when leveraging TSX for fault-tolerant execution. As an optimistic and best-effort synchronization mechanism, the eventual successful execution of a transaction cannot be guaranteed. This can lead to regions in the application code containing unfriendly instructions, which cannot be executed in a transaction. Additionally, transactions may overflow easily if the L1 cache exceeds due to its limited associativity. The fixed hardware implementation of TSX causes some limitations, which must be handled by the instrumentation. Since TSX uses the L1 cache to hold back data which is not yet committed, a transaction must be aborted in case of a full cache or cache-set. This can happen frequently, since the L1 cache is eight-way set-associative.

A transaction may abort not only due to conflicting memory accesses, but also due to unfriendly instructions or other system events, like interrupts. Most unfriendly instructions modify processor flags or control registers, and thus rarely occur in user space code. In case of an abort due to exceptions or interrupts, the transaction usually commits after a few tries. However, TSX does not guarantee that a transaction commits eventually, and some instructions always lead to a transaction abort. If our library detects repeated aborts of the same transaction, the affected block must be executed without a transaction. In fact, the execution of this specific block is then vulnerable. Error detection is still possible, but the non-transactional execution prevents a rollback. This reduces the fault-tolerant coverage of the application, but the instrumentation of the program can be optimized to lower the number of always aborting transactions, e.g. by splitting blocks to shorten transactions. Further, TSX transactions cannot be paused in a way that would allow to escape the transaction. Escape actions would allow to use transactions in both processes and to compare the signatures within the same transaction. In case of a rollback, the leading process would not be required to be killed, since it still would be possible to rollback the faulty block. As a workaround, the interleaved execution with signature exchange through a FIFO queue was implemented. However, this makes rollback complicated, since the leading process has to be killed and newly forked.

The presented approach is currently not capable of instrumenting multi-threaded programs, due to the difficulty of organizing the program execution of multiple redundant threads, synchronization in between, and assurance of correct execution after error recovery. This challenging topic will be part of our future work.

For a complete sphere of replication, calls to external functions and system calls require interception. Currently, external functions are executed without instrumentation in both processes to ensure the same functionality as the original, non-instrumented application. However, this prevents I/O on the same file handle. With an enhanced sphere of replication, redundant processes become transparent for their environment. External functions then are executed only once, with their result being provided to both redundant process. This is also required to support synchronization in redundant parallel applications.

7   Conclusion

In this paper, we proposed a software/hardware hybrid fault-tolerant execution on an Intel Xeon "Broadwell-EP" multi-core CPU. Transient errors can be detected by redundant execution and signature-based process comparison. By leveraging the checkpointing and rollback mechanisms of Intel's hardware transactional memory, an efficient method for error recovery and containment was presented.

Binary instrumentation enhances already compiled programs without requiring modifications of the source code. This allows a wide range of applications for fault-tolerant execution with full coverage of the program code. The resulting execution time overhead of redundant and fault-tolerant execution was shown to be 140% on average on existing hardware. Signature generation and transactional execution are the main contributors to the increased execution time. However, hardware enhancements and the integration of advanced techniques for signature creation and exchange reduce the average run time overhead to 47%.

References

1. Bernick, D., Bruckert, B., Vigna, P.D., Garcia, D., Jardine, R., Klecka, J., Smullen, J.: NonStop® advanced architecture. In: Proceedings of the International Conference on Dependable Systems and Networks (DSN), pp. 12–21 (2005)
2. Fetzer, C., Felber, P.: Transactional memory for dependable embedded systems. In: Proceedings of the International Conference on Dependable Systems and Networks Workshops (DSN-W), pp. 223–227 (2011)
3. Haas, F., Weis, S., Metzlaff, S., Ungerer, T.: Exploiting Intel TSX for fault-tolerant execution in safety-critical systems. In: Proceedings of the International Symposium on Defect and Fault Tolerance in VLSI and Nanotechnology Systems (DFT), pp. 197–202 (2014)
4. Haas, F., Weis, S., Ungerer, T., Pokam, G., Wu, Y.: POSTER: fault-tolerant execution on COTS multi-core processors with hardware transactional memory support. In: Proceedings of the International Conference on Parallel Architecture and Compilation Techniques (PACT), pp. 421–422 (9 2016)
5. Hammarlund, P., Martinez, A.J., Bajwa, A.A., Hill, D.L., Hallnor, E., Jiang, H., Dixon, M., Derr, M., Hunsaker, M., Kumar, R., et al.: Haswell: the Fourth-Generation Intel Core Processor. IEEE Micro **34**(2), 6 20 (2014)
6. Henning, J.L.: SPEC CPU2006 benchmark descriptions. ACM SIGARCH Comput. Archit. News **34**(4), 1–17 (2006)
7. Herlihy, M., Moss, J.E.B.: Transactional memory: architectural support for lock-free data structures. In: Proceedings of the International Symposium on Computer Architecture (ISCA), pp. 289–300 (1993)
8. Kuvaiskii, D., Faqeh, R., Bhatotia, P., Felber, P., Fetzer, C.: HAFT: hardware-assisted fault tolerance. In: Proceedings of the European Conference on Computer Systems (EuroSys), pp. 25:1–25:17 (2016). http://doi.acm.org/10.1145/2901318.2901339
9. LaFrieda, C., Ipek, E., Martinez, J.F., Manohar, R.: Utilizing dynamically coupled cores to form a resilient chip multiprocessor. In: Proceedings of the International Conference on Dependable Systems and Networks (DSN), pp. 317–326 (2007)
10. Laurenzano, M.A., Tikir, M.M., Carrington, L., Snavely, A.: PEBIL: efficient static binary instrumentation for Linux. In: Proceedings of the International Symposium on Performance Analysis of Systems and Software (ISPASS), pp. 175–183 (2010)
11. Mukherjee, S.: Architecture Design for Soft Errors. Morgan Kaufmann Publishers Inc., San Francisco (2008)
12. Reinhardt, S.K., Mukherjee, S.S.: Transient Fault Detection via Simultaneous Multithreading. In: Proceedings of the International Symposium on Computer Architecture (ISCA), pp. 25–36 (2000)
13. Reis, G.A., Chang, J., Vachharajani, N., Rangan, R., August, D.I.: SWIFT: software implemented fault tolerance. In: Proceedings of the International Symposium on Code Generation and Optimization (CGO), pp. 243–254 (2005)

14. Shye, A., Blomstedt, J., Moseley, T., Reddi, V.J., Connors, D.A.: PLR: a software approach to transient fault tolerance for multicore architectures. IEEE Trans. Dependable Secure Comput. (TDSC) **6**(2), 135–148 (2009)
15. Yalcin, G., Unsal, O.S., Cristal, A.: Fault tolerance for multi-threaded applications by leveraging hardware transactional memory. In: Proceedings of the International Conference on Computing Frontiers (CF), pp. 4:1–4:9 (2013)

Accelerators

OpenCL-Based 6D-Vision on Heterogeneous System on Chips

Michael Bromberger[1]([⊠]), Steffen Ehrle[1], Michael Scharrer[1,2],
Lukas Erlinghagen[2], and Jens Schick[2]

[1] Chair of Computer Architecture and Parallel Processing,
Karlsruhe Institute of Technology, Karlsruhe, Germany
bromberger@kit.edu
[2] MYESTRO Interactive GmbH, Karlsruhe, Germany

Abstract. Object tracking is an important task in many applications. 6D-Vision circumvent drawbacks of approaches solely based on sequences of images. But 6D-Vision is computationally very expensive, hence most approaches rely on non-embedded hardware or even on hardware acceleration to enable a high-performance execution. This work considers 6D-Vision on a low-power heterogeneous System on Chip for the first time. Therefore, we present a powerful 6D-Vision pipeline that fully exploits the capabilities of a FPGA-based System on Chip. We reduce the complexity of the design using OpenCL and introduce different optimizations in order to implement a high-performance calculation of a 6D field. Our 6D-Vision pipeline processes 24 frames per second and provides useful information about a traffic scene. Moreover, we have successfully integrated the design for a gesture control application.

1 Introduction

Detecting, tracking, and classifying moving objects is a significant task for many applications, especially for mobile systems. Autonomous driving or gesture control often relies on tracking moving objects in accordance with minimum framerate, maximum power, and maximum cost constraints. A 6D-Vision system describes each point in a scene by a 3D position and a 3D velocity vector, hence it allows tracking and classifying of objects. 6D-Vision is a key technology for intelligent vehicles and provides knowledge about the current car situation [6]. Knowing the movement of an object, which is represented as a cluster of 6D points, an estimate of the likelihood for a collision can be given. Sequences of stereo camera images are used to calculate a 6D field [4].

Reliable tracking of moving objects based on 6D-Vision requires a certain density of the 6D field. Furthermore, dense fields make the system more robust against inaccurate 6D vectors. Most of the current approaches rely on high-end hardware, since the main parts, i.e. stereo vision and optical flow are computationally very intensive. Implementations of such algorithms, which calculate 6D fields of sufficient quality, are too slow on low-power embedded CPUs as our

© Springer International Publishing AG 2017
J. Knoop et al. (Eds.): ARCS 2017, LNCS 10172, pp. 33–46, 2017.
DOI: 10.1007/978-3-319-54999-6_3

investigation reveals. But for many applications including autonomous cars, common desktop or high-end hardware are too expensive or too power-consuming. Moreover, mobile systems should include multiple 6D-Vision systems in order to achieve redundancy and a surround view.

Heterogeneous System on Chips (SoCs) are promising platforms for such tasks, since they make hardware acceleration possible while also allowing CPU implementations. Stereo vision greatly benefits from such an acceleration. Most of the work in 6D-Vision is mainly focused on density and accuracy of 6D fields instead of low-power and low-cost solutions. A proposed heterogeneous 6D-Vision system offers a performance of 20 frames per second for images of size 320 × 240, but it uses a high-end GPU and it is not clear which FPGA is used [1]. The work of Sahlbach et al. [11] is most related to our work, but has several drawbacks. Firstly, the allowed maximum disparity as well as displacement between positions over time is limited, hence it prevents the usage for real-world scenarios. Secondly, the image size is small and it uses a high-end FPGA. Finally, the design is implemented using a hardware description language which is error-prone and time-consuming. But the main drawback of their paper is that an evaluation about the quality is missing. Therefore, we address following issues regarding the state-of-the-art:

1. FPGAs are suitable as part of a high-performance 6D-Vision system, but require low-level programming
2. Few approaches have its focus on high-performance 6D-Vision
3. No approach considers an entire solution on a low-power heterogeneous SoC for 6D-Vision

To overcome the first issue, we exploit the arise of OpenCL to implement FPGA designs. Based on OpenCL, we analyze, design, and implement components that are required by a 6D-Vision system. Due to hardware limitations, concessions have to be made regarding the density and accuracy of the 6D field. We describe several design choices that enable a processing of these components on a low-power heterogeneous SoC. Our main contributions in this work are:

- We outperform the most related work, i.e. [11] in terms of performance, supported disparities as well as flow displacements. We also provide an evaluation of the accuracy.
- We apply several optimizations, i.e. a multi iteration approach and introduce a sorting step which better fits to a FPGA, and make several design choices which drastically reduces resource consumption and increases the performance.
- We analyze the performance of the entire 6D-vision pipeline for different use-cases. The resulting 6D-Vision data provide valuable information about traffic scenes. Furthermore, we show that a gesture control system successfully works using our low-power 6D-Vision design.
- This is the first work that considers the reduction of the design complexity for high-performance 6D-Vision using OpenCL.

2   Preliminaries

Our goal is a 6D-Vision system that provides reasonable performance for different applications. Moreover, our design goals comprise reducing resources as far as possible and focusing on a low power and low-cost solution, while we target to maximize the accuracy of a 6D field under those hardware constraints. This is especially important for mobile systems where hardware costs and energy consumption play a mayor role during the design phase. Minimizing the design effort is equally important, hence we exploit a high-level hardware language, i.e. OpenCL. Above design goals prevent us from using variational methods for 6D-Vision, which are commonly used, hence we rely on another solution. We use an approach for computing 6D vectors which is based on pixel correspondences from multiple images that are taken from different positions and instances in time. Using corresponding pixels in four frames of two stereo pair images, we can calculate an estimation for a 6D vector regarding the current considered point in the scene. In Fig. 1, l and r present the current stereo image, while l' and r' present the previously taken image. To calculate a 6D vector for a certain point, we have to find a 4-pixel correspondence, which needs three correspondence pairs. Two pairs are calculated via stereo vision (green lines) and the other using optical flow (orange line). The major issue with the approach above is that if one of the three correspondence pairs is undefined, no 6D vector can be constructed. Stereo Vision allow to calculate a 3D position vector of a certain point in an image. Optical flow calculates the position of the same point, but at the time of the previous frame. Hence, we have enough information to calculate a 3D velocity vector. The two 3D vectors form the final 6D vector of a point in the scene. Hence, we divide the problem of calculating 6D data into two sub problems.

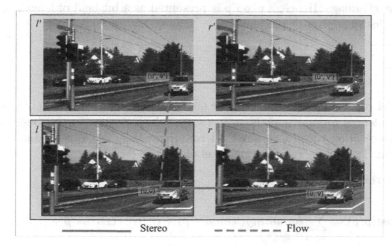

Fig. 1. Fusion of stereo and optical flow. Image from [10]. (Color figure online)

The computation complexity of stereo vision is reduced to a 1D search problem by using warped images. Such theoretical restrictions are not possible or optical flow, because points can move in any direction. Therefore, we use two different algorithms for optical flow and stereo matching, which is different to the design in [11]. This allows to reduce significant amount of resources for stereo vision as well as optical flow, since we integrate different optimizations which would not be possible else. In the following, we discuss the design decisions for stereo vision and optical flow.

2.1   Stereo Vision

Semi-global method (SGM) approaches rely on high bandwidth and huge memory resources, which limits the usage of low cost FPGAs as well as the performance [7]. Since our focus is on a solution which uses less resources and offers a high performance, we decide to consider local methods. There are two main local approaches, Sum-of-Absolute-Differences (SAD) and sum of hamming distances (SHD). Applying preprocessing methods on the input image, e.g. sobel and census transform, enables to increase the accuracy of the matching.

We did an extensive evaluation of different approaches with the result, that for SAD in combination with a sobel preprocessing step the accuracy is increased by using a larger region around a pixel, i.e. block, but the FPGA resource utilization drastically increases with the number of possible disparities. Using SHD with census transformation, resources are drastically reduced, since less adders are required due to hamming operations. Moreover, a line matcher which exploits a census transform pattern similar to min census [8] provide similar accuracy compared to block matchers for SHD, which further reduces resources.

Filter. A min census transform, $lcensus$ and $rcensus$, is applied to the left $l()$ and right $r()$ image. Hence, a pixel p is presented as a bit field of length n. $a(i)$ defines a list of n pixel displacements.

$$lcensus/rcensus_i(p)_{i=1,..,n} = \begin{cases} 1, \text{if } l(p+a(i)) > l(p) \\ 0, \text{otherwise} \end{cases} \tag{1}$$

Stereo Matcher. As cost function, we use SHD within a 1×9 region of possible correspondences around a pixel $p = (u,v)$, which results in the best choice between execution time, accuracy, and resource consumption according to our evaluation. The best corresponding pixel of p is

$$corresp(p) = \arg\min_{\bar{p} \in A_p} cost(p, \bar{p})$$

$$cost(p, \bar{p}) = \sum_{i=-4}^{4} hamming(lcensus(p) + (i, 0)), rcensus(\bar{p} + (i, 0))) \tag{2}$$

The distance regarding the dimension u of the image between p and $\bar{p}$ presents the disparity value of p.

Sub-pixel Matching. A single pixel difference means often a large real-world distance, hence it is useful to exploit the sub-pixel domain. Therefore, we use linear interpolation which is suitable for the above task and has low resource impact on the FPGA compared to more computationally intensive interpolation approaches, since low resource utilization is one of our most important design goals.

Post-processing. We apply two steps to reduce the amount of false matches, which impacts density but increases the accuracy of matches. Firstly, we use a uniqueness criterion. Since camera images include noise, it is quite possible that the lowest value is not the best match. But often the lowest and second lowest value are also similar, even with sub-pixel matching. Therefore, we accept a match only, if the difference between the lowest and the third lowest value is greater than a pre-defined minimum, which is determined empirically. Secondly, we exploit left-right consistency check [7]. Disparity values are only accepted, if matching from left to right and right to left returns only a small difference for the disparity of a certain position.

2.2   Optical Flow

As already mentioned, most optical flow approaches are based on total variational methods, but they do not allow sufficient performance on resource-limited architectures. Local approaches for optical flow require to search correspondence pixels in a 2D region around a certain pixel and use, e.g. SAD. But as our evaluation for SAD approaches reveals, such an approach is very resource intensive, hence limits supported flow displacements. This aspect strongly influences the accuracy. Therefore, we apply an approach which is based on an unique match approach [12], which avoids the usage of adders and has no limit for supported flow displacements.

Generating Features. The first part of the algorithm generates unique features for each pixel in the right and left image individually. Each feature consists of an image position (u, v) and a 24-bit key. The key is generated from a 7×7 pixel region around the current pixel by exploiting a variant of a census transform. It was shown that such keys have a low probability to be equal for two different pixels, if they do not represent the same point in scene. But still, there are collisions because of recurring patterns in the scene, hence to avoid false correspondences we have to filter them out. Since filtering results in a low density, we only filter out keys which occur on more than 16 different positions.

Matching Features. In this step, equal keys in both images are identified, in case there are multiple features using the same key, the closest ones regarding the pixel position are chosen. This approach is reasonable because very large displacements are unlikely, if the recording rate is low. In [12], the authors use hash tables for finding matches. This has several drawbacks for a FPGA execution. Assuming the entries of the hash table are a single bits, where a bit states the existence of a key in the other frame, the hash table has a size of $2^{24}\, bits = 2\,\mathrm{MB}$ which is too large for the on-chip memory resources of low-cost FPGAs. This is even worse in our case where several positions have to be stored in the hash table. Hence, it requires the usage of off-chip memory and storing and loading data from this memory in a random access way. Since the hash is generated on the FPGA, we have a backward dependency because the current memory access depends on the previous one and a load requires up to hundreds of cycles. Therefore, we need a different solution to efficiently port the above algorithm to a FPGA. Our novel solution is to sort features according to the key for both images. After sorting, above described matching becomes an easy task.

Post-processing. To remove likely incorrect matches, we apply two different post-processing steps. We discard all matches having an unrealistic large displacement and accept correspondences only, if there is a certain number of matches in the neighborhood.

3   Related Work

In this section, we summarize current work in 6D-Vision. Additionally, we also give a brief overview about optical flow and stereo vision, since it is part of our 6D-Vision approach.

3.1   6D-Vision

Vogel et al. [14] propose a variational approach, but despite the high accuracy the computational complexity rule out solutions on low-cost hardware. 6D data based on monocular camera images requires to solve an optimization problem and high computing power [15]. A high-performance approach running on a common consumer laptop was proposed in [2]. A system exploiting heterogeneous hardware resources relies on high-end GPUs and FPGAs which are too power-consuming for many embedded applications [1]. The most related work to our work is too limited regarding allowed disparity and possible flow displacements [11]. Moreover, their solution relies on the resource hungry SAD approach and share the same resources for optical flow and stereo vision which limits performance. They also do not apply any post processing steps and do not provide an evaluation about the accuracy of the resulting 6D-field. It must be noted, that 6D vision is used in commercial cars but details are not publicity available. Therefore, we present the first 6D vision approach focusing on a low-resource and low-cost design.

3.2   Stereo-Vision

Approaches resulting in highly accurate depth maps are based on a global or SGM which are very time-consuming [7]. SGM requires high memory bandwidth and high internal resources. A recent approach exploits convolutional neural networks, but it is also very compute-intensive [17]. Most high-performance approaches are based on hardware accelerators, e.g. FPGAs and GPUs, and use local approaches, e.g. SAD, which are easier to parallelize. Similar to [8], we implement a variant of the mini census transform method as stereo vision core on a FPGA, but our method supports more disparities. Additionally, our design easily enables a trade-off between resource consumption and execution time by an iterative approach.

3.3 Optical Flow

Variational approaches are the basis for most optical flow algorithms [16]. Such approaches rely on optimizing a global energy function which is highly non-convex. While the quality of the result is promising, the complexity hampers high-performance execution. Such global algorithms are accelerated by orders of magnitude using FPGAs, but even if they provide enough performance for above described applications the resource consumption is significant high [3]. This is mainly caused by the warping stage required for the hierarchical app-roach. Our focus is on a low resource consuming design, however above method could be integrated into our design for the optical flow matcher as well. Local approaches based on unique features like the one which is used in our work, provide a high frame rate on modern desktop CPUs [12]. A reduced version was optimized for a FPGA execution [5], but the small allowed maximum displace-ment between frames limits the usage for real-world applications, e.g. self-driving cars, and their solution requires more internal memory resources, since they do not apply min census. An important filter for ambiguous features, which reduces false matchings, is missing. In [13], they propose a FPGA-based approach requir-ing a two-dimensional search which doubles execution time and highly increase resource consumption but calculates more accurate flow maps.

4   FPGA-Based SoC for Supporting 6D-Vision

Our system architecture is shown in Fig. 2. As input a stereo image recorded by a stereo camera or simulation data are used. Both images will be warped, i.e. rectified, and used to calculate a disparity and a flow map afterward. The Stereo Matcher and the Optical Flow Matcher are performed on a FPGA,

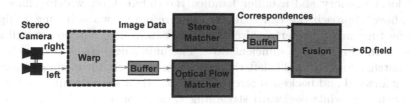

Fig. 2. Pipeline for generating 6D data.

while the Fusion, which is not computationally expensive, are executed on a CPU. All modules form a macro pipeline. The Stereo Matcher and the Optical Flow Matcher run data-parallel, hence in the same pipeline step. As writing to random memory addresses is significantly slower compared to contiguous access patterns (up to ten times on our evaluation system), we reduce random accesses to a minimum.

4.1 Warp

Warping is an important step for stereo vision, since it reduces the correspondence problem to 1D. Usually, so-called reverse warping is performed, but it demands two data-dependent lookup operations. We test a CPU version of the reverse warping algorithm but no real-time execution is feasible. Therefore, we use pre-rectified images as input which is quite common in literature and consider warping in future work.

4.2 Stereo Matcher

A census transform is applied to the warped left and right frame, hence two census transform units are implemented on the FPGA for performance reasons. We exploit a large shift register to implement (1) efficiently. The core part of the stereo matcher, i.e. finding the best correspondence per position, gets the census transformed frames as input. Again we use a shift register to implement the function $corresp(p)$. Since the resource consumption linearly grows with the amount of considered disparities $|A_p|$ and the required amount for most applications is high, it would be impossible to implement the Stereo Matcher and the Optical Flow Matcher on a low-end FPGA. Therefore, the used approach for the Stereo Matcher is to split the task into multiple iterations, where each iteration considers only a certain amount of possible disparities. The design of the Stereo Matcher is shown in Fig. 3a. interpolate applies a moving average on the right frame. By running the Stereo Matcher once with interpolation and once without, we achieve half-pixel matching. Afterwards, the basic stereo matcher described above estimates the best disparity on the current disparities under consideration. This optimum is compared to the previously calculated optimum. The calculated disparity and minimum cost values are buffered in the local off-chip RAM of the FPGA and used to choose the best disparity in the following iteration. After the last iteration only the disparity values are transferred to the local memory and a buffer handles the different bit widths efficiently. Using above approach, we can reduce FPGA resources while having a higher execution time and a higher required memory bandwidth, but we are still able to process the frames in a sufficient rate. The uniqueness check is done in the stereo matcher core. To enable left-right consistency check, the memory streamer supports forward and backward streaming. A left-right depth map requires forward streaming, while backward streaming is used for a right-left depth map, but the disparities are reversed in the memory. The actual check is performed

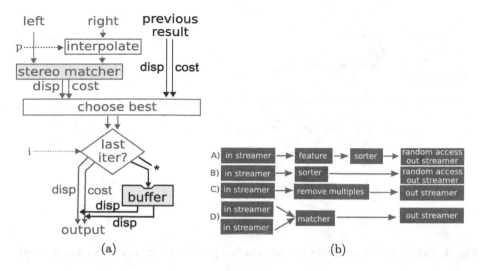

Fig. 3. Stereo matcher core including half-pixel matching and exploiting the multi-iteration approach (a). Different steps of the `Optical Flow Matcher` (b).

on the CPU because it is computationally less expensive and requires random access on a row-wise scheme.

4.3 Optical Flow Matcher

In order to calculate the final flow map, we perform several steps (A, B, C, and D) as shown in Fig. 3b. Each step is performed on the FPGA sequentially. We place buffers before the `random access out streamers` in order to collect data as far as possible, which enables memory burst transfers. The first step A generates the features according to Sect. 2.2 for the current image and applies a preprocessing for the sorting task. The second step B performs the sorting according to the 24-bit keys. We consider different sorting algorithms which are potentially suitable for a FPGA execution. A combination of block sort and merge sort is well suited [9], but it requires large block sizes to achieve a good performance. Hence, it consumes a large amount of resources and makes it impossible to implement it together with other steps on a low-end FPGA. Moreover, reconfiguration of the FPGA using OpenCL is not possible since it requires roughly 200 ms as we measured and rules out real-time execution. Therefore, we apply radix sort (see Fig. 4). Radix sort applies a bucket sort on a portion of the bits in the key in several iterations, e.g. starting with the 2 least significant bits then using the next two bits and so on. The parameter i specifies the current iteration, hence states which bits are considered for sorting. These bits select the buffer to store the current feature. If a buffer is full, it is written to memory. Counters enable to have a contiguous chunk of data where each bucket is adjacent to his neighbor without a gap, hence the correct starting address for each bucket in the memory has to be known to avoid fragmentation. This is achieved by counting the elements per bucket in advance (left part of Fig. 4a). For the first iteration,

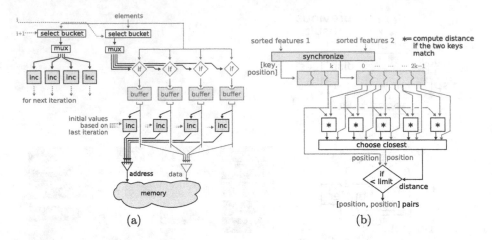

(a)   (b)

Fig. 4. Kernel for the radix sort (a). Matcher as part of the `Optical Flow Matcher` (b).

it is done in Step A. Because of the used sorting, step B has to be performed several times according to the considered bits of the key. The resource consumption exponentially grows with the number of considered bits, while the execution time only linearly decreases.

Step C removes keys that occur more than 16 times by using a shift register of size 16. Finally, Step D performs the matching of features (see Fig. 4b). The `Synchronize` unit takes care that always elements from the stream which have a lower key will be read until keys are equal in both streams. Then all following equal keys are transfered to two shift registers which are of size $k = 16$. Padding is used to invalidate elements in case one stream has more equal keys following. Since moving data to operators causes additional logic resources by the OpenCL tool flow, we perform more operations to avoid moving the data. A key of the reference frame can occur at any position starting from 15 elements before and 15 elements afterwards in the other stream. Between each pair the Euclidean distance is calculated by using DSP blocks. Additionally, the equality of keys is considered to avoid false matches. In case, more points having the same key the ones with the closest distance are selected. If the distance is lower than a certain limit as discussed earlier, they are transfered to the local memory. Since sorting (step B) is the performance bottleneck, implementing the `Optical Flow Matcher` as pipeline on the FPGA only causes additional resource overhead with less performance improvement.

4.4   Fusion

Bad matches are removed by taking the values of neighboring pixels into account. This is computationally simple enough in order to run it on the CPU. Combining the depth and flow map to a 6D field needs random memory accesses and low computational effort, hence FPGA acceleration is not required even under high-performance scenarios. Therefore, we map this task to the CPU.

5   Evaluation Setup

We use the SoCrates II board as platform of choice. The SoCrates uses a Cyclone V FPGA, which combines two ARM Cortex A9 running at 800 MHz, a reconfigurable FPGA fabric with an external clock of 100 MHz, and 1 GB DDR3 RAM at a frequency of 333 MHz. There are 41910 Logic Array Blocks (LABs), 112 Digital Signal Processors (DSPs), and 5 662 720 Memory Bits on the FPGA. The CPUs and the FPGA share the RAM. The board offers several interfaces like USB or Ethernet and runs a full-fledged Linux operating system. We measure the power consumption of the board while running a fully booted but otherwise idle operating system and get 2 W. The maximum power consumption is around 6 W for computing stereo-vision. We implemented all algorithms in OpenCL, taking advantage of PC OpenCL drivers and the Altera emulation environment for fast development and testing reiteration. All OpenCL kernels are put into Altera's OpenCL compiler, which generates Verilog code. Thus, each kernel is synthesized into a specialized IP core for the FPGA. Kernels are connected via so-called channels, which are hard-coded in the design. A single work item is executed per kernel (using `enqueueTask()`). Out-of-order queues allow a parallel execution of kernels, which are controlled by event objects. These cores are combined with the FPGA system project and synthesized into a single bitstream. At runtime, the OpenCL drivers on the SoC's ARM Linux host take care of reconfiguring the FPGA with the correct bitstream for the required kernels.

6   Evaluation

In this section, we evaluate the performance and resource consumption of the different kernels running on the FPGA or CPU. Afterwards, we use the KITTI-Benchmark [10] to consider the quality of the 6D field.

6.1   Performance and Resource Consumption

In Table 1, we show the resource consumption and performance of different components inside the 6D-Vision system. As input we use images of size 640 × 480. Additionally, we compare the performance against a CPU execution on a core of the ARM Cortex A9. We use equivalent algorithms, but we optimize them for CPU execution, e.g. we apply an 8-bit radix sort because it performs best on CPU. All execution times include OpenCL overhead. The memory accesses of the kernel itself are part of the kernel execution, hence are included in the measurements. While Stereo Matching and calculating flow features massively benefit from a FPGA-based acceleration, sorting is only slightly faster. An execution of the `Stereo Matcher` requires ∼3.6 ms and supports 32 disparities in half-pixel resolution. "Stereo total" comprises 8 calls of the `Stereo Matcher` because we consider 128 possible disparities and perform matching from both sides for the consistency check. "Flow total" includes 3-bit radix sort, because it offers the best trade off between resource consumption and execution time.

Table 1. Resource consumption and performance of different components.

Component	Time [ms] FPGA	CPU	Speed-Up
Stereo Total	28.7	3771.2	131
Flow Total	41.6	1067.7	25.7
Flow Features	3.6	867.6	241
Sort 2 bit	46.8	83.2	1.7
Sort 3 bit	32.3	83.2	2.5
Sort 4 bit	25.1	83.2	3.31
Flow Remove	3.6	18.4	5.6
Flow Match	2.1	107.3	56.1

Resource	Amount	Utilization
LABs	31,321	75%
DSP blocks	21	19%
Memory Bits	~1,011k	18%
RAM blocks	234	42%
Frequency	100 MHz	

The remaining CPU tasks such as fusion and filtering are much faster than tasks running on the FPGA. According to the performance measures, the optical flow is the slowest component of the 6D pipeline, hence each pipeline stage processes 24.0 frames per second. The latency of each frame is 78 ms.

Unfortunately, the current version of the OpenCL framework for the SoCrates II board has problems with scheduling too many OpenCL kernels in a short time which causes unexpected crashes. Despite the shared memory data have to be transfered between OpenCL buffers, which is not efficient yet. Some of above issues are resolved in the next version of the OpenCL framework. However, we are able to successfully use our design for gesture control. The goal is to find a dominant moving object in the scene as well as determining direction and speed (see Fig. 5a). Therefore, we calculate 6D points using our system and cluster them on the CPU. The cluster with the highest movement is considered as the dominant object i.e. the hand.

(a)   (b) Scene   (c) Resulting 6D field

Fig. 5. Detecting moving hand (a). A real-world traffic scene [10] (b+c). (Color figure online)

6.2   KITTI Benchmark

We use example sequences from the KITTI benchmark [10] to evaluate the density of the 6D field. In order to use our pipeline, we crop the original images of KITTI to size 640 × 375. Interestingly, the 6D field has a similar density than the flow map, hence stereo information was most of the time obtained where flow correspondences are found. The KITTI evaluation tool analyzes the quality of a totally dense 6D field, and applies simplistic interpolation for submitted fields

Table 2. Comparison of different approaches.

Method	Performance	Platform	KITTI benchmark				
			Rank	D1-all	D2-all	SF-all	Time
PRSM	–	1 core @ 2.5 GHz	1	4.26%	7.28%	9.43%	300 s
PCSF	–	GPU @ 2.0 GHz	7	8.46%	22.80%	33.02%	0.09 s
HWBSF	–	4 cores @ 3.5 GHz	10	20.12%	34.46%	46.02%	7 min
VSF	–	1 core @ 2.5 GHz	12	26.28%	57.08%	67.08%	125 min
Our approach	24 fps (640 × 480)	Socrates II	13	28.91%	80.64%	83,81%	0.08 s
[11]	20.15 fps (512 × 384)	Virtex 5	–	–	–	–	–
[1]	20 fps (320 × 240)	FPGA/GeForce GTX 480	–	–	–	–	–

that have a lower density. Therefore, it does not distinguish between points for that no 6D data is found and wrong results. D1 states the quality of the depth map, D2 of the flow map and SF for the 6D field. Low values are better. While we perform at least for stereo vision in a similar range compared to low-ranked desktop solutions, we perform poor for the 6D field because of the poor optical flow density (cf. Table 2). But only our approach in the KITTI ranking enables a high-performance execution on an embedded system, while the only similar one in terms of performance requires a high-end GPU.

An issue with KITTI benchmark is that accuracy is stated independent from found objects, hence there is no difference between points which are part of the row, and points that are part of obstacles. Approaches that uses smoothing can miss small objects in the scene but get a high accuracy value in the benchmark. This is caused by the small penalty for missing small objects. Therefore, we do a qualitative analysis which shows that our approach is useful for providing information about a traffic scene (see Fig. 5b, c). Objects in the scene can be found in the 6D field using a clustering of similar 6D vectors. A line connects points in the current frame with the same point seen at the previous frame and the color presents the distance, hence the velocity. Therefore, the relatively fast movement of the black car (red circle) is seen as red lines. Our approach is able to find the critical objects in the scene.

Compared to [11], our solution has a higher performance despite a slower clock rate and requires less power (10.56 W against 6 W). As they provide no accuracy evaluation, comparing the accuracy is not possible. Our approach also outperforms the solution of Wedel et al. in terms of performance. Results are difficult to compare, since they have not applied it on the KITTI benchmark.

7 Conclusion

In this paper, we have presented a high-performance 6D-Vision pipeline on a heterogeneous FPGA-based System on Chip. We discussed and introduced optimizations that allow to implement time critical tasks on a low-cost FPGA. Our pipeline processes stereo images at 24 frames per second. The resulting 6D field provides useful information about a traffic scene and is successfully used for gesture control.

References

1. Wedel, A., et al.: Stereoscopic scene flow computation for 3D motion understanding. Int. J. Comput. Vis. **95**(1), 29–51 (2011)
2. Badino, H., Kanade, T.: A head-wearable short-baseline stereo system for the simultaneous estimation of structure and motion. In: MVA, pp. 185–189 (2011)
3. Barranco, F., Tomasi, M., Diaz, J., Vanegas, M., Ros, E.: Parallel architecture for hierarchical optical flow estimation based on FPGA. IEEE Trans. Very Large Scale Integr. (VLSI) Syst. **20**(6), 1058–1067 (2012)
4. Rabe, C., Müller, T., Wedel, A., Franke, U.: Dense, robust, and accurate motion field estimation from stereo image sequences in real-time. In: Daniilidis, K., Maragos, P., Paragios, N. (eds.) ECCV 2010. LNCS, vol. 6314, pp. 582–595. Springer, Heidelberg (2010). doi:10.1007/978-3-642-15561-1_42
5. Claus, C., Laika, A., Jia, L., Stechele, W.: High performance FPGA based optical flow calculation using the census transformation. In: Intelligent Vehicles Symposium, pp. 1185–1190. IEEE (2009)
6. Franke, U., Rabe, C., Badino, H., Gehrig, S.: 6D-vision: fusion of stereo and motion for robust environment perception. In: Kropatsch, W.G., Sablatnig, R., Hanbury, A. (eds.) DAGM 2005. LNCS, vol. 3663, pp. 216–223. Springer, Heidelberg (2005). doi:10.1007/11550518_27
7. Hirschmüller, H., Buder, M., Ernst, I.: Memory efficient semi-global matching. ISPRS Ann. Photogramm. Remote Sens. Spat. Inf. Sci. **3**, 371–376 (2012)
8. Jin, M., Maruyama, T.: A fast and high quality stereo matching algorithm on FPGA. In: 22nd International Conference on Field Programmable Logic and Applications (FPL), pp. 507–510. IEEE (2012)
9. Koch, D., Torresen, J.: FPGASort: a high performance sorting architecture exploiting run-time reconfiguration on FPGAs for large problem sorting. In: Proceedings of the 19th ACM/SIGDA International Symposium on Field Programmable Gate Arrays, pp. 45–54. ACM (2011)
10. Menze, M., Geiger, A.: Object scene flow for autonomous vehicles. In: Conference on Computer Vision and Pattern Recognition (CVPR) (2015)
11. Sahlbach, H., Whitty, S., Ernst, R.: A high-performance dense block matching solution for automotive 6D-vision. In: Design, Automation Test in Europe Conference Exhibition, pp. 268–271, March 2012
12. Stein, F.: Efficient computation of optical flow using the census transform. In: Rasmussen, C.E., Bülthoff, H.H., Schölkopf, B., Giese, M.A. (eds.) DAGM 2004. LNCS, vol. 3175, pp. 79–86. Springer, Heidelberg (2004). doi:10.1007/978-3-540-28649-3_10
13. Tanabe, Y., Maruyama, T.: Fast and accurate optical flow estimation using FPGA. SIGARCH Comput. Archit. News **42**(4), 27–32 (2014)
14. Vogel, C., Schindler, K., Roth, S.: 3D scene flow estimation with a piecewise rigid scene model. Int. J. Comput. Vis. **115**(1), 1–28 (2015)
15. Xiao, D., Yang, Q., Yang, B., Wei, W.: Monocular scene flow estimation via variational method. Multimed. Tools Appl., 1–23 (2015). doi:10.1007/s11042-015-3091-6
16. Xu, L., Jia, J., Matsushita, Y.: Motion detail preserving optical flow estimation. IEEE Trans. Pattern Anal. Mach. Intell. **34**(9), 1744–1757 (2012)
17. Zbontar, J., LeCun, Y.: Stereo matching by training a convolutional neural network to compare image patches. CoRR abs/1510.05970 (2015). http://arxiv.org/abs/1510.05970

Hardware-Accelerated Radix-Tree Based String Sorting for Big Data Applications

Christopher Blochwitz[1][✉], Julian Wolff[1], Jan Moritz Joseph[3], Stefan Werner[2], Dennis Heinrich[2], Sven Groppe[2], and Thilo Pionteck[3]

[1] Institute of Computer Engineering, Universität zu Lübeck, Lübeck, Germany
{blochwitz,wolff}@iti.uni-luebeck.de
[2] Institute of Information Systems, Universität zu Lübeck, Lübeck, Germany
{werner,heinrich,groppe}@ifis.uni-luebeck.de
[3] Hardware-Oriented Technical Computer Science, Universität Magdeburg, Magdeburg, Germany
{jan.joseph,thilo.pionteck}@ovgu.de

Abstract. In this paper, a scalable hardware architecture for string sorting in the application field of Big Data is presented. Current hardware architectures focus on the acceleration of sorting small sets of data with a maximum string length. In contrast, we propose an FPGA-accelerated architecture based on Radix-Trees, which has the ability to sort large sets of strings without practical limitation of the string length. The Radix-Tree is parameterizable and so is the design, which enables the adaptation for application-specific properties, such as diversity of strings and size of the used alphabet. The scalable design has a hierarchical processing and memory architecture, which operate in parallel. Optimal parameters and configurations are evaluated by using a dataset of the Semantic Web, as an example of Big Data applications. The results are analyzed with a focus on throughput, memory requirement, and utilization. The hardware design is faster for all values of the radix parameter and achieves a maximum speed-up factor of 2.78 compared to a software system.

Keywords: Radix-Tree · Big data · Dictionary generation · Semantic web · String sorting · Field-programmable gate array

1 Introduction

The concept of Big Data is usually based on a huge amount of data produced by research, medicine, humans, etc. In most Big Data applications, string handling, storage, and sorting are important parts. For example the Semantic Web [13], where so called triples consisting of three unique Uniform Resource Identifiers (URI) are combined on the basis of string matching. However, the handling of such big data sets is very time-consuming and the software systems require many hardware resources for processing, analysis, and storage. For instance, the generation of a Semantic Web Database consisting of the btc-2009 datasets [1] with 830 million triples requires 30 h on a cluster of 6 Intel Core2Quad Q9400

© Springer International Publishing AG 2017
J. Knoop et al. (Eds.): ARCS 2017, LNCS 10172, pp. 47–58, 2017.
DOI: 10.1007/978-3-319-54999-6_4

computers and consumes about 100 GB of storage [6]. Therefore, efficient data handling and data structures are required.

One possibility of sorting strings is a tree-based data structure. Blochwitz et al. [2] propose a hardware-optimized Radix-Tree which has a simplified structure for a hardware compatible use case. The nodes have a well-defined structure with a fixed maximum number of children and fixed length of content. A hierarchical and scalable hardware design for Radix-Tree generation is proposed, which addresses Big Data applications. The time-consuming task of tree generation is accelerated by the hardware domain, which is evaluated by sorting datasets of the Semantic Web.

In this paper, we focus on a flexible and pipelined hardware architecture for string sorting, which uses internal and external memory, controller units, and two main processing units. The first processing unit builds small Radix-Trees in parallel and is called *Radix-Tree-Engine*. Afterwards, the Radix-Trees are merged by the second processing unit, called *Merge-Engine*. We use different memory types in a hierarchical structure: fast but small memory for local operations of the *Radix-Tree-Engine* and relatively slow but big memory (DDR4) for storing the merged Radix-Tree. The number of engines, number of memories, size of memories, and width of interfaces are parameterizable and designed to process the hardware-optimized Radix-Tree on a Xilinx Virtex Ultrascale. Different memories such as Block RAM, DDR, and SATA-SSD can be used for a scalable design. Therefore, a flexible and defined interface is required, which is realized by the integration of AXI-Interfaces. We evaluate the design on performance, memory requirement, and utilization, using a dataset of the billion triple challenge.

The paper is structured as follows: First, we provide an overview of related work, focusing on string sorting and tree generation for hardware architectures. Then, we summarize the essentials of the hardware-optimized Radix-Tree. Afterwards, we propose our hardware design, the main processing units (*Radix-Tree-Engine* and *Merge-Engine*), additional modules, interfaces, and parameters. Finally, we evaluate our design and discuss the results regarding performance and utilization for different parameters for the Radix-Tree and design.

2   Related Work

For some decades, there have been well-established string sorting trees for software systems. Morrison [10] initially presents a new algorithm for sorting strings in an alphanumerical order called: PATRICIA – Practical Algorithm To Retrieve Information Coded in Alphanumeric. This is the first publication dealing with a specialized data structure for sorting strings. He claims that the response is $O(n)$ with n equal to the size of the searched string and independent of the number of stored strings. Because trees require a lot of memory, Ferragina and Grossi [4] introduce a String B-Tree, which sorts strings by storing pointers to an external memory, where the string is stored. Because of the balanced B-Tree and the lightweight storing of pointers, the required memory accesses are reduced by a factor of 8. An adaptive Radix-Tree is described by Leis et al. [8], where only the required memory of the data structure is allocated without reservation for future data. The search performance is comparable with hash tables reducing the required memory by half.

There is also some work in the field of hardware-based string sorting for different types of applications and problem sizes. Marcelino et al. [9] compare different sorting algorithms for hardware implementations. For small data, the speed-up factor is about 80. Because of the limited number of internal memory, larger data sets must be processed by a hybrid system, which has a speed-up factor of 20 in contrast to a software approach on a Xilinx Microblaze softcore. Harkins et al. [7] also analyze different sorting algorithms on an FPGA system and the results show a gain of a factor of up to 2.75 compared to a node with two Intel Xeon 2.8 GHz CPUs and 1 GB main memory. A high performance hardware design for large-scale sorting for Big Data streaming applications is introduced by Srivastava et al. [11]. They use a hybrid sorting network consisting of serial merge networks and bitonic merge units in higher stages, which use internal memory. They theoretically analyze maximum throughput and latency of the sorting network. In comparison to the state-of-the-art implementation, they are 1.2 times faster, have a lower latency, and a better memory efficiency.

3   Radix-Tree

This work is part of a larger project in the field of Semantic Web Databases as an example of a Big Data application, where string sorting is important. The fundamental unit of the Semantic Web is a triple consisting of a subject, predicate, and object. A semantic context or graph is generated by combining triples. Typically, triples have a Uniform Resource Identifier (URI) style, which ensures a unique identification of the triple's components and are realized by string literals.

A Semantic Web Database is processed by specialized engines, which typically consist of two components. First, the database itself, where the triples are stored and, second, the query engine, which is responsible for queries. The generation of the database and the query processing evolve a huge amount of comparisons of triples. Hence, many read/write operations on the memory are required. The effort of comparing strings with an arbitrary length is high for hardware as well as for software systems. Therefore, it is important to convert the strings to a data structure with a fixed length, which will also reduce the number of memory accesses. Furthermore, the data structure must represent the alphanumerical order of the URIs. Therefore, integers are established, which map the set of strings to an incremental set of integers with a fixed bit width. This allows an efficient processing on hardware compared to the ASCII string representation with a variable length. Due to the string-integer mapping, a dictionary is needed for encoding and decoding.

3.1   An Optimized Radix-Tree

As mentioned above, the dictionary generation for a Semantic Web Database consisting of string-integer pairs in an alphanumerical order is very time-consuming and an efficient sorting is needed. For this, algorithms as well as data structures with a sorting ability are suitable. Well-established sorting data structures are trees. Especially for strings, the Radix-Tree is used. For two strings with a prefix length of n, the tree is forked and two child nodes are created, which is illustrated in Fig. 1a. One of the main benefits of the trees is the good compression especially for strings of the Semantic Web because URIs of the same context have long identical prefixes. For example, the prefix, as shown in Fig. 1a.

For software systems, tree-based data structures are common and well-known. A node has an unlimited content size and pointers to its child nodes. For a hardware design, nodes with a fixed maximum length m of the content and a defined number of children are required. The hardware-optimized Radix-Tree [2] has the required abilities and is based on a traditional Radix-Tree. As shown in Fig. 1b, the first node is split after the maximum content length of $m = 10$ into. The radix, which is the numeral base of the used alphabet defines the atomic block-size of bits which can not be split. Implicitly, it defines the number of children, because for every member of the alphabet, a fork is possible. The number of children is equal to 2^{radix}. As illustrated in Fig. 1c, the bit size of an ASCII character is 7-bit, which is a prime and, therefore, no multiple of the $radix = 2$. Hence, not all characters of a string are convertible into the block-size, and at the end, there are some remaining bits. In the example of string b, the remainder is 0 and for c, it is 1. All strings without a remainder are represented

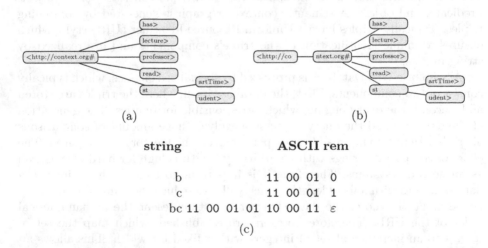

(a)   (b)

string	ASCII				rem
b	11	00	01		0
c	11	00	01		1
bc	11 00 01	01	10 00	11	ε

(c)

Fig. 1. (a) A Radix-Tree with six elements. (b) A hardware-optimized Radix-Tree with six elements and a maximum content length of $m = 10$. (c) Example strings, their meaning in ASCII coding grouped by two bits as the $radix = 2$. The bits marked in bold are not elements of the alphabet. This remainder is stored in the node data structure in the *isEndFlag* [2].

with the end-symbol ε, as shown in Fig. 1c for the string *bc*. For this reason, a node of the hardware-optimized Radix-Tree has $2^{radix} - 1$ *isEndFlag* bits. This also means that one end node can include multiple strings. Both the radix as well as the maximum content length m are parameterizable and, therefore, can be used for different use cases, scalable for different memories and processing units.

4   Hardware Architecture

The proposed design provides string sorting for Big Data applications, which offloads the hard workload of the generation of Radix-Trees to the hardware. The design has a pipelined architecture with two stages. First, the *Radix-Tree-Engine*, which generates Radix-Trees out of the received strings. Multiple *Radix-Tree-Engines* can be implemented, which work in parallel and increase the throughput. The *Radix-Tree-Engines* are connected to Block RAM modules to store the trees. The Block RAM modules can be bound flexibly on the engines and work as a buffer between *Radix-Tree-Engine* and *Merge-Engine*. Second, the *Merge-Engine*, which is connected to a large external memory merges small Radix-Trees from the Block RAM modules into the large memory. The input data of the merging process consists of nodes and, therefore, only node-based operations such as splitting are required and a high percentage of the time is used to copy sub-trees by fast bursts. Both *Radix-Tree-Engine* and *Merge-Engine* are independent and work in parallel.

The design overview is given in Fig. 2, where the data flow is from the left to the right side. At first, there is the Xillybus PCIe interconnect [3], which manages the data from the host system followed by the first main unit, the *Radix-Tree-Engine*. The next unit is a crossbar for Block RAM modules with a controller, which manages the control signals to the engines. On the other port of the dual port Block RAM, an AXI-Controller is implemented, which is connected to an AXI-Interconnect and, therefore, to the second main unit, the *Merge-Engine*. Finally, the external memory (e.g. DDR4) is connected to the right side of the *Merge-Engine*, where the final Radix-Tree is stored. The number of *Radix-Tree-*

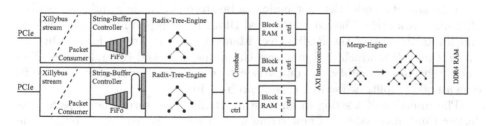

Fig. 2. An overview of the pipelined and scalable design. The *Radix-Tree-Engine* of the first stage is placed on the left. In the middle the internal Block RAM and interconnects and on the right, the *Merge-Engine* as the second stage is shown.

Engines and Block RAM modules is parameterizable, which allows a scalable and flexible design.

4.1   Xillybus and Packet-Consumer

The communication between the host system and the FPGA is realized by a PCIe connection. The used IP core is called Xillybus [3] and provides multiple FIFOs for different datastreams, which allows an independent and flexible use of the *Radix-Tree-Engines*. In our use case, a FIFO is connected to a *Packet-Consumer* (Fig. 2), which belongs to a dedicated *Radix-Tree-Engine*. The *Packet-Consumer* manages the flow control of the FIFO, extracts the packet, and hands over the string to the *Radix-Tree-Engine*. This design allows to send packets to a *Radix-Tree-Engine* consisting of a single string and the string's length.

4.2   String-Buffer Controller

The *String-Buffer Controller* is placed between the *Packet-Consumer* and the *Radix-Tree-Engine* consisting of a FIFO and a shift register, as shown in Fig. 2. The FIFO adapts the width of the Xillybus stream to the content length m, which is required by the *Radix-Tree-Engine*. At any time, only one string is stored in the *String-Buffer FIFO*, which is assigned by the *Packet-Consumer*. The *Radix-Tree-Engine* consumes various leading characters with a maximum size of m, the content length. Therefore, a shift register is required which shifts the string by the size of the consumed substring. The size of the FIFO is given by the longest string, which must be stored. In our case, the data set of the billion triple challenge is used whose longest string has a size of 65.244 characters [5].

4.3   Radix-Tree-Engine

The *Radix-Tree-Engine* is one of two main units. It generates small Radix-Trees out of strings. The Radix-Tree is stored in the Block RAM module, which can be seen in Fig. 2 on the left side. The Block RAM provides memory access in every clock cycle and, therefore, a low latency and high throughput. The width of the Block RAM module is parametrized with e.g. 256 bit, which is equal or greater than the size of a node. Hence, a node can be stored in one line and is accessible after one clock cycle. The size of the used Block RAM is parameterizable as well and limits the size of the Radix-Tree. Memory accesses are performed by the *rd/wr Controller*, which also manages the filling level and free addresses. The clock frequency is doubled in comparison to the *Radix-Tree-Engine* because in case a node is split, two write accesses are required.

The insertion of a string in an existing Radix-Tree starts when the *String-Buffer Controller* receives a new string and provides the leading m bits to the *Radix-Tree-Engine*, which is called further *compare string*. The engine reads the root node from the Block RAM and calculates the prefix length of the node's content and the *compare string*. If it is a prefix of the *compare string*, the next child node is read and the *compare string* is shifted by the *String-Buffer Controller* by the value of the prefix length. The comparison is repeated child by child until the comparison is false. The remaining string is inserted in new nodes and, if needed, an existing node is split. Afterwards, the *String-Buffer Controller* is ready to receive a new string.

4.4 Merge-Engine

The second main unit is the *Merge-Engine*, which merges smaller Radix-Trees into a bigger one. In Fig. 2 on the left side of the *Merge-Engine*, the Block RAM modules are illustrated, which store small Radix-Trees, and on the right side, the bigger destination memory is shown. The memories on the left and right side are connected to separate controllers via the AXI-Interface. The AXI-Interface provides a flexible and scalable integration of different Intellectual Property Cores especially memory controllers for Block RAM, DDR, and SATA. The address spaces are managed by Xilinx's Vivado. The *Merge-Engine* has two stack memories, which are used to traverse each of the two radix trees. The size of the stack is defined by the depth of the Radix-Tree and contains the nodes from the root up to the current node. Also a memory for translation between the two address domains of the left and right memory is implemented as well as a unit, which manages the free space on the right memory.

The process of merging starts by assigning a new Block RAM to the *Merge-Engine*, which contains a Radix-Tree. The root node of both sides are read and stored into the two associated stacks. The node's content is compared and if it is unequal, one of these two strings is split at the position of the calculated prefix length. Otherwise and after the split, the end flags and children are merged. To merge children, there are two possible cases: First, the node on the right side has no children at this specific position. Then, the children with their full sub-tree of the left side can be copied by a fast burst. In the second case, the position of the children is occupied, then, both children will be read and put on the stacks. This process is performed recursively until the left Radix-Tree is merged completely into the right one.

5 Evaluation

For a structured evaluation of the design, this section starts with a description of the used parameters, configurations, and data set. Afterwards, the performance and memory requirements of the design are evaluated and finally the device utilization is presented. The performance of the hardware is compared to a lightweight C++ implementation of a Radix-Tree without a limitation in the string length and only one end flag per node. The software implementation uses the standard character and string operations. Hence, an ASCII coding with a $radix = 8$ is used. We evaluate a random part of a real dataset from the billion triple challenge 2014 [12]. The full data set consists of 4 billion triples and 1.1 TB of unzipped data. We use datasets with a size between 100 and 1 million strings and an 8 bit ASCII coding.

The server where the Semantic Web Database engine and benchmarks are processed consists of an Intel Xeon E3-1226v3 with 4x 3.30 GHz, 32 GB of DDR3 memory, and the Xilinx FPGA VCU108 Evaluation Kit with a Virtex UltraScale XCVU095 FPGA, 144 MB RLDRAM3, 2x 2.5 GB DDR4 memory (only 2 GB are accessible, the remaining 0.5 GB are reserved for ECC), a PCIe Gen3 x8 connector, and other peripherals. The operating system is CentOS 7 and Xilinx Vivado 2016.2 is used for synthesis. Software benchmarks are repeated 100 times to eliminate side effects like scheduling and background tasks and processed on a single core.

5.1　Evaluated Parameter

In a previous work, we proposed the hardware-optimized Radix-Tree and found optimal candidates of parameters for the Semantic Web application. It shows that a small $radix = 1$ to 4 is good and the *maximum content length* can be chosen by other constraints such as required bit width of interfaces or device utilization.

Hence, we create multiple test systems with different parameters of the radix and fix the *content length* to $m = 128$ for a fair comparison of the radix in performance and utilization. The required space for a single node with the content from radix 1 to 4 is 210, 224, 312, and 448 bits, which results in a bit width of 224, 256, 320, and 448 of the interface of the internal Block RAM.

5.2　Design Configuration

As mentioned above, the design is flexible and scalable and consists of two stages, which work in parallel. The execution time is measured with a custom and cycle accurate timing module. For an optimal evaluation, both the *Radix-Tree-Engine* and the *Merge-Engine* are evaluated separately. The memory requirements for a Radix-Tree are recorded by the memory controller of each engine. The latency of the PCIe core is negligible because of the streaming characteristic of the design. The two configurations for evaluation are designed as follows:

Radix-Tree-Engine: The *Radix-Tree-Engine* is implemented as shown in Fig. 2 on the left. The data path to the host is realized by PCIe and the engine is connected to an internal Block RAM with a depth of 65 k.

Merge-Engine: In this case, the configuration of the *Radix-Tree-Engine* is extended by the external DDR4 memory with 2 GB. As illustrated in Fig. 2, the *Merge-Engine* is connected to the second port of the Block RAM module and the DDR4 memory via a separate *AXI controller*.

5.3　Performance Radix-Tree-Engine

In this section, the *Radix-Tree-Engine* with different values of the $radix = \{1, 2, 3, 4\}$ is compared with a lightweight software implementation of a Radix-Tree. The number of inserted strings is up to 100 k and is limited by the number of lines of the *Block RAM Module* of 65 k. As mentioned in Sect. 2, the time

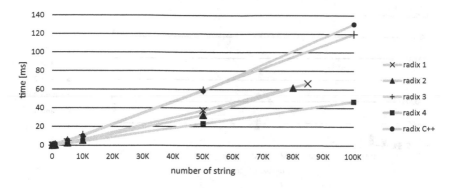

Fig. 3. Time of Radix-Tree generation in relation to the string number

complexity of a single string insertion into a Radix-Tree is $O(1)$ and the generation of a full Radix-Tree with n strings is $O(n)$. In Fig. 3, the execution time in μs is compared to the number of inserted strings of a dataset of the billion triple challenge. It can be seen, that the expected linear dependence between execution time and string number is present. For any configuration and string number, the hardware-optimized Radix-Tree is faster than the software implementation. The counted clock cycles are decreasing the higher the radix, because the tree is flat and, therefore, the number of steps to the last node respectively the memory accesses are fewer. When taking frequency (see Table 1) into account, the differences become smaller between $radix = \{1, 2, 4\}$. The $radix = 3$ is significantly slower, because the clock frequency is nearly halved. That is caused by a couple of VHDL processes of the prefix calculation, where division and multiplication is used. For a radix equal to 2^n, shifts can be used, which is much faster.

5.4 Performance Merge-Engine

The performance of the *Merge-Engine* depends mainly on three things: First, the characteristic of the Radix-Tree, which is evaluated in Subsect. 5.3. Second, the bit width of the Block RAM module. Hence, the AXI interface has a fixed width and the data must be serialized, which requires additional clock cycles. Third, the percentage of disjunction of the Radix-Trees. The tested dataset has no big percentage of presorted strings and, therefore, the generation time increases linearly. This behavior is demonstrated in Fig. 4. Because of a higher AXI latency and clock frequency, the time difference between the hardware implementations is smaller. The influence of the radix parameter on performance is not as big as on the *Radix-Tree-Engine*. Further, to achieve a higher speed-up, presorting strategies must be evaluated.

5.5 Memory Requirement

In Fig. 5, the required memory of a Radix-Tree in relation to the number of strings is shown. For comparison, the required space of the software Radix-

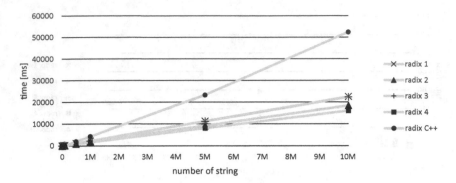

Fig. 4. Time of merging Radix-Trees in relation to the string number

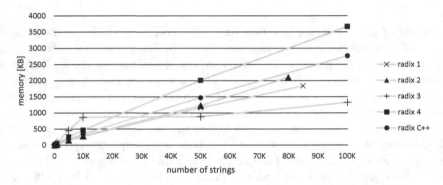

Fig. 5. Memory requirement of radix trees in relation to the string number

Tree is also included. The software implementation uses dynamic data structures for storing child-pointers and, therefore, a minimum of memory is required. As expected, the size of the tree grows linearly with the number of strings, except for the hardware-optimized Radix-Tree with a $radix = 3$. As mentioned above, the maximum content length is fixed to $m = 128$ for all configurations. Therefore, only the radix influences the memory requirement of a hardware-optimized Radix-Tree. In general, a higher radix requires more memory because of the additional child-pointers and *isEndFlags*, which can be seen in Fig. 5. In comparison to the software implementation, a $radix = \{1, 2\}$ requires less memory and in contrast, a tree with a $radix = 4$ requires more than the software. The unexpected behavior of the memory requirement of a $radix = 3$ is caused by the characteristic of the hardware-optimized Radix-Tree, which has multiple *isEndFlags*. This is the only configuration where the radix is no divider of single characters, which has 8 bit. Therefore, multiple *isEndFlags* of one node are used in parallel and not only the ε of the *isEndFlags*. This characteristic of the hardware-optimized Radix-Tree allows a better memory requirement by choosing a good value of the radix in dependency to the the used data. The used

Table 1. Utilization of the Radix-Tree-Engine ($m = 128$) and clock frequency.

Radix	LUT		FlipFlop		Block RAM		Clk MHz
	abs	%	abs	%	abs	%	
Total	537,600		1,075,200		1,728		
1	8,459	1.57	2,341	0.22	15.5	0.9	94.5
2	8,730	1.62	2,545	0.24	15.5	0.9	90.9
3	11,417	2.12	2,951	0.27	15.5	0.9	44.6
4	12,458	2.32	4,084	0.38	15.5	0.9	84,7

Table 2. Utilization of the Merge-Engine

Radix	LUT		FlipFlop		Block RAM		Clk MHz
	abs	%	abs	%	abs	%	
Total	537,600		1,075,200		1,728		
1	13825	2.6	4008	0.4	103	6.0	120.6
2	18483	3.4	4781	0.4	109	6.3	111.5
3	24569	4.6	6428	0.6	120	6.9	79.6
4	37586	7.0	9720	0.9	141	8.2	70.3

strings are part of the billion triple challenge and are very similar to each other. Therefore the probability for storing multiple ends in a node is very high.

5.6 Utilization

The utilizations for a *Radix-Tree-Engine*, *Merge-Engine*, and interface modules are analyzed by choosing different values of the radix parameter, which influences the required interface width and, therefore, the register and operator size in hardware. Table 1, shows the utilization of a *Radix-Tree-Engine* for different values of the radix. The total amount of resources of the FPGA is given in Table 1, as well as the absolute and relative used resource. The utilization of LUT and register increases linearly with the radix parameter and the Block RAM is constant because the input buffer and a FIFO in the *PacketConsumer* only depends on the maximum content length, which is fixed to $m = 128$.

The utilization of the *Merge-Engine* is shown in Table 2. Overall, the required resources are higher compared to the *Radix-Tree-Engine*. Also the increasing of resources is higher and non linear. The reason could be the higher influence of the node size, in the engine as well as in the AXI controllers. The address mapping of the *Merge-Engine* requires a relatively high number of Block RAMs but is constant. The stacks are also realized by Block RAMs, which are increasing with the radix, because the nodes to store are wider.

6   Conclusion

In this paper, we presented a scalable hardware architecture for string sorting in the field of Big Data applications based on the hardware-optimized Radix-Tree. The engine is faster for higher radix values and achieves a maximum speed-up is 2.78 for a $radix = 4$. The required memory for a Radix-Tree is optimal for a $radix = 3$, because the feature of multiple *isEndFlags* are used. For the other cases, the required memory is increasing with the radix. An optimal radix parameter can be chosen by a low memory requirement ($radix = 3$) or high performance ($radix = 4$). For the field of Big Data, a high performance is important and therefore, we will focus on a $radix = 4$ and expand our design with multiple *Radix-Tree-Engines* and a hierarchical design with multiple external memories. The integration of multiple *Radix-Tree-Engines* allows different data streams, for example a disjunct set of strings. Therefore, the *Merge-Engine* can process in the fast copy mode more often.

References

1. Harth, A.: Billion triples challenge data set (2012)
2. Blochwitz, C., Joseph, J.M., Backasch, R., Pionteck, T., Werner, S., Heinrich, D., Groppe, S.: An optimized radix-tree for hardware-accelerated dictionary generation for semantic web databases. In: 2015 International Conference on ReConFigurable Computing and FPGAs (ReConFig), pp. 1–7 (2015)
3. Billauer, E.: Xillybus (2016)
4. Ferragina, P., Grossi, R.: The string B-tree: a new data structure for string search in external memory and its applications. J. ACM **46**(2), 236–280 (1999)
5. Grimnes, G.A.: (Still) Nothing clever – Billion Triple Challenge (2009)
6. Groppe, S.: Data Management and Query Processing in Semantic Web Databases. Springer, Heidelberg (2011)
7. Harkins, J., El-Ghazawi, T., El-Araby, E., Huang, M.: Performance of sorting algorithms on the SRC 6 reconfigurable computer. In: 2005 IEEE International Conference on Field-Programmable Technology, pp. 295–296 (2005)
8. Leis, V., Kemper, A., Neumann, T.: The adaptive radix tree: ARTful indexing for main-memory databases. In: 2013 29th IEEE International Conference on Data Engineering (ICDE 2013), pp. 38–49 (2013)
9. Marcelino, R., Neto, H.C., Cardoso, J.M.P.: A comparison of three representative hardware sorting units. In: IECON 2009–35th Annual Conference of IEEE Industrial Electronics (IECON), pp. 2805–2810 (2009)
10. Morrison, D.R.: PATRICIA–practical algorithm to retrieve information coded in alphanumeric. J. ACM **15**(4), 514–534 (1968)
11. Srivastava, A., Chen, R., Prasanna, V.K., Chelmis, C.: A hybrid design for high performance large-scale sorting on FPGA. In: 2015 International Conference on ReConFigurable Computing and FPGAs (ReConFig), pp. 1–6 (2015)
12. Käfer, T., Harth, A.: Billion triples challenge data set (2014)
13. World Wide Web Consortium. Semantic Web - W3C (2011)

Boosting Java Performance Using GPGPUs

James Clarkson$^{(\boxtimes)}$, Christos Kotselidis, Gavin Brown, and Mikel Luján

School of Computer Science, University of Manchester, Manchester, UK
{james.clarkson,christos.kotselidis,gavin.brown,
mikel.lujan}@manchester.ac.uk

Abstract. In this paper we describe Jacc, an experimental framework which allows developers to program GPGPUs directly from Java. The goal of Jacc, is to allow developers to benefit from using heterogeneous hardware whilst minimizing the amount of code refactoring required. Jacc utilizes two key abstractions: *tasks* which encapsulate all the information needed to execute code on a GPGPU; and *task graphs* which capture both inter-task control-flow and data dependencies. These abstractions enable the Jacc runtime system to automatically choreograph data movement and synchronization between the host and the GPGPU; eliminating the need to explicitly manage disparate memory spaces. We demonstrate the advantages of Jacc, both in terms of programmability and performance, by evaluating it against existing Java frameworks. Experimental results show an average performance speedup of 19x, using NVIDIA Tesla K20m GPU, and a 4x decrease in code complexity when compared with writing multi-threaded Java code across eight evaluated benchmarks.

1 Introduction

Heterogeneous programming languages, such as CUDA [2] and OpenCL [3], enable developers to execute portions of their code on specialized hardware. Typically, this involves offloading work from a *host* onto a *device* such as a GPGPU, and doing this requires developers to be mindful of the different *contexts* their code may execute on. Hence, the developer is burdened with writing the application and the extra code to manage its execution over disparate devices. This paper describes a programming framework (JIT compiler and run-time system), which has been designed to eliminate, or automate, a large amount of this responsibility to help reduce the burden placed on developers.

Current established heterogeneous programming languages, such as CUDA and OpenCL, require developers to logically separate their applications into code that runs either on the host or on the device (known as a *kernel*). As a consequence, these approaches require additional code to co-ordinate execution between the host and kernels.

This paper describes a simplified heterogeneous programming model in the context of the Java language. We make use of implicit parallelism and task-based parallel execution. The **J**ava **Acc**eleration system, hereafter Jacc, is inspired by and shares many similarities with directive-based approaches such as OpenMP

© Springer International Publishing AG 2017
J. Knoop et al. (Eds.): ARCS 2017, LNCS 10172, pp. 59–70, 2017.
DOI: 10.1007/978-3-319-54999-6_5

4.0 [15]. However, the true benefits of Jacc are derived from the Java programming language: modular, statically typed code and dynamic compilation. Thus, a Jacc application does not need to be ported across different operating systems or hardware devices and it is possible to compose complex processing pipelines from existing code. Overall the paper makes the following contributions:

(1) Provides an overview of Jacc, its components, and design rationale.
(2) Discusses how Jacc can be used to write concise data-parallel code in Java and the sub-set of the Java language supported.
(3) Analyzes the implementation of the internal components of Jacc. The Jacc JIT compiler, unlike most prior work, compiles Java bytecode directly to PTX code which can be executed directly by NVidia drivers.
(4) Provides an in-depth comparative performance analysis of Jacc and standard Java multi-threaded benchmarks.

2   The Jacc Framework

Jacc is a Java based framework which simplifies the programming of heterogeneous hardware. At present, we have been able to use Jacc to program a wide range of devices such as multi-core processors, Xeon Phi, and both embedded and discrete GPGPUs. In this paper we describe our initial prototype that has been developed to program CUDA enabled GPGPUs. As depicted in Fig. 1, the two major components of Jacc are: its API and the runtime system.

The Jacc API has been designed to make possible the creation of high performance data-parallel code without forcing developers to, unnecessarily, change their software engineering practices. In order to support the API, Jacc has a runtime system that is able to manage the execution of application code on disparate hardware. This typically requires support for generating and executing

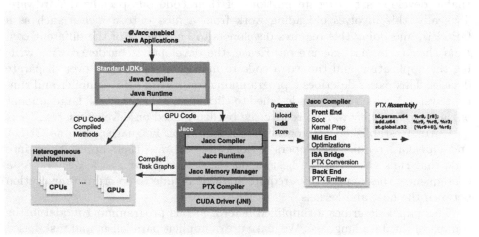

Fig. 1. Jacc system overview.

code, moving data between devices, and synchronization. Using both components together, Jacc is able to automate and optimize many common housekeeping tasks involved in writing heterogeneous code; relieving the developer from a number of burdens that exist in languages such as CUDA and OpenCL.

The API is built on top of two basic abstractions: the *task* and the *task graph*. A task encapsulates all the information needed to perform some action on a disparate hardware device such as code execution, data transfers or synchronization. Hence, a task which executes some code will encapsulate: a reference to the code, references to all the data accessed by the code and some *meta-data*. The meta-data is used to pass task specific parameters to the runtime system - such as the device it should execute on, the number of threads, or the size of each thread group, allowing dynamic adaption of those parameters during runtime.

Tasks which perform data transfers and synchronization are implicitly handled by the runtime system - leaving the developer responsible for defining only those which execute code. These tasks can be created from any method in the application. Furthermore, their meta-data contain a mapping which associates each one of them with the device it should execute on. Typically, this mapping is defined when a task is inserted into a task graph, but as it is just an entry in their meta-data it can also be updated dynamically.

Executing tasks on a GPGPU requires a number of actions to be performed: compilation, data movement to the GPGPU, execution on the GPGPU, and data movement back to the host. Although this can be done synchronously, it is inefficient to execute tasks in this manner - especially when multiple tasks operate on shared data. To make task execution more efficient, Jacc provides the *task graph* abstraction - a mechanism which allows the runtime system to optimize task execution through lazy evaluation. After a task graph is created, the runtime system uses its meta-data to build an executable *directed acyclic graph* (DAG). Once built, the runtime system is able to optimize the DAG by inspecting task meta-data to remove redundant data transfers and re-organize the order in which tasks are executed.

Jacc exploits many features of the Java platform in order to simplify the development workflow. The GPGPU code is directly generated from Java bytecode which avoids the need to either: embed source code inside the application, like OpenCL, or re-parse the source code. This means that the code running on the GPGPU is created using a single type system, unlike OpenCL which introduces a second type system to the developer.

2.1   Writing Data Parallel Code

There are two ways in which developers can write parallel code: explicitly or implicitly. Although the Jacc framework supports both, implicit parallelism is strongly encouraged since the code will produce the same result whether executed serially or in parallel. This provides Jacc with the option to revert back to serial execution if an error is encountered whilst offloading onto the GPGPU.

Jacc provides an annotation based API, similar to OpenMP, which allows developers to statically define task meta-data. However, unlike OpenMP this meta-data can also be provided or adapted dynamically at runtime. For instance, information such as the parallelization strategy and type of variable access, specified by the @Jacc, @Read, @Write and @ReadWrite annotations, is better defined statically. In certain circumstances it may be beneficial to override these settings - for example to ensure data is always fetched from the host and not cached on the GPGPU or if a specific device responds better to a different parallelization scheme. The only aspects of the API which cannot be overridden are the ones which directly influence code generation, such as @Atomic or @Shared, as they are embedded directly into Java bytecode.

To produce data-parallel code, the Jacc compiler has the ability to re-write certain classes of loop-nests so that each iteration of a loop is executed by a different thread. This can be done by adding to a method the @Jacc annotation and setting the iterationSpace parameter. The iteration space parameter defines how many levels of the loop-nest should be re-written. (e.g. A value of 2 will re-write the two outermost loops.) Since it is not possible to use annotations at a sub-method granularity in Java 7, the Jacc compiler will only parallelize the first loop-nest encountered in a method[1].

As some loop-nests communicate data between iterations, Jacc provides the ability to perform inter-thread communications via shared memory atomics. A field can be declared as @Atomic which forces the compiler to use atomic operations when reading from and writing to this field. To support reduction operations, it is possible to specify an operation that can be applied in each update of the field. In this case, the field is initialized with a default value at the start of execution and then updated with the result of applying the operation to the existing and incoming values.

In cases where it is impossible to express a kernel using a single loop-nest, the developer has two choices: to split functionality across multiple kernels or to manually parallelize the code similarly to CUDA and OpenCL. The advantage of the latter approach is that developers can create highly optimized parallel code for a specific device. Unfortunately, this comes at the expense of reduced code re-use as Java applications cannot readily use this code.

Figure 2 (right) provides an example of how the data-parallel code is written while Fig. 2 (left) demonstrates how a task is created and scheduled using a task-graph. Initially, we want each iteration of the outermost loop to be executed by independent threads — each thread will read a single element of the array and accumulate the value in result. To achieve this, a parallelization strategy is selected in line four, using the @Jacc annotation, to specify that only the outermost loop should be parallelized. Finally, to handle the accumulation of partial results in the result variable, line 11, we use the @Atomic annotation which instructs the compiler to update this variable atomically.

In order to execute this code on a GPGPU, we need to define a task, add it to a task-graph, and schedule it. This is shown in Fig. 2 (left) where the task is defined in lines 1–11. In this case, the task-graph consists of a single task which has been mapped onto the GPGPU. The number of threads used and the

---

[1] This problem is resolved in Java 8.

```
1  DeviceContext gpgpu =                    public class Reduction {
2   Cuda.getDevice(0).createContext();        @Atomic(op=ADD) float result;
3
4  Reduction r = new Reduction(...);         @Jacc(iterationSpace=ONE_DIMENSION)
5  Task task = Task.create(                  public void reduction(
6     Reduction.class,methodName,              @Read float[] array) {
7     new Dims(array.length),                   float sum=0;
8     new Dims(BLOCK_SIZE));                     for(int i=0;i<array.length;i++) {
9                                                  sum+=array[i];
10 task.setParameters(r, data);                 }
11 tasks = new TaskGraph() {                    result=sum;
12   @Override                                }
13   public void create() {                 }
14     executeTaskOn(task, gpgpu);
15   }
16 }
17 tasks.execute();
```

Fig. 2. Left: Reduction by generating a TaskGraph, Right: Reduction operation using implicit parallelism.

dimensions of each thread group are defined in lines 7–8, where `array.length` threads are specified - one for each iteration of the loop. On invoking the `execute` method of the task-graph, the runtime system will: compile the code for the GPGPU, move data to the GPGPU, execute the code, and synchronize the data between the host and the GPGPU.

2.2 Current Subset of Java Supported for Execution on GPGPUs

Objects: Jacc provides object support and is able to freely access fields and invoke methods on objects or classes[2]. Jacc is not integrated directly with the garbage collector and, thus, it only supports the manipulation of existing objects on the GPGPU. However, due to escape analysis, stack allocated objects can be freely accessed. In practise, we have found that most tasks amenable for GPGPU offloading perform some form of volume reduction and object creation is often not needed. At present we do not maintain object headers in order to reduce storage requirements and improve serialization times. Consequently, we do not yet support reflection or the `instanceof` keyword[3].

Arrays: Use of arrays of primitives, objects and multi-dimensional arrays is supported as long as the element type is not an interface.

Virtual and Static Method Calls: Practically, the aggressive use of inlining removes all method calls except polymorphic calls which introduce indirection into the generated code. Tasks can be created from either static or virtual methods. The only difference between these two, is that the developer must remember to insert the `this` object reference as the first task parameter. The advantage of virtual methods is that the `this` object reference neatly encapsulates state that needs to be shared among multiple kernels.

---

[2] However, this can easily lead to a large number of indirect-memory accesses in the generated code - which will degrade performance on a GPGPU.

[3] There is no technical reason why support can not be added at a later date.

Memory Allocations: Jacc is able to support the new keyword under certain circumstances. The compiler will try to inline the constructor and any memory is allocated on the stack. Additionally, the use of inlining enables the elimination of a number of field accesses using scalar replacement. If the developer wishes to allocate memory in a certain memory space, the variable must be declared as a field with the declaration using the annotation specifying the memory space.

Assertions and Exceptions: Jacc has the ability to handle assertions and some limited exception checking on the GPGPU. Exception checks such as null pointer and array index out of bounds can be inserted by the compiler. If the runtime system detects that an exception has been thrown, it will attempt to run the same code within the JVM to produce a valid stack trace.

3   Runtime System

3.1   JIT Compiler

The Jacc JIT compiler, shown in Fig. 1, unlike most prior work compiles Java bytecode directly to PTX code which can be executed directly by NVidia drivers. The compiler is organized in three layers: the front-end - responsible for parsing bytecode; the mid-end - responsible for transforming and optimizing the code for data-parallel execution; and the back-end - responsible for emitting the GPGPU specific machine-code. The front-end of the compiler has been implemented using the SOOT framework [17]. It generates various levels of IR from Java bytecode and leverages a number of advanced optimizations (e.g. common sub-expression elimination, loop invariant code motion, copy propagation, constant folding, straightening, and dead code elimination).

Initially, the IR is augmented with information about kernel entry points, exception handlers, and sets up accesses to the different memory spaces. Next, an optional transformation performs parallelization - this involves searching for loop-nests and updating the schedule of their induction variables so that iterations are assigned to different threads. This update is dependent on the value of the iterationSpace parameter specified in the meta-data of each task[4]. After parallelization, the remainder of the mid-end aims to generate high quality data-parallel code through a set of optimizations.

To optimize away costly functions calls, we search the IR for call-sites which map directly onto hardware instructions and replace them with appropriate intrinsics. If it is not possible to substitute a specific call-site, the compiler then tries to inline the code. If inlining is deemed infeasible the compiler will generate the code to support the call. If the compiler is unable to determine the actual method invoked at a particular call-site, the compilation will be terminated with an exception. Additionally, the compiler tries to minimize the number of branches in the IR. For example, it attempts to fully exploit the fact that PTX

---

[4] In our experience, the majority of kernels that we could not auto-parallelize using this scheme was due containing multiple loop-nests.

supports predicated execution by replacing simple branch statements with predicated instructions.

The mid-end is also responsible for handling code which access variables that are stored in different memory spaces or use shared memory atomics. Data-flow analyses are used to discover which loads/stores access a particular memory space and templated code is used to handle the initialization and update of variables accessed using atomics.

After passing through the mid-end, the IR goes through a lowering process which converts each statement of the IR into lower-level IR statements which generate one or more PTX instructions — this is marked as the ISA bridge. Finally, the PTX emitter converts each statement into valid PTX instructions.

3.2 Memory Management

As a prerequisite to execution, data must be pre-loaded into the GPGPU memory by a memory manager (an instance is assigned to each device). To enable Jacc to target as many devices as possible, we have taken the decision that the Jacc runtime should be responsible for explicitly managing GPGPU memory; opposed to using CUDA's unified memory — as it is not yet available on all devices. This also has the secondary advantage of allowing Jacc to optimize data layout on a per-device basis. Typically, Jacc is able to avoid copying un-used data and minimizes the number of indirect memory accesses in the code. Hence, the memory manager is responsible for maintaining a custom data layout scheme. The format used is built dynamically, in concert between the memory manager and the compiler, and is communicated to the compiler and data serializer via a *data schema*. The generated schema maps each element of a composite type onto a specific memory location (relative to a given address). If the runtime system wishes to transfer data to the GPGPU it must serialize each object according to the schema provided by the memory manager.

A key design goal of Jacc is the ability to allow data to persist on the GPGPU. This feature makes possible to have multiple tasks or even task-graphs operate on the same data - avoiding the continual need to transfer data between host and device. However, as Jacc is unable to determine whether an object has been modified on the JVM, the developer is responsible for maintaining the state of persistent data. Typically, Jacc ensures shared state remains consistent by blocking until the task-graph has finished executing, at which point the memory managers will have synchronized any modified data with the host.

Generally, variables or arrays of primitive types can be copied "as-is" and composite types are laid out according to the data schema provided by each device manager. In order to tackle the data serialization process of objects, we developed a novel compiler driven approach that dynamically builds data schemas during compilation. A schema starts empty, and as compilation progresses and new composite-types are discovered, dynamic new data schemas are built with on-demand object references. This minimizes the number of objects transferred to the device during data serialization[5].

4   Evaluation

The experimental hardware platform used has two Intel Xeon E5-2620 processors (12 cores/24 threads total @2.0 GHz), 32 GB of RAM and a NVIDIA Tesla K20m GPGPU with 5 GB of memory. Regarding the experimental software stack, CentOS 6.5, CUDA 6.5 and Java SDK 1.7.0_25 were used. All CUDA implementations are taken from the CUDA SDK except the matrix multiplications: SGEMM is taken from the cuBLAS library and SPMV from cuSPARSE. The benchmarks used for the performance evaluation are:

Vector Addition adds two 16,777,216 element vectors (300 iterations).

Reduction performs a summation over an array of 33,554,432 elements (500 iterations).

Histogram produces frequency counts for 16,777,216 values placing the results into 256 distinct bins (400 iterations).

Dense Matrix Multiplication of two 1024×1024 matrices (400 iterations)[6].

Sparse Matrix Vector Multiplication performs a sparse matrix-vector multiplication using a 44609×44609 matrix with 1029655 non-zeros (The bcsstk32 matrix from Matrix Market) (400 iterations).

2D Convolution of a 2048×2048 image with a 5×5 filter (300 iterations).

Black Scholes is an implementation of the Black Scholes option pricing model. The benchmark is executed to calculate 16,777,216 options over 300 iterations and is supplied as an example in the APARAPI source code.

Correlation Matrix is an implementation of the Lucene OpenBitSet "intersection count". The benchmark is executed using 1024 Terms and 16384 Documents and is supplied as an example in the APARAPI source code. Only a single iteration is performed.

Jacc is compared against: serial Java, multi-threaded Java, OpenMP, CUDA and the more mature APARAPI [1] framework that uses OpenCL [3]. The performance of each benchmark is calculated by measuring the time to perform the specified number of iterations of the performance critical section of the benchmark. Each quoted performance number is an average across a minimum of ten different experiments. The reported Jacc execution times are inclusive of a single data transfer to the device and a single transfer to the host but exclusive of JIT compilation times. This is done in order to demonstrate both the peak-performance of Jacc generated code and the low-overheads of the runtime system. In terms of programmability, we take the stance that code complexity is proportional to code size and that code can be accelerated, using a GPGPU, without

---

[5] The schema also tracks which fields are accessed and modified by the code, to minimize the cost of synchronizing data with the host after a task has been executed.

[6] The OpenMP implementation uses the OS supplied `libatlas` library.

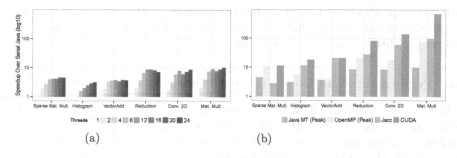

(a)   (b)

Fig. 3. Left: The speedups obtained using multi-threaded Java code only, Right: The performance of GPGPU accelerated implementations normalized to the performance of the serial Java implementation.

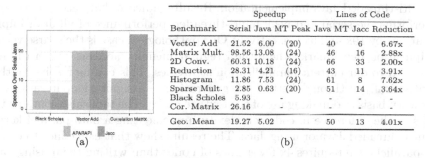

	Speedup			Lines of Code		
Benchmark	Serial	Java MT	Peak	Java	MT Jacc	Reduction
Vector Add	21.52	6.00	(20)	40	6	6.67x
Matrix Mult.	98.56	13.08	(24)	46	16	2.88x
2D Conv.	60.31	10.18	(24)	66	33	2.00x
Reduction	28.31	4.21	(16)	43	11	3.91x
Histogram	11.86	7.53	(24)	61	8	7.62x
Sparse Mult.	2.85	0.63	(20)	51	14	3.64x
Black Scholes	5.93	-		-	-	-
Cor. Matrix	26.16	-		-	-	-
Geo. Mean	19.27	5.02		50	13	4.01x

(a)   (b)

Fig. 4. Left: Speedup obtained by APARAPI and Jacc over serial Java implementations, Right: A comparison of Jacc against Java based implementations.

requiring any significant increase in code complexity over a multi-threaded implementation. We assess this by measuring the number of source code lines required to express the data-parallel kernel(s).

4.1   Java Multi-threaded Performance

Figure 3a shows the speedups achieved by converting from serial to multi-threaded Java implementations. The results show that these benchmarks scale with increased thread counts. In this scenario, the largest performance increases are observed when the number of threads used is equal to or less than the number of physical cores in the system (up to 12 threads). Figure 4b provides a summary of the peak performances of each benchmark and the number of threads used.

Figure 3b compares the same benchmarks against the Jacc implementations running on the GPGPU. As a sanity check, we have also implemented all benchmarks in OpenMP 3.2 and CUDA. By comparing the multi-threaded Java and OpenMP implementations, we see that our Java implementations have a number of inefficiencies. However, with the exception of the sparse matrix vector multiplication benchmark, Jacc still outperforms the OpenMP implementations. Furthermore, in order to provide a strong comparison point, the OpenMP version of

SGEMM is provided by `libatlas`. Results indicate that even in this case Jacc is still able to outperform OpenMP, albeit by a reduced margin in comparison to Java multi-threaded implementations.

4.2 Performance and Code Size in Heterogeneous Environment

In terms of performance, Jacc is evaluated against: serial Java, multi-threaded Java, multi-threaded OpenMP and CUDA. The effect on programmability is studied by comparing the lines of code required to implement data-parallel code on the GPGPU against that required to write multi-threaded Java code.

Figure 4b summarizes the speedups obtained by Jacc against our Java implementations. We have normalized the speedups with the performance of two different Java implementations: a serial Java implementation and the peak performing multi-threaded Java implementation. Results indicate that Jacc, on average, outperforms the serial and peak multi-threaded performance of all Java implementations by 19x and 5x respectively. Our pathological case is the sparse vector multiplication benchmark, where the irregular memory accesses pattern is not well suited to our current parallelization strategies. This can be resolved either algorithmically or through better code generation — assigning loop iterations on a per warp basis and making use of the texture cache. The table also contains the results of the difference in code complexity implementing a data-parallel kernel in multi-threaded Java or using Jacc. The results show that using Jacc to create data-parallel code requires 4x fewer lines of codes than writing them using Java threads.

Additionally, we compare against APARAPI [1], an alternative Java based framework, using three of their benchmarks: Vector addition, Black Scholes, and Correlation Matrix. A comparison of the results is shown in Fig. 4. To understand the impact of JIT compilation on performance, we conducted experiments that are both inclusive and exclusive of compilation times. Comparing the geometric mean of these speedups, we observe that both frameworks are very similar in terms of performance; APARAPI just incurs less overheads due to its faster JIT compilation.

In contrast to our approach, APARAPI is built upon OpenCL and uses source-to-source translation to generate OpenCL C from Java bytecode. This approach provides APARAPI with two advantages: consistently low-compilation times, around 400 milliseconds, and a high quality of generated code. As our compiler matures, the cost of our JIT compilation will fall, so that it is comparable with APARAPI.

In the Correlation Matrix benchmark, Jacc significantly outperforms APARAPI because of its ability to easily tune the number of threads in each work group[7] and to replace an entire method with a single PTX instruction — `popc`.

---

[7] We found that changing Jacc's work group size, to match that of APARAPI, severely reduced performance but remained faster than APARAPI.

5   Related Work

Most prior work focuses on embedded support for heterogeneous programming inside existing languages targeting GPGPUs, FPGAs, vector units, and multi-core processors [1, 5, 8–10, 12–14, 16, 18]. Jacc is different from the majority of these efforts since it does not rely on translating bytecode into CUDA or OpenCL C to generate code for the GPGPU. Instead it generates PTX code which can be JIT compiled by the GPGPU driver. To the best of our knowledge, the most complete attempt at enabling the use of GPGPUs from Java is APARAPI [1] which translates Java bytecode into OpenCL C. We improve over APARAPI since we impose less restrictions on developers while making it easier to build complex multi-kernel codes. Jacc does not force developers to separate data-parallel code into singleton classes and our task-graph abstraction enables a series of runtime optimizations that are not possible in APARAPI. This work was being used as inspiration for the now defunct OpenJDK Sumatra project [4].

Rootbeer [16] is another attempt at exposing GPGPUs to Java developers. In contrast to APARAPI, it uses ahead of time code generation by extending SOOT [17] with support for emitting CUDA code. Other projects [5, 6, 10, 12, 13] use supersets of Java which include special syntax and language features to simplify the writing of data-parallel code, or advocate the use of a functional style programming on a specialized array class. Finally, projects such as [7, 11] use a new intermediate language (IL) which is enriched with support for parallel execution allowing the JIT to be embedded in domain-specific dynamic programming languages. Jacc is different from these approaches as we use an existing IL, Java bytecode, and we aim to support general purpose programming in Java.

6   Conclusions

Heterogeneous programming allows developers to improve performance by running portions of their code on specialized hardware resources. In this paper we have introduced the Jacc framework and shown how it is possible to write concise data-parallel code and execute it on GPGPUs. Moreover, our task-based programming model and runtime system means that a large amount of tedium associated with programming heterogeneous devices can be automated. Our experimental results demonstrate that Jacc is able to generate code which outperforms serial Java code by 19x on average and that it requires 4x less code than a multithreaded Java implementation.

Acknowledgments. This work is supported by the AnyScale Apps and PAMELA projects funded by EPSRC EP/L000725/1 and EP/K008730/1. Dr. Luján is supported by a Royal Society University Research Fellowship.

References

1. Aparapi. http://developer.amd.com/tools-and-sdks/opencl-zone/aparapi/
2. CUDA. http://developer.nvidia.com/cuda-zone
3. OpenCL. https://www.khronos.org/opencl/
4. Project Sumatra. http://openjdk.java.net/projects/sumatra/
5. Auerbach, J., Bacon, D.F., Cheng, P., Rabbah, R.: Lime: a java-compatible and synthesizable language for heterogeneous architectures. In: Proceedings of the ACM International Conference on Object Oriented Programming Systems Languages and Applications (OOPSLA 2010). ACM (2010)
6. Catanzaro, B., Garland, M., Keutzer, K.: Copperhead: compiling an embedded data parallel language. In: Proceedings of the 16th ACM Symposium on Principles and Practice of Parallel Programming (PPoPP 2011). ACM (2011)
7. Chafi, H., Sujeeth, A.K., Brown, K.J., Lee, H., Atreya, A.R., Olukotun, K.: A domain-specific approach to heterogeneous parallelism, p. 35. ACM Press (2011)
8. Chafik, O.: ScalaCL: faster scala: optimizing compiler plugin+GPU-based collections (openCL). http://code.google.com/p/scalacl
9. Dotzler, G., Veldema, R., Klemm, M.: JCudaMP. In: Proceedings of the 3rd International Workshop on Multicore Software Engineering (2010)
10. Fumero, J.J., Steuwer, M., Dubach, C.: A composable array function interface for heterogeneous computing in java. In: Proceedings of ACM SIGPLAN International Workshop on Libraries, Languages, and Compilers for Array Programming (ARRAY 2014). ACM (2014)
11. Garg, R., Hendren, L.: Velociraptor: an embedded compiler toolkit for numerical programs targeting CPUs and GPUs. In: Proceedings of the 23rd International Conference on Parallel Architectures and Compilation (PACT 2014). ACM (2014)
12. Hayashi, A., Grossman, M., Zhao, J., Shirako, J., Sarkar, V.: Accelerating habanero-java programs with openCL generation. In: Proceedings of the 2013 International Conference on Principles and Practices of Programming on the Java Platform: Virtual Machines, Languages, and Tools (2013)
13. Herhut, S., Hudson, R.L., Shpeisman, T., Sreeram, J.: River trail: a path to parallelism in javascript. In: Proceedings of the 2013 ACM SIGPLAN International Conference on Object Oriented Programming Systems Languages Applications (OOPSLA 2013). ACM (2013)
14. Nystrom, N., White, D., Das, K.: Firepile: run-time compilation for GPUs in scala. In: Proceedings of the 10th ACM International Conference on Generative Programming and Component Engineering (GPCE 2011). ACM (2011)
15. OpenMP Architecture Review Board: OpenMP Specification (version 4.0) (2014)
16. Pratt-Szeliga, P., Fawcett, J., Welch, R.: Rootbeer: seamlessly using GPUs from java. In: Proceedings of 14th International IEEE High Performance Computing and Communication Conference on Embedded Software and Systems (2012)
17. Vallèe-Rai, R., Hendren, L., Sundaresan, V., Lam, P., Gagnon, E., Phong, C.: Soot - a java optimization framework. In: Proceedings of CASCON 1999 (1999)
18. Yan, Y., Grossman, M., Sarkar, V.: JCUDA: a programmer-friendly interface for accelerating java programs with CUDA. In: Sips, H., Epema, D., Lin, H.-X. (eds.) Euro-Par 2009. LNCS, vol. 5704, pp. 887–899. Springer, Heidelberg (2009). doi:10.1007/978-3-642-03869-3_82

System and Application Performance

A Low Noise Unikernel
for Extrem-Scale Systems

Stefan Lankes[1]([✉]), Simon Pickartz[1], and Jens Breitbart[2]

[1] E.ON Energy Research Center,
Institute for Automation of Complex Power Systems,
RWTH Aachen University, Aachen, Germany
{slankes,spickartz}@eonerc.rwth-aachen.de
[2] Bosch Chassis Systems Control, Stuttgart, Germany
jens.breitbart@de.bosch.com

Abstract. We expect that the size and the complexity of future supercomputers will increase on their path to exascale systems and beyond.
Therefore, system software has to adapt to the complexity of these systems to simplify the development of scalable applications. In cloud environments, the activity of a virtual machine on a neighboring core may
decrease performance due to issues such as cache contamination (noise
neighbor problem). In this paper, we present the unikernel operating system *HermitCore* coming up with predictable runtimes, which improves
the scalability. It extends the multi-kernel approach with unikernel features while providing better programmability and scalability for hierarchical systems. In addition, the same binary can be used to run as unikernel within virtual machines. By using a unikernel, the memory footprint
of Virtual Machines (VMs) is decreased, which reduces the pressure on
the cache system and improves the overall performance. We prove the
predictable runtime of the design via micro benchmarks by taking the
example of *HermitCore* on the upcoming manycore architecture *Knights
Landing*.

1 Introduction

System noise is considered a major challenge for the application scalability across
nodes on exascale systems [1] as the impact of the noise is linearly proportional
to the job size [2]. This property becomes critical for extreme scale systems utilizing thousands of nodes. Upcoming manycore CPU architectures such as Intel's
Knights Landing require high intra-node scalability for the efficient utilization of
shared memory within a node, i.e., one of the rather slow cores can easily block
a large portion of the remaining cores. Unikernels are an attractive approach for
the development of scalable and secure Operating Systems (OSs) [3]. These are
single-address-space kernels constructed by using library OSs which are tailored
to the needs of the respective application. They are typically built by compiling
(high-level) programming languages directly into specialized machine images. As
a result, system calls are replaced by common function calls promising a faster
handling of resources.

© Springer International Publishing AG 2017
J. Knoop et al. (Eds.): ARCS 2017, LNCS 10172, pp. 73–84, 2017.
DOI: 10.1007/978-3-319-54999-6_6

In previous works we introduced the High-performance Computing (HPC) kernel HermitCore which extends the multi-kernel approach by using unikernel features [4]. Our kernel runs HPC workloads bare-metal by using a library OS alongside Linux. This approach reduces the OS complexity and enhances application performance due to lower OS noise. Furthermore, it eases the software development process as HermitCore itself deals with the complexity that arises from Non-Uniform Memory Access (NUMA). HermitCore is integrated into the GCC toolchain and supports C/C++, Fortran, Pthreads, and OpenMP.

In this paper we present the extension of HermitCore that enables the stand-alone execution as unikernel within a VM and also bare-metal on real hardware. This makes HermitCore an attractive choice for cloud and real-time environments, due to the reduced memory footprint. This implicitly reduces the pressure on the cache system and promises a predictable runtime behavior.

In addition, HermitCore now supports Intel's recent manycore architecture Knights Landing (KNL). HermitCore can be easily integrated into the existing infrastructure by the registration of a proxy which is then able to start the HermitCore applications bare-metal on pre-defined cores or within a VM. HermitCore provides less noise compared to Linux on both traditional Intel multicore CPUs, but also Intel's KNL.

The rest of this paper is structured as follows: In Sect. 2, we start with a discussion of the related work in the design of operating systems for high-performance computing. Subsequently, we present the new design of the unikernel HermitCore in Sect. 4. Afterwards, we conclude the paper in Sect. 5 with a performance evaluation and finally in Sect. 6 with a summary.

2   Related Work

The specialization of the OS to the needs of HPC applications is common practice as only a subset of the features provided by standard OSs is required in this domain. The employment of standard OS kernels results in an increased pressure on the cache and interrupt system which is also referred to as system or OS noise. A notable reduction of the application performance is the result. Dan Tsafrir et al. provide a probabilistic argument showing that the effect of OS noise is linearly proportional to the size of the cluster [2], e.g., the probability of a single-node delay of a petascale machine possessing tens of thousands of nodes should not exceed 10^{-6} to keep the probability of suffering from noise at a reasonable level. Hence, the noise generated by OS layer is a key aspect for upcoming systems and should be kept as low as possible.

There is a lot of ongoing research towards a reduction of the system noise with the goal of increasing the scalability. The following three approaches are most common: (1) Full-Weight Kernels (FWKs) stripped down to the features required to run HPC workloads, (2) Light-Weight Kernels (LWKs) abolishing full compatibility to common FWKs such as Linux, and finally a relatively recent development: multi-kernels combining the advantages of FWKs and LWKs.

Cray's Extreme Scale Linux [5], Catamount [6] and ZeptoOS [7] are common representatives for FWKs tailored to the needs of HPC. However, their maintenance imposes challenges as new features and bug fixes of the upstream kernel have to be back-ported. With Kitten[1] and Blue Gene's CNK [8] there are two examples for the LWK approach. Although they are able to provide excellent performance and facilitate the maintenance due to the small code basis, they are restricted with respect to the compatibility to the underlying hardware. Device drivers usually have to be written from scratch or back-ported from existing kernels. FusedOS [9], mOS [10], and McKernel [11] are representatives of the multi-kernel approach. They employ a standard kernel such as Linux on a small subset of cores for the provision of basic services, e.g., the file system. The remaining cores run a LWK fulfilling the demands of HPC applications. To allow for the execution of traditional applications on the top of this LWK, system calls have to be delegated to the FWK which provides full support for the Portable Operating System Interface (POSIX) API.

HermitCore extends the multi-kernel approach by combining Linux with a unikernel [3], i.e., a single-address-space kernel constructed by using a library operating system. These specialized kernels target at a minimal overhead to the application's execution by replacing system calls with common function calls. This promises a more efficient handling of resources. By using this technique, HermitCore guarantees maximum performance and scalability while Linux provides support for common interfaces to the OS layer and non-performance critical tasks. In contrast to the works presented above, a majority of the system calls is directly handled by the unikernel. Since HermitCore focuses on HPCs programming models such as Message Passing Interface (MPI) and OpenMP, it lacks full POSIX compliance for the sake of performance and a small code basis.

3 KNL

We conducted all our experiments on Intel's latest generation Xeon Phi processors codename KNL which is extensively described by Jeffers et al. [12]. The Xeon Phi product line comprises CPUs especially designed for HPC that are considered manycore CPUs. In contrast to the standard Xeon product line, Xeon Phi products sacrifice single core performance to allow for more cores on a chip. The KNL cores are based on a modified Intel's Silvermont micro-architecture, which is typically used for Intel Atom processors. Compared to a modern Xeon CPU core, the KNL core for example uses:

- wider vector units/registers supporting up to 512 bit, i.e., a single instruction is sufficient for the modification of a whole cache line.
- supports 4-wide Simultaneous Multithreading (SMT) (called Hyperthreading by Intel).

---

[1] https://software.sandia.gov/trac/kitten.

Currently, the KNL is only available as a self-booting processor, but may also be released as a PCIe card. The self-booting processor supports two memory flavours: well-known DDR-4 DRAM (up to 384 GiB) and 16 GiB of Multi-Channel DRAM (MCDRAM). The latter is 3D-stacked DRAM that is put close to the processor and thereby provides higher bandwidth. In a stream benchmark, DRAM only provides about 90 GiB/s whereas MCDRAM provides over 400 GiB. The memory latency differs based on the (bandwidth) utilization of the memory type. In an idle state, DRAM provides a slightly lower latency compared to MCDRAM but that evens out once the bandwidth utilization increases. The KNL possess two memory controllers for DRAM (on opposing sides of the chip) and 8 for MCDRAM (two available in each quarter of the chip.). The on-chip MCDRAM can be configured in three ways by modifying the BIOS settings accordingly:

flat. It is exposed explicitly as part of the address space (via its own NUMA domain) and can be directly accessed by read/write instructions.

cache. It is configured as a cache for DRAM and not visible to the OS.

hybrid. A portion of the MCDRAM is directly accessible while the remaining part serves as a cache.

Using MCDRAM as a cache results in a rather high cache-miss latency since accesses to MCDRAM has about the same latency as DRAM. There is no on-chip L3 cache as it is available in current Xeon CPUs. However, the KNL provides a directory based L2 cache (1 MiB shared by two cores each) and a core-local L1 cache (32 KiB for data). As a result, L1 cache misses are served from the local L2 if possible, or the on-chip tag directory must be queried for the state of the requested address. Depending on the result, the data is provided by another L2 cache or MCDRAM cache is queried (if enabled) In case the data is not available in any cache, it must be provided by MCDRAM/DRAM depending on the actual location of the data. The processor can be split into 4 virtual clusters for a reduction of the latency and congestion of memory accesses. With enabled cluster mode, the tag directories are guaranteed to be in the same quadrant of the L2 cache responsible to cache the data, however the memory controller responsible may not be in the same quadrant. This option is transparant to the software stack. To further reduce the latency, sub-numa-clustering (SNC) can be enabled. This mode exposes the four virtual clusters to the software via NUMA domains including four additional NUMA domains containing the MCDRAM local to each cluster (in case flat/hybrid mode is enabled). As a result, the software can explicitly store data in local DRAM or MCDRAM.

Our measurement were run on an Intel Xeon Phi 7210 with 64 cores exposing 256 hyperthreads in total. These cores are clocked at 1.3 GHz, equipped with 96 GiB DDR4 RAM and 16 GB MCDRAM. We deactivated the turbo mode to avoid any side effects.

4 Design of HermitCore

In previous works we introduced the first version of HermitCore [4] while mainly focusing on HPC workloads in common multi-core clusters. We extended our objectives by the support for upcoming many-core architectures such as Intel's KNL. Furthermore, we added standalone support for running our kernel without Linux alongside, e.g., such setups can be used to guarantee predictable runtimes in cloud computing environments. Now the same binary is executable within a virtual machine as traditional unikernel or directly on the hardware as single-/multi-kernel.

Consequently, HermitCore targets at an improved programmability and scalability of HPC systems, but also at the building of virtual clusters that can be easily started, stopped, and migrated within a real cluster. Virtual clusters ease the creation of checkpoints since the application including all dependencies is encapsulated within an isolated environment. Thereby, the resiliency of current and future HPC systems can be improved. For the same reason, load balancing is facilitated since virtual machines provide means for migrations across the cluster [13].

In case of the multi-kernel approach, every NUMA node runs an individual HermitCore instance only managing local resources such as memory and CPU cores (cf. Fig. 1). This hides the hardware complexity by presenting the application developer a traditional Uniform Memory Access (UMA) architecture. Inter-kernel Communication (IKC) among the HermitCore instances is realized by means of a virtual IP device based on Light-weight IP (LwIP)[2] or by the message passing library iRCCE [14,15]. In multi-kernel environments HermitCore requires a special loader that is capable of handling a slightly modified Executable and Linking Format (ELF). This identifies HermitCore applications by a magic number in the binary's header and launches a proxy (cf. Fig. 2) for the communication with the outside world. The application itself is then booted on an exclusive set of cores which is unregistered from the running Linux kernel.

For cloud environments, the proxy is able to boot HermitCore directly within VMs without the need for a Linux kernel running alongside. Therefore, QEMU is used which comes with support for the *Multiboot Specification*[3]. Thereby, OS kernels can be directly booted that come in the ELF format. The communication to the outside world is realized over an IP connection between HermitCore and the Linux proxy which is initialized on the startup of QEMU. The boot loader *grub* also supports the *Multiboot Specification* and the same technique can be used to boot the kernel as single-kernel directly on the hardware. Device drivers for typical network interfaces are already part of HermitCore. As a consequence, the same binary can be used in a multi-kernel environment together with Linux, as unikernel within a VMs, or as unikernel bare-metal on the hardware.

---

[2] http://savannah.nongnu.org/projects/lwip/.
[3] https://www.gnu.org/software/grub/manual/multiboot/multiboot.html.

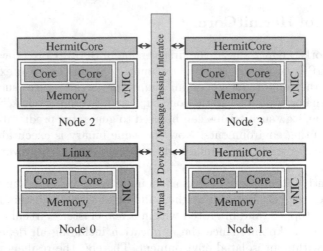

Fig. 1. A NUMA system with one satellite kernel per NUMA node (from [4]).

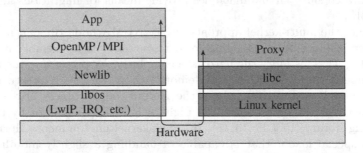

Fig. 2. The software stack of HermitCore in a multi-kernel setup (from [4]).

HermitCore is implemented as library OS which enables the implementation of all system calls as common function calls. This guarantees a small overhead and promises an excellent runtime behavior in HPCs and real-time environments. The design requires that the initialization routines of the library OS has to be located on predictable address and is accessible at boot time. For a simplification of the boot process, the kernel is stored in a special section and located at the beginning of the application (cf. Fig. 3).

Functionality which is currently not supported by our kernel, can be provide in multi-kernel setups by Remote Procedure Calls (RPCs) to the Linux kernel via the IP connection to the proxy. In [4], we propose a technique, where HermitCore is able to directly access hardware devices such as InfiniBand. Although most system calls are directly handled by HermitCore, the RPC mechanism offers backward compatibility at the expense of peak performance.

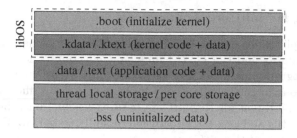

Fig. 3. Memory layout of a HermitCore application

4.1 Support for Intel's Xeon and Xeon Phi Architectures

HermitCore is a small 64 bit kernel providing basic OS functionalities, i.e., memory management and priority-based round-robin scheduling. It is designed with focus on Intel's 64 bit processors and comes with support for SMT, SSE4, AVX2, and AVX512. The maximal number of threads in the system is defined at compile time as HPC applications typically start an amount of threads equivalent to the number of cores. Consequently, static arrays can be used for internal data structures such as the process control block and the ready queue. This promises fast and cache-aware accesses. HermitCore still provides a scheduler, since garbage collection of managed programming languages or performance monitoring may result in more threads than available cores. Currently, this does not support load balancing since explicit thread placement is favoured over automatic strategies in HPC.

HermitCore employs a dynamic timer, i.e., the kernel does not interrupt computation threads which run exclusively on a certain core and do not use any timer. This does not only reduce the scheduling overhead to a minimum but also results in a reduction of the OS noise. The MCDRAM of the KNL is supported by means of new memory allocation functions and is already used for the IKC facilities within HermitCore. Therefore, we ported iRCCE [14, 15] to serve as communication layer between the HermitCore isles. This is a non-blocking communication extension to the RCCE Communication Library [16] which was designed for Intel's Single-Chip Cloud Computer (SCC). In case of HermitCore, the on-die memory is emulated by shared memory regions between the HermitCore isles. The behavior of the SCC is similar to HermitCore's target platforms. In case of the SCC, each core has its own on-die memory and is able to share the memory with the other cores. The access to the local on-die memory is faster than a remote access. This fits the behavior of a NUMA architecture which is HermitCore's target platform. Consequently, each HermitCore isle, i.e., each NUMA node, exports a local memory region as virtual on-die memory to the other isles and hence provides a similar behavior to that of the SCC. If case of Knights Landing, the virtual on-die memory is located in the MCDRAM which is close the NUMA node. With these modifications, we are able to use SCC-MPICH [17] without modifications on the top of HermitCore, which was designed for the SCC and based on the communication layer iRCCE.

4.2   Building HermitCore Applications

HermitCore applications can be built by using a cross toolchain which is based on the *GNU binutils* and the *GNU Compiler Collection*. Thereby, HermitCore supports all programming languages which are supported by gcc requiring minimal modifications to the original GNU toolchain. It was sufficient to integrate the support of the target for HermitCore (*x86_64-hermit*) into the cross configure script of binutils and gcc. We already successfully tested Go, Fortran, C, and C++ code on the top of HermitCore.

In addition to our previous works [4], we ported the complete Go runtime to HermitCore by removing all methods related to process creation or inter-process communication. As single address-space kernel, HermitCore does not support the execution of more than one process at a time. We already successfully tested web-services written in Go in conduction with our unikernel.

Furthermore, it is possible to use other C/C++ compilers (e.g., Intel's C compiler) instead of our cross compiler suite. In this case, the compilers have to use the header files of HermitCore instead of the Linux headers. The resulting object files have to be converted to HermitCore objects, as the compilers generated Linux objects per default. Therefore, we provide an adapted version of *elfedit* as part of HermitCore's toolchain.

5   Performance Evaluation

For all benchmarks we used KNL's SNC mode with four NUMA nodes using DDR4 RAM and MCDRAM. We used an adapted 3.10 Linux kernel on a CentOS 7 installation and compiled the micro benchmarks by using gcc with enabled hardware-independent[4] and hardware dependent[5]) optimizations. All micro benchmarks, which run on the unmodified CentOS system, are compiled with the gcc 4.8.5, which is part of the CentOS's software distribution, while benchmarks on the HermitCore kernel used the gcc 5.3.1.

For an estimation of the OS noise, we performed measurements using the Linux kernel's *isolcpu*[6] feature. This allows for the exclusion of a set of cores from the balancing and scheduling algorithms for user-tasks. Isolcpu promises lower OS noise but demands for the explicit allocation of the respective cores via the CPU affinity calls.

5.1   Operating System Micro-benchmarks

At first, the overhead of a system call and a reschedule are evaluated. The used benchmark, which we already published in [4] and is part of Hermit-Core's software distribution[7], calls up 10 000 times the system calls getpid and

---

[4] Hardware-independent optimization flags: -O3.

[5] Hardware-dependent optimization flags: -march=native -mtune=native.

[6] https://www.kernel.org/doc/Documentation/kernel-parameters.txt.

[7] http://www.hermitcore.org.

sched_yield after a cache warm-up. getpid is the system call with smallest runtime and represents nearly the overhead of a system call. The system call sched_yield checks if another task is ready and switches to them. In our case, the system is idle and consequently the system call returns directly after the check of the ready queues. Table 1 summarizes the results as average number of CPU cycles for Linux and HermitCore.

To allow for a comparison of a KNL-based and a Haswell-based system, we also add the results from our previous works [4], which based on Intel Haswell CPUs (E5-2650 v3). The overhead of HermitCore is clearly smaller because in a library operating system the system calls are mapped to common functions. The gap between HermitCore and Linux is clearly larger on Knights Landing because the system activities utilizes only a single core and the single-core performance is clearly lower in contrast to the Haswell processor. This proves also the demand on an efficient operating system design to improve overall performance. Furthermore, the difference between getpid and sched_yield is on HermitCore smaller, which proves the small overhead of HermitCore's scheduler.

Table 1. A performance comparison of HermitCore and Linux regarding basic system services on two different architectures. The results are given in CPU cycles. (based on [4])

System activity	KNL		Haswell	
	HermitCore	Linux	HermitCore	Linux
getpid()	15	486	14	143
sched_yield()	197	983	97	370
malloc()	3051	12806	3715	6575
First write access to a page	2078	3967	2018	4007

Finally, the memory allocation and initialization are evaluated. On both operating systems malloc reserves a space on the heap. The first access to the reserved memory region triggers a pagefault and the exception handler maps a page frame to the virtual address space. The used benchmark allocates 1024 arrays with an array size of 1 MiB. Afterwards the benchmark writes on each allocated page 1 Byte. By writing this small number of bytes, the first write access is dominated by handling of the pagefault. Both, the memory allocation and the pagefault handling is on HermitCore (cf. Table 1) clearly faster in contrast to Linux.

5.2   Hourglass Benchmark

To determine the OS noise, we use the *Hourglass* benchmark [18]. It was introduced for the analysis of the time slices assigned by the operating system to multiple processes. In this work, the concept was used for determining the *gaps* in the execution time caused mainly by the operating system. In principle, the benchmark continuously reads the time stamp counter of the processor. Besides some blocked system service, the benchmark runs exclusively on the system and is bound to a specific core. Consequently, if a larger gap between two read operations occurs, the kernel of the operating system steals some time from the user application to maintain the system (e.g., scheduling or interrupt handling).

Figure 4 presents the results of the hourglass benchmark showing gaps larger than 234 cycles to filter cache misses [1]. As expected, the results reveal that a standard Linux system has the most and the largest gaps (cf. Fig. 4a) in comparison to the other configurations. The isolation feature of the Linux kernel has

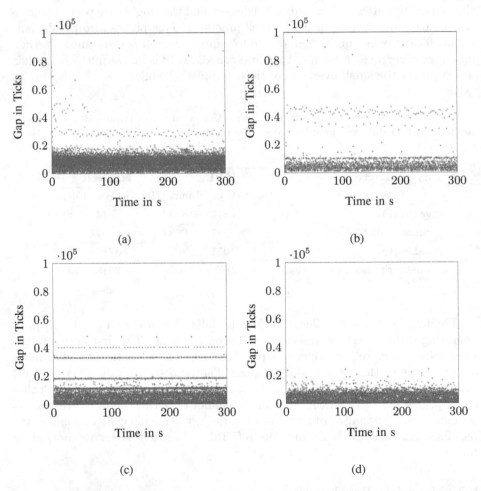

Fig. 4. Scatter plot of observing the hourglass benchmark for 1 min on Core 16 in four different configurations: (a) Standard Linux, (b) Linux with enabled *isolcpus* and *nohz* on all cores but Core 0, and (c) HermitCore, and (d) HermitCore without IP thread.

only a limited effect. It reduces the number of gaps but the gap size remains on a high level as kernel threads are still scheduled on the isolated cores.

Besides the idle loop and the application threads, HermitCore creates only one additional thread for the handling of IP packets, which could induce OS noise. The results of the core, which handle the IP threads, is shown in Fig. 4c. The OS noise is noticeable but the gap size is smaller compared to Linux. All other cores are exclusively assigned to thread and are not interrupted by an interrupt. Consequently, the results of these cores (cf. Fig. 4d) shows the smallest OS noise. But it is not completely noise-free because hyperthreading induces a latency when switching between the threads.

6 Conclusion

In this paper, we present a new operating system design. On the one hand it supports the traditional unikernel approach while on the other hand the same binary can be employed in multi-kernel setups. A single-address-space kernel promises minimal overhead, excellent scalability, and a low operating system noise. We achieve promising preliminary results with respect to the system noise.

HermitCore already supports AVX-512, Knights Landing's MCDRAM, a message passing interface, Intel's OpenMP runtime, and a fully integrated GNU cross toolchain. For future work we plan a comprehensive evaluation of the performance by using application benchmarks to compare these results with traditional operating systems.

References

1. Hoefler, T., Schneider, T., Lumsdaine, A.: Characterizing the influence of system noise on large-scale applications by simulation. In: SC (2010)
2. Tsafrir, D., Etsion, Y., Feitelson, D.G., Kirkpatrick, S.: System noise, OS clock ticks, and fine-grained parallel applications. ACM (2005)
3. Madhavapeddy, A., Mortier, R., Rotsos, C., Scott, D., Singh, B., Gazagnaire, T., Smith, S., Hand, S., Crowcroft, J.: Unikernels: library operating systems for the cloud. In: Proceedings of the Eighteenth International Conference on Architectural Support for Programming Languages and Operating Systems (ASPLOS 2013), pp. 461–472. ACM, New York (2013)
4. Lankes, S., Pickartz, S., Breitbart, J.: HermitCore: a unikernel for extreme scale computing. In: Proceedings of the 6th International Workshop on Runtime and Operating Systems for Supercomputers (ROSS 2016), pp. 4:1–4:8. ACM, New York (2016)
5. Oral, S., Wang, F., Dillow, D.A., Miller, R., Shipman, G.M., Maxwell, D., Henseler, D., Becklehimer, J., Larkin, J.: Reducing application runtime variability on Jaguar XT5. In: Proceedings of Cray User Group (CUG 2010) (2010)
6. Kelly, S.M., Brightwell, R.: Software Architecture of the Light Weight Kernel, Catamount. In: In Cray User Group, pp. 16–19 (2005)
7. Yoshii, K., Iskra, K., Naik, H., Beckman, P., Broekema, P.C.: Characterizing the performance of big memory on Blue Gene linux. In: Proceedings of the 2nd International Workshop on Parallel Programming Models and Systems Software for High-End Computing (P2S2 2009), pp. 65–72 (2009)

8. Giampapa, M., Gooding, T., Inglett, T., Wisniewski, R.W.: Experiences with a Lightweight supercomputer kernel: lessons learned from Blue Gene's CNK. In: 2010 International Conference for High Performance Computing, Networking, Storage and Analysis (SC), pp. 1–10, November 2010

9. Park, Y., Van Hensbergen, E., Hillenbrand, M., Inglett, T., Rosenburg, B.S., Ryu, K.D., Wisniewski, R.W.: FusedOS: fusing LWK Performance with FWK functionality in a heterogeneous environment. In: SBAC-PAD, pp. 211–218 (2012)

10. Wisniewski, R.W., Inglett, T., Keppel, P., Murty, R., Riesen, R.: mOS: an architecture for extreme-scale operating systems. In: Proceedings of the 4th International Workshop on Runtime and Operating Systems for Supercomputers (ROSS 2014), New York, pp. 1–8. ACM Request Permissions, June 2014

11. Shimosawa, T., Gerofi, B., Takagi, M., Nakamura, G., Shirasawa, T., Saeki, Y., Shimizu, M., Hori, A., Ishikawa, Y.: Interface for heterogeneous kernels: a framework to enable hybrid OS designs targeting high performance computing on many-core architectures. In: 2014 21st International Conference on High Performance Computing (HiPC), pp. 1–10 (2014)

12. Jeffers, J., Reinders, J., Sodani, A.: Intel Xeon Phi Coprocessor High Performance Programming, 2nd edn. Morgan Kaufmann Publishers Inc., San Francisco (2016)

13. Pickartz, S., Lankes, S., Monti, A., Clauss, C., Breitbart, J.: Application migration in HPC - a driver of the exascale era? In: 2016 International Conference on High Performance Computing Simulation (HPCS), pp. 318–325, July 2016

14. Clauss, C., Lankes, S., Reble, P., Galowicz, J., Pickartz, S., Bemmerl, T.: iRCCE: a non-blocking communication extension to the RCCE communication library for the Intel single-chip cloud computer - version 2.0 iRCCE FLAIR. Technical report, Chair for Operating Systems, RWTH Aachen University Users' Guide and API Manual (2013)

15. Clauss, C., Lankes, S., Reble, P., Bemmerl, T.: New system software for parallel programming models on the Intel SCC many-core processor. Concurr. Comput. Pract. Exp. **27**(9), 2235–2259 (2015)

16. Mattson, T.G., van der Wijngaart, R.F., Riepen, M., Lehnig, T., Brett, P., Haas, W., Kennedy, P., Howard, J., Vangal, S., Borkar, N., Ruhl, G., Dighe, S.: The 48-core SCC processor: the programmer's view. In: 2010 International Conference for High Performance Computing, Networking, Storage and Analysis (SC), pp. 1–11, November 2010

17. Clauss, C., Lankes, S., Reble, P., Bemmerl, T.: Recent advances and future prospects in iRCCE and SCC-MPICH. In: Proceedings of the 3rd Symposium of the Many-core Applications Research Community (MARC), Ettlingen. KIT Scientific Publishing Poster Abstract, July 2011

18. Regehr, J.: Inferring scheduling behavior with hourglass. In: Proceedings of the USENIX Annual Technical Conference, FREENIX Track, Monterey, pp. 143–156, June 2002

A New Approach to Detecting Execution Phases Using Performance Monitoring Counters

Saman Khoshbakht[✉] and Nikitas Dimopoulos

Department of Electrical and Computer Engineering,
University of Victoria, Victoria, BC, Canada
{samankh,nikitas}@ece.uvic.ca

Abstract. In this paper, a new hierarchical view of the workload phase classification problem is introduced. Execution phases are the continuous pieces of execution that show consistent behaviour in terms of performance and power. To the best of our knowledge, this is the first work which uses a hierarchical approach to collect and cluster the performance monitoring counters in order to detect macroscopic phases in an application. Our results show the ability of our model to differentiate between execution phases according to the processor power behaviour. Furthermore, we investigate the power consistency inside each phase. The results show the effectiveness of our proposed methodology in classifying phases with similar power behaviour. This information can be used by the system to control and maintain power bursts, increasing the data centre's power efficiency by reducing the maximum-to-average power ratio.

1 Introduction

Having insight into current and near future behaviour of the workload gives the system the opportunity to better manage the available resources. Although recent processors tend to have several power management strategies such as Intel SpeedStep, Turbo Boost and Running Average Power Limit (RAPL), current schedulers do not speculate about the near-future demands of the running jobs in terms of resources such as power, memory or CPU time.

On the other hand, our observations along with those of previous works [1,2] show benchmarks to have distinct sections of execution where the behaviour of the software in terms of the monitored feature (power, resource usage, etc.) stays consistent. These continuous portions of the execution are referred to as **Execution Phases** (or **Phases**). Our work is motivated by the observations that firstly the execution trace comprises several phases each of which are considerably long. Secondly we observed that these phases show repeating patterns with similar power and performance behaviour. In this work we introduce a new methodology to classify each time stamp of the execution into one of the phases.

By having a-priori knowledge about the resource demands of each phase, the system can strive for a more uniform power by modifying the processor frequency according to the power currently needed by the software. It is more desirable for data centers to utilize the available power headroom as much as possible

© Springer International Publishing AG 2017
J. Knoop et al. (Eds.): ARCS 2017, LNCS 10172, pp. 85–96, 2017.
DOI: 10.1007/978-3-319-54999-6_7

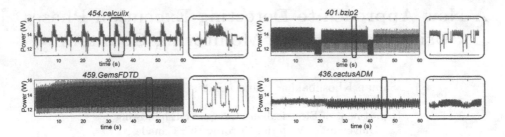

Fig. 1. Snippets of some SPEC CPU2006 benchmark power patterns

by reducing the $max(power) - mean(power)$ factor during the execution of the workload [3] which results in a smoother power trace for each workload. The goal of this work is to provide the system with the information about the phase power demands of the workload in order to lower the $max(power) - mean(power)$ factor.

Figure 1 shows some examples of the repeating patterns in some SPEC CPU2006 [4] benchmarks. Most of the benchmarks we chose show power patterns seen either in very large periods (e.g. *calculix*) or tighter repeating patterns (e.g. *GemsFDTD*). Some benchmarks show distinct behaviour along different times through whole runtime. An example of this type is *bzip2*. The third group consist of benchmarks showing uniform power or indistinct phases (e.g. *cactusADM*). This is an exploratory work in order to develop a method for phase classification. Our ultimate goal is to develop a hardware-assisted speculative component which will be responsible to speculate the near-future power demands of the workload based on its current performance behaviour utilizing the phase information. For this purpose, we chose 9 of the SPEC CPU2006 benchmark suite for preliminary testing. From the benchmarks we managed to manually compile, we tried to choose the ones showing the most power variance. As our method aims to reduce the $max(power) - mean(power)$ factor, it will not be of much use when applied to flat-powered workloads. The benchmarks chosen for this work are as follows: *bzip2, cactusADM, calculix, gcc, GemsFDTD, gobmk, gromacs, lbm* and *namd*.

1.1 Related Work

Some approaches to phase detection look at phases from the software point of view by dividing the execution into high-level phases, using the program trace. Benomar et al. [2] use a shortened version of the trace to create a phase history based on a heuristic genetic algorithm. This work focuses on the high-level footprint of the software to determine the phases from the software point of view. JIVE [5] and AMIDA [6] use a similar approach to divide and categorize Java codes into phases using the method call graphs. As software trace collection is intrusive to workload flow, the accuracy of the above methods is compromised.

Other approaches use the hardware-implemented Performance Monitoring Counters (PMC) to detect the workload phase. These techniques have the advantage of incurring lower overhead to the system. Isci and Martonosi [7] compare PMC-based phase classification to Basic Block Vector (BBV)-based approaches with regards to workload's power demands. They implemented both techniques using Intel Pin and showed PMC-based results to provide an average 33% less power characterization error than BBV approaches. Zhang and Chang [8] used PMCs to divide the execution trace into two major phases: memory-intensive and CPU-intensive by determining the amount of L2 cache misses. They use this information to lower the processor frequency in order to save energy in memory intensive phases. Cochran et al. [9] made use of these counters to determine the execution phase in each 100 ms time sample by clustering the data into separate phases and showed to be able to detect future IPCs within a 10% error. Similar to [8], the goal of this work was to differentiate between two major software phases: low-power and high-power stable sections. One of the advantages of our methodology over [7–9] is the two-level hierarchical approach to phase classification, which provides lower noise in phase detection in addition to fine timing granularity. Additionally, the number of phases in our method is estimated dynamically, whereas above works assumes a static number of phases in all benchmarks (i.e. 5 phases in [7] and 2 phases in [8,9]).

All of the models mentioned above utilize a fixed-time sampling rate and the data in each sample is used in order to determine the phase of that sample. Using this approach, increasing the length of the sampling period would lead to loss of fine details while reducing it introduces unwanted artefacts and noise to the system. Our model introduces a novel hierarchical view to classify and analyse the workload execution. We also investigated the effects of utilizing a secondary derived parameter (i.e. power proxy) in our model to increase the accuracy of the results. In short, our contributions can be summarized as:

- Using PMC information, designed a low-overhead methodology for classifying the program execution into phases.
- Developed a hierarchical view of the execution in order to provide coarse-grain phase analysis while retaining fine details for each time sample.
- Utilized a secondary power model to improve power-oriented phase detection.

In the next section, the developed methodology for detecting phases is described. Section 3 summarizes the results this method provides when applied to a number of SPEC CPU2006 benchmarks and Sect. 4 covers the future works and concludes the paper.

2   Methodology

After a short warm-up period of $1sec$, we collect the information from the first 10% of the execution. The collected data is used as the **training set** in our method. To test our methodology, we apply the phase model created using the training set to the whole benchmark in order to score our phase results.

In order to achieve high timing precision in detecting phases, choosing a high sampling rate is necessary. However, shortening the time slices decreases the accuracy of phase detection by adding noise and unwanted artefacts induced by the operating system in the performance counter values. Our proposed method approaches this dilemma in a new way. We collect the input data in short time intervals (1 ms) but by considering the value of the counters in the previous samples, we include the history of the counters in our phase calculations. Using this approach, we use the history along with each time slice's data in order to detect the phase of each time stamp.

2.1   Collecting PMC Data

Figure 2 shows the overall architecture of our proposed methodology. We use the PAPI tool [10] to collect the Performance Monitoring Counter (PMC) information. The system lets us collect up to five performance counter values each time. As this work mainly focuses on power behaviour in execution phases, we consulted a number of previous works which used a selection of performance counters for modeling power [11–13]. After choosing a number of PMC candidates, we determined the correlation between each performance counter and power while calculating the cross-correlation between each counter pair. We selected the counters based on maximum correlation to measured power while having minimal cross-correlation. The counters we selected are the total number of cycles, number of stalled cycles, number of L1 and L2 instruction cache misses and number of L3 total cache misses.

2.2   Data Preparation

We used a low-overhead, in-house developed profiling tool [14] for synchronously collecting the PMC information along with the real processor power and the RAPL energy estimates in 1 ms intervals. Our tool incurs less than 1% timing overhead to the system. We use the training set to create the benchmark-specific phase model for each benchmark. We then use the model to analyse the rest of the benchmark based on the training set, using the same sampling frequency of 1 ms. We normalize the data using the "standard score" based on a previously collected sample run of benchmarks. Although our framework can also perform a Principal Component Analysis on the inputs, we have elected not to use this capability for the present work as the number of descriptors are quite small.

2.3   Execution Phase and Sub-phase Detection

Clustering is traditionally used to detect major behaviour classes. However, in our case, the behaviour of the workload may change very rapidly, or it may enter a sustained pattern of distinctive and successive behaviour states. Our approach is tailored to identify sustained and consistent behaviour.

We have adapted a two-stage approach. The first stage clusters the states of computation as exemplified by the values of the PMC counters plus potentially

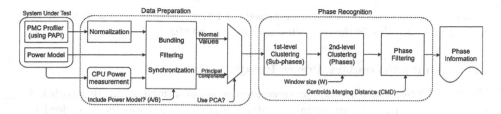

Fig. 2. Our proposed methodology

other parameters (such as derived power). The second stage tries to identify
sustained patterns in the succession of behavioural states classified through first-
stage clustering. We denote the classes resulted from the first-stage clustering of
the PMC values as **Sub-phases**. We denote the classes identified as sustained
during the second stage of our approach as **Execution Phases** (or "Phases"
in short). Figure 3 shows an example of phases and sub-phases for *calculix*. In
detail, we proceed as follows:

After collecting the information from the first 10% of the benchmark we use
kmeans, or Lloyd's, algorithm to cluster each time slice into one of N_1 clusters
based on the five PMC values in each time slice. N_1 is a predefined value. Our
tests showed that using $N_1 = 10$ clusters leads to enough distinction while
providing acceptable clustering overhead. The assigned sub-phase for each time
slice t is denoted as $S(t) \in \{1, 2, ..., N_1\}$. The maximum number of iterations for
this step is set to 1000, and the initial seeds for centroids are chosen using the
kmeans++ algorithm.

To determine the execution phases we use a sliding window with length W.
Within this time window, we count the number of time slices associated with a
particular sub-phase and annotate the current time with this information. We
define the buffer B as a vector of N_1 values where N_1 is the number of sub-
phases. We use $N_1 = 10$ for our tests. At any given time T, each component B_i
of vector B is calculated as

$$0 \le B_i(T) = \frac{\sum_{t=T-W}^{t=T} C_{i,t}}{W} \le 1 \qquad i = 1, ..., N_1 \qquad (1)$$

where $C_{i,t} = 1$ if $S(t) = i$ and 0 otherwise. $B_i(T)$ denotes the share of sub-phase
i during the time window $T - W$ to T. The subsequent clustering of $B_i(T)$
in every time slice T will determine the phase in each time slice. To choose
the number of phases for each benchmark, we adopt the "Elbow method" [15].
After determining the number of clusters for the benchmark, we use kmeans for
clustering in this step, using the same configuration as the first stage. The results
from this step are the raw phase data which represent the corresponding phase
for each time slice. We then filter the phase data in order to merge any closely
detected phases and remove empty clusters if needed. Finally, we determine the
radius for each phase as $Mean + 2 * stddev$ of distances between each member
and the centroid within the phase. Ultimately, any data point outside of this

radius is considered "Background Phase". Figure 3 shows an example of the phases and sub-phases detected in a section of *calculix*.

2.4 Using a Secondary Power Proxy

We propose two different models to create the phase information. In **Model A**, only the performance monitoring counter information is collected and used for the first level clustering. This model does not need any information regarding power and is simpler to implement. We propose a second model, **Model B**, which uses a power model as a sixth descriptor for each time slice. We expect this model to show improvement in differentiating between slices which exhibit the same behaviour in the collected PMCs, but different power dissipation. There are many previous works which provide different models for estimating the power dissipation of the processor [11,12,16,17]. We compared the models which could be used in our system, including Intel's RAPL energy estimate model. Among the tested models, RAPL showed to be the most accurate power model, therefore we elected to use RAPL as the sixth descriptor in our tests.

3   Experimental Results

This section provides the information we obtained from each benchmark. As an example, Fig. 3 shows the phasing results for a portion of *calculix* benchmark. In the following sections we shall report the coverage of our methodology and analyse whether the results obtained during the training phase are applicable to the whole execution. Further, we shall analyse whether a phase maintains its behaviour as time progresses by comparing all instances of each phase along the runtime of the execution.

The tests were conducted on a Dell Optiplex 7010 tower PC, running on an Intel Core i7-3770 processor. We used CentOS Linux release 7.1.1503 and

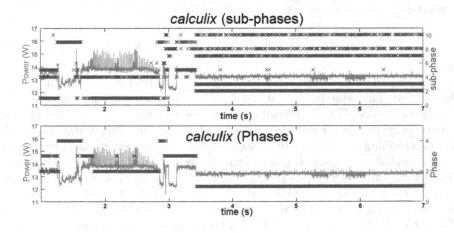

Fig. 3. Detected sub-phases and phases in *calculix* using Model B

stripped down the OS from unwanted services and processes in order to reduce power and performance artefacts. In order to have full control on the environment in which the tests were conducted, we switched off all but one of the processor's cores as well as dynamic voltage and frequency controlling (DVFS) mechanisms. This is done in order to validate the effectiveness of the methodology independent of current power-control mechanisms, as we aim to provide a software-aware replacement for current OS-controlled power management techniques. The power is measured by a secondary system using a non-invasive current clamp. The framework designed by the authors [14] includes a power profiler developed in Labview and implemented in a NI PXIe-1062Q data acquisition system. The results reported are the average scores of **20 runs** where we apply our methodology to each benchmark under both models. Having chosen 9 benchmarks for our tests, we performed a total of **360 separate experiments**.

3.1   Coverage Results

The phasing stage either maps each time-stamp within the workload with one of the phases, or classifies it as the *"background phase"* as discussed in Sect. 2.3. We define C_P or **Coverage** as the ratio between all time stamps with a reported phase value (not including *"background phase"* time stamps) over all time stamps collected. Additionally, we want to know how much of the execution time consists of phases longer than a certain minimum length. These phases (referred to as "Long phases") are of importance since any change to the system parameters (e.g. processor frequency control, rescheduling, etc.) incurs a non-trivial overhead. We define LPC_l or the **Long Phase Coverage** as the sum length of all phases longer than l divided by the whole runtime of the workload. Table 1 shows coverage (C_P) and Long Phase Coverage (LPC_l) for $l = 11$ ms for all benchmarks. We chose $l = 11$ ms as it is the round-robin time slice in the operating system. The results show slightly lower coverage in both factors in Model B compared to Model A, which can be explained by the addition of the sixth input (i.e. the derived power) introducing variance in the clustering space.

On average, the overall coverage (C_P) for our two models are 99% and 96% respectively, while the average LPC_{11} is 96% and 94% respectively.

3.2   Power Estimate Validation

To show how much we can depend on the first 10% of the benchmark to be the representative of the power behaviour of the phases, we compare the power histograms of real phase power for the whole benchmark with the estimated phase power derived from performing a weighted sum of the power histogram recorded for each sub-phase of the training set (i.e. the first 10%). We use cross-correlation analysis to compare two histograms.

To calculate the overall **Estimated Power Score** (P_{est}) for the benchmark we perform a weighted sum of the power correlation of each phase to its estimate. Our results show the estimate and real phase power histograms to correlate closely. As an example, Fig. 4 shows this correlation for *calculix*.

Table 1. Coverage (C_P), Long Phase Coverage (LPC_{11}), estimated power score (P_{est}), phase power improvement (P_σ) and phase power consistency $(S_\lambda$ and $S_\sigma)$ results using models **A** and **B**.

Benchmark	C_P		LPC_{11}		P_{est}		P_σ		S_λ		S_σ	
	A	B	A	B	A	B	A	B	A	B	A	B
calculix	1.00	1.00	0.99	0.99	0.99	0.99	1.22	1.39	0.034	0.024	0.58	0.36
GemsFDTD	1.00	1.00	0.98	0.98	0.98	0.98	1.49	1.73	0.024	0.021	0.17	0.18
gobmk	1.00	1.00	0.96	0.98	0.97	0.98	1.18	1.18	0.012	0.012	0.47	0.46
gromacs	0.99	0.99	0.95	0.98	0.99	0.99	1.11	1.26	0.012	0.012	0.64	0.55
bzip2	0.97	0.99	0.94	0.96	0.95	0.97	1.09	1.26	0.035	0.022	0.67	0.68
cactusADM	0.98	0.70	0.97	0.69	0.99	0.95	1.03	1.32	0.019	0.011	0.62	0.41
zeusmp	1.00	1.00	0.95	0.96	0.96	0.90	1.06	1.52	0.032	0.020	0.95	0.75
namd	1.00	1.00	0.98	0.99	0.99	0.99	1.19	1.16	0.008	0.011	0.92	0.97
gcc	0.99	0.99	0.94	0.94	0.98	0.97	1.19	1.27	0.027	0.026	0.45	0.46
Average	**0.99**	**0.96**	**0.96**	**0.94**	**0.98**	**0.97**	**1.17**	**1.34**	**0.023**	**0.018**	**0.61**	**0.54**

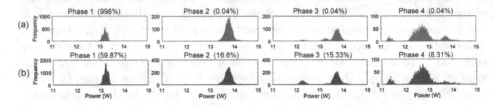

Fig. 4. (a) Estimated and (b) measured **power histogram** of phases in *calculix*, along with each phase's respective size in the (a) training set and (b) whole benchmark

Table 1 shows the results for P_{est} for all benchmarks. It can be seen that there is a strong correlation between estimated and real power histograms of the benchmarks, showing the power recorded for the phases from the first 10% of the runtime can be a good representative of the benchmark, even for benchmarks with varying behaviour along the runtime (e.g. *bzip2* in Fig. 1).

3.3   Phase Power Differentiation

To measure the ability of our methodology in separating the execution into phases based on the power behaviour of each phase, we define **Phase Power Improvement** (P_σ) as the ratio between the standard deviation of the power along the whole benchmark (H_{BM}) and the weighted sum of the standard deviation of power within each phase, as follows:

$$P_\sigma = \frac{\sigma(H_{BM})}{\sum_{p=1}^{p=NC_2} W_p * \sigma(H_p)} \qquad (2)$$

Where H_p is the power distribution within phase p and W_p is the share of phase p from the whole runtime. $\sigma(H_{BM})$ is the standard deviation of power

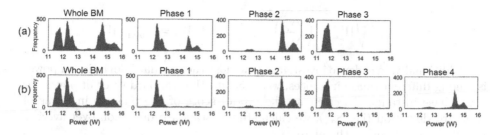

Fig. 5. Power histogram of phases in *459.GemsFDTD*, showing phase power separation for (a) model A and (b) model B

along the whole benchmark. This factor is used to show how successful the method is in separating phases according to their power attributes. The working assumption is that the power within each phase is consistent and hence its density function (i.e. the power histogram) is narrower as compared to that of the entire benchmark. A value of $P_\sigma = 1$ does not show any improvement in this criteria, while larger values show improved results.

As it is shown in Fig. 5, which shows the power histogram for each phase of *GemsFDTD* (under both models) compared to the histogram of the whole benchmark shown in the leftmost graphs, the power histogram of the whole benchmark is separated among the benchmark's phases. As Table 1 shows, on average, using Model A improves this factor by 17% while Model B provided 34% improvement in P_σ. The improvement resulted by using the power estimate in Model B is expected as we introduce the power estimate as the sixth input to the sub-phase clustering stage.

3.4   Phase Power Consistency

The main goal of our proposed methodology is to detect and classify similar consistent phases throughout the execution. We expect the power distributions of the instances of a phase to be similar. To validate this claim, we compare all instances within a phase in terms of their *mean* and *standard deviation* of measured power. In order to score each phase in this aspect, we first collect the mean and standard deviation of each phase instance. We define λ_{p_i} as the mean and σ_{p_i} as the standard deviation of power in instance i of phase p. We define λ_{λ_p} as the average of all mean powers in phase p and σ_{λ_p} as the standard deviation of the all mean powers in phase p.

$$\lambda_{\lambda_p} = \frac{\Sigma_{i=1}^{M_p} \lambda_{p_i}}{M_p} \quad and \quad \sigma_{\lambda_p} = \sqrt{\frac{1}{M_p} \Sigma_{i=1}^{M_p} (\lambda_{p_i} - \lambda_{\lambda_p})^2} \tag{3}$$

In order to score each phase, we compare σ_{λ_p} with λ_{λ_p} to calculate the standard error for mean power of each phase p. To analyse the whole benchmark in terms of **Phase Power Consistency**, we report S_λ as the weighted geometric mean of $\frac{\sigma_{\lambda_p}}{\lambda_{\lambda_p}}$ among all phases of the benchmark

$$S_\lambda = \sqrt[W_s]{\Pi_{p=1}^{p=N_2} \left(\frac{\sigma_{\lambda_p}}{\lambda_{\lambda_p}}\right)^{W_p}} \quad where \quad W_s = \Sigma_{p=1}^{p=N_2} W_p \tag{4}$$

Additionally, in order to investigate how close the standard deviation of power is among different phase instances, we calculate the standard error of power for each phase instance. To calculate the overall score of the phase p in terms of standard deviation (i.e. S_{σ_p}), we calculate the standard deviation over average for all instances within the phase p.

$$S_{\sigma_p} = \frac{\sqrt{\frac{1}{M_p} \cdot \sum_{i=1}^{M_p}(S_i - \bar{S}_{\sigma_p})^2}}{\bar{S}_{\sigma_p}} \quad where \quad S_i = \frac{\sigma_{p_i}}{\lambda_{p_i}} \tag{5}$$

Where $\bar{S}_{\sigma_p}$ is defined as the average of S_i among all instances in the phase. We report S_σ as the geometric mean of the standard error of the standard deviation of power in all phase instances.

The smaller the values of S_λ and S_σ are, the better our methodology performs, with zero being the ideal score. Table 1 shows S_λ and S_σ for all benchmarks. According to this table, using our methodology, we can achieve an average of 2.3% error in terms of S_λ value, using model A. This score is improved even more in model B, leading to 1.8% error on average. The S_λ scores verify that all instances of a phase have nearly the same mean power (within about 2% error). The S_σ score shows the phase instances consistency in terms of their standard deviation. Our methodology scores 61% for model A and 54% when using model B. The S_σ score signifies the presence of noise. It shows the standard deviation of the instances to vary as much as 61% in average indicating the contribution of noise to our measurement.

3.5   Power Management Utilizing Phase Results

Creating the phase information model for the benchmark is the first step in controlling the execution in order to control the overall power dissipation of the system. To show an example of how the phase information can be used to manage power, we manually created a frequency management trace for two benchmarks (*calculix* and *GemsFDTD*) based on their phase results to be used to control the CPU frequency in later executions. We utilized a frequency control daemon we developed for this purpose. Creating an automated tool which responds to the phase data and controls the CPU frequency in an online manner is a part of our future works.

Figure 6 shows the result of this technique. In this figure the normal power traces are shown on the left (Fig. 6(a) and (c)) while frequency-controlled power traces are shown on the right (Fig. 6(b) and (d)). In case of *GemsFDTD* the power control mechanism was switched on at $t = 1600$ ms to provide a comparable trace in this figure. The intervals shown in this figure correspond to the same sections of execution with or without power control. The maximum power dropped from 15.4 W to 14.4 W (6.5%) in *calculix* and from 14.98 W

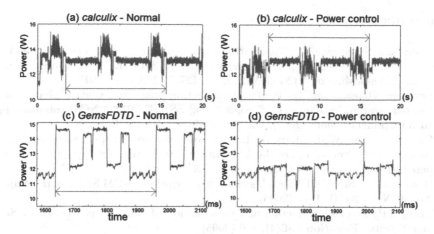

Fig. 6. Measured power traces of (a) *calculix* normal execution - (b) *calculix* with Power control - (c) *GemsFDTD* normal execution - (d) *GemsFDTD* with Power control

to 12.65 W (15.5%) in *GemsFDTD*. We also reduced the average power from 13.2 W to 12.76 W (3.3%) in *calculix* and from 13.25 W to 11.85 W (10.6%) in *GemsFDTD*. The frequency drop decreased the performance of *calculix* and *GemsFDTD* by 2.7% and 6.9% respectively. Using our method, the overall $max(power) - mean(power)$ parameter dropped from 2.20 W to 1.64 W (25%) in *calculix* and from 1.74 W to 0.8 W (54%) in *GemsFDTD*.

4   Conclusions and Future Works

In order to provide the system with information about the current conditions of the workload, we proposed a new hierarchical methodology for classifying the execution into distinct phases. Using current and previously read processor performance counter values, our method maps each time slice into one of dynamically created execution phases. We showed our model's ability to separate the benchmark's phases in terms of their power histogram using a portion of the execution as the training set. We compared only using the performance counter values (i.e. model A) with utilizing an additional secondary power derivative (i.e. model B). We investigated the consistency of phase instances in terms of their power behaviour and achieved an average of **2.3% or 1.8%** error in consistency of mean power in phase instances, based on the chosen model. Using the secondary power model improves the phase consistency scores (S_λ and S_σ) and the phase power improvement factors (P_σ) while it does not meaningfully affect coverage (C_P and LPC_i) or the phase power estimation results (P_{est}). As for further expansions of this work, we are developing a methodology to use the phasing data to forecast near-future phases and automatically manage the CPU frequency accordingly.

References

1. Srinivasan, S., Kumar, R., Kundu, S.: Program phase duration prediction and its application to fine-grain power management. In: 2013 IEEE Computer Society Annual Symposium on VLSI (ISVLSI), pp. 127–132, August 2013
2. Benomar, O., Sahraoui, H., Poulin, P.: Detecting program execution phases using heuristic search. In: Goues, C., Yoo, S. (eds.) SSBSE 2014. LNCS, vol. 8636, pp. 16–30. Springer, Cham (2014). doi:10.1007/978-3-319-09940-8_2
3. Fan, X., Weber, W.-D., Barroso, L.A.: Power provisioning for a warehouse-sized computer. In: Proceedings of the 34th Annual International Symposium on Computer Architecture. ISCA 2007, pp. 13–23. ACM (2007)
4. Henning, J.L.: SPEC CPU2006 benchmark descriptions. ACM SIGARCH Comput. Archit. News **34**(4), 1–17 (2006)
5. Reiss, S.P.: Dynamic detection and visualization of software phases. ACM SIGSOFT Softw. Eng. Notes **30**(4), 1–6 (2005)
6. Ishio, T., Watanabe, Y., Inoue, K.: AMIDA: A sequence diagram extraction toolkit supporting automatic phase detection. In: Companion of the 30th International Conference on Software Engineering, pp. 969–970. ACM (2008)
7. Isci, C., Martonosi, M.: Phase characterization for power: evaluating control-flow-based and event-counter-based techniques. In: HPCA 2006, pp. 121–132 (2006)
8. Zhang, Z., Chang, J.M.: A cool scheduler for multi-core systems exploiting program phases. IEEE Trans. Comput. **63**(5), 1061–1073 (2014)
9. Cochran, R., Reda, S.: Thermal prediction and adaptive control through workload phase detection. ACM Trans. Des. Autom. Electron. Syst. (TODAES) **18**(1), 7 (2013)
10. Mucci, P.J., Browne, S., Deane, C., Ho, G.: PAPI: A portable interface to hardware performance counters. In: Proceedings of the Department of Defense HPCMP Users Group Conference, pp. 7–10 (1999)
11. Sun, Y., Wanner, L., Srivastava, M.: Low-cost estimation of sub-system power. In: International Green Computing Conference (IGCC), pp. 1–10. IEEE (2012)
12. Kim, Y., Park, S., Cho, Y., Chang, N.: System-level online power estimation using an on-chip bus performance monitoring unit. IEEE Trans. Comput. Aided Des. Integr. Circuits Syst. **30**(11), 1585–1598 (2011)
13. Bartalos, P., Blake, M.B.: Green web services: modeling and estimating power consumption of web services. In: 2012 IEEE 19th International Conference on Web Services (ICWS), pp. 178–185. IEEE (2012)
14. Khoshbakht, S., Dimopoulos, N.: SAPPP: the software-aware power and performance profiler (under Review)
15. Hardy, A.: An examination of procedures for determining the number of clusters in a data set. In: Diday, E., Lechevallier, Y., Schader, M., Bertrand, P., Burtschy, B. (eds.) New Approaches in Classification and Data Analysis. Studies in Classification, Data Analysis, and Knowledge Organization, pp. 178–185. Springer, Heidelberg (1994). doi:10.1007/978-3-642-51175-2_20
16. Bircher, W.L., John, L.K.: Complete system power estimation using processor performance events. IEEE Trans. Comput. **61**(4), 563–577 (2012)
17. Rodrigues, R., Annamalai, A., Koren, I., Kundu, S.: Scalable thread scheduling in asymmetric multicores for power efficiency. In: 2012 IEEE 24th International Symposium on Computer Architecture and High Performance Computing (SBAC-PAD), pp. 59–66. IEEE (2012)

Memory Systems

Adaptive and Scalable Predictive Page Policies for High Core-Count Server CPUs

Tameesh Suri[✉] and Aneesh Aggarwal

Intel Corporation, 2200 Mission College Boulevard, Santa Clara, CA 95054, USA
{tameesh.suri,aneesh.aggarwal}@intel.com

Abstract. Increasing datacenter compute requirements has led to tremendous growth in the cadence of CPU cores on chip-multiprocessors. With large number of threads running on a single node, it is critical to achieve high memory bandwidth efficiency on large scale CMPs to support continued growth in the number CPU cores. In this paper, we present several mechanisms that improve the memory efficiency by improving the page hit rate for multi-core processors. In particular, we present memory page-policies that dynamically adapt to the runtime workload characteristics and use thread awareness to reduce contention between different memory address streams from the different threads. Unlike contemporary DRAM page policies such as static or timer-based, the proposed framework profiles the memory stream at runtime and uncovers opportunities to close or keep DRAM pages open, resulting in reduced page-conflicts and improved efficiencies. We implement the proposed policies in a cycle-accurate performance model simulating an 8-core processor. Our results show that the proposed adaptive page policies increase performance of high memory bandwidth workloads in SPECint2006 by up to 3%, and can attain 83% average performance relative to a "perfect" page prediction policy. We further show that the performance improvement from the techniques increases with the number of cores and with making the policies thread-aware in a many-core processor. The implementation cost of our techniques is extremely low, an area overhead of only 69 bits, making them extremely attractive for real-life products.

1 Introduction

We are seeing tremendous growth in the data center capacities, driven in large part by the exponential growth in internet connections and data storage requirements. The data center capacities are increasing in terms of both the number of nodes deployed in the data centers as well as the number of cores within each node. This has resulted in the current many-core data center CPUs, with the expectation that the number of cores will increase significantly in every new generation. However, the memory channels that a vendor can integrate in a CPU is many times limited by other constraints such as package size, pin-out limitations, etc. Hence, each memory controller in these many-core CPUs is expected to handle high memory bandwidths from the multiple cores. Furthermore, the memory traffic observed by a memory controller is a mix of streams from the multiple cores and the overall traffic mix is highly dependent on each application's stream.

© Springer International Publishing AG 2017
J. Knoop et al. (Eds.): ARCS 2017, LNCS 10172, pp. 99–110, 2017.
DOI: 10.1007/978-3-319-54999-6_8

The page policy implemented in the memory controllers decides whether to keep a page open or close the page after it has been accessed. The page policy that will work the best will be different for different workloads. For instance, some workloads may prefer an open-page policy whereas other workloads may prefer a closed-page policy. The optimal page policy may also differ between the different phases within a single workload. Furthermore, different DRAM banks within a single phase may prefer different page policies.

The current DRAM page policies implemented in the memory controllers are mostly static in nature [7]. These policies either close the page on every access or keep the page open for a time before closing it if there are no further accesses to that page [2, 3, 7]. Such "one size fits all" policies do not adapt the page open/close policy to the current memory traffic stream observed by the memory controller, so as to minimize the memory access time and maximize the bandwidth.

To show the importance of having a page policy that adapts to the applications' memory streams, we experimented with two static policies with some intelligence built into the policies that looks ahead at the other commands in the pipe. Intelligent page open (IPO) policy keeps a page open on an access by default, but closes the page if there is a conflicting page to the same bank pending in the queue. Intelligent page close (IPC) policy closes the page by default but keeps it open if there is another access to the same page pending.

To further motivate adaptive page policies, we modeled a "perfect" page policy. Perfect page policy keeps a page open if a subsequent memory transaction to the bank is a page-hit, and closes the page if the subsequent transaction to the bank accesses a different DRAM row. No additional penalties are incurred in the perfect page policy to predict whether to close the page or to keep the page open. The experimental setup is discussed in Sect. 4.

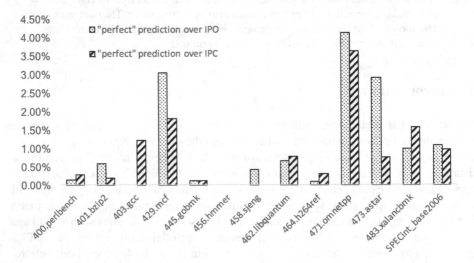

Fig. 1. SPECintrate2006 performance increase using "perfect" page prediction policy over baseline IPO and IPC policies

Figure 1 shows performance improvement using "perfect" page predictor over baseline IPO and IPC policies. Firstly, note that for memory intensive components such as *mcf* and *omnetpp*, IPC performs slightly better than IPO because bank contention due to multiple threads prefers closing the page. In contrast, there are other components, mainly *gcc* and *xalancbmk*, for which IPO performs better than IPC. This illustrates the importance of adapting the page policy to the behavior of the applications.

Secondly, the high memory bandwidth components of the SPECInt Suite, such as *mcf* and *omnetpp*, observe 3–4% performance gains with perfect page prediction policies. This motivates the need to accurately predict whether to close a page or keep it open. Even though we experiment with an 8-core processor, we expect that adaptive page-policies will perform better with more cores. However, such predictive page policies need to adapt to several factors, including workload phases, number of threads, and inter-arrival transaction rate (dictated primarily by the choice of interconnect).

In this paper, we propose a mechanism to dynamically predict and optimize the page open/close policy for the current behavior of the application. The high level architectural details for the proposed page-policies are also presented in a recently granted US patent [1]. Our experiments show that the proposed mechanisms give up to 3% better performance for memory intensive applications running on an 8-core processor with 2 memory channels. We further show that with enough pages per core, there is almost no benefit with any adaptive page policies, but as number of cores increase, the benefit of adapting the page policies increases. For instance, for the same intensive applications on 2-channel CPU, the improvement of adaptive policies reduces to 1% for 4 cores, 0.5% for 2 cores. If we go beyond 8 cores, the improvement is expected to be higher. We also propose using thread-awareness along with memory access history pattern to further optimize the policy for each thread. Thread-awareness leads to the most optimal page-policy decisions in a many-core system and results in higher memory efficiency and better performance. Our best case page-policy can achieve 83% of "perfect" page policy performance with an additional area overhead of only 69 bits.

The rest of the paper is organized as follows. Section 2 gives a brief background on DRAM page policies and incurred latencies for different page modes. Section 3 describe the proposed adaptive page policies, including thread-aware schemes. Section 4 presents the evaluation methodology and results from different schemes. Section 5 summarizes the related work, and finally, Sect. 6 presents our conclusions.

2   DRAM Organization

Contemporary DRAM used in server systems are available commercially as dual in-line memory modules (*DIMMs*). Each *DIMM* is typically a collection of one or more *ranks*, and depending on the DRAM bus width (usually 64-bits), *rank* may constitute multiple DRAM chips. Each *rank* is further organized into several memory *banks*, where each *bank* supports concurrent memory request from the memory controller. Data is read out from the memory *bank* in DRAM page granularity (also referred as *rows*) and are stored in *row buffers*.

DRAM *row buffer* supports three states: *open*, *close* and *empty*. Before read or write transactions are issued, DRAM *row* (where transaction resides) is required to be in *open* state. Each bank supports at most one *open page* in the *row buffer*, and subsequent transactions to this bank addressed to another page require a *precharge* operation to close the current page, and an *activate* operation to open the new page before the read or write *CAS* transaction. This process is termed as page conflict, and results in highest latency penalty for the memory transaction. If a *row buffer* is *empty*, i.e. no page is opened, before memory transaction is issued, an *activate* operation is needed to open the addressed row – known as *page empty*. In comparison, if subsequent memory transactions are addressed to the same *open row*, read or write CAS operation can be directly issued. This results in best case latency for any memory transaction, and is called *page hit*.

Table 1 shows the latency penalty for different page status for memory transactions. General practice is to use open page policy (i.e. keep the page open on every access) if the memory stream demonstrates locality and close page policy for irregular traffic. These are (mostly) static in nature, and configured during boot time.

Table 1. DDR timing for page hits, page misses and page conflicts.

Page status	DDR timing	DDR3-1600 (dclks)
Page conflict	tRP + tRCD + tCL	33
Page miss	tRCD + tCL	22
Page hit	tCL	11

CPU cores continue to increase rapidly, while memory channel growth is severely limited, primarily by package I/O pin constraints and overall chip costs. This leads to exponential increase in contention on each memory bank, resulting in increased latencies and reduced memory efficiencies. Static policies and look-ahead schemes in memory controller which generally worked for single-core or smaller CMPs are ineffective with the increased thread contention. As an example, a dual channel DDR3 memory controller supporting dual-rank DIMMS provides a total of 32 independent banks, or parallel memory address streams, while 50 + core chips are soon becoming a common-place [16].

3   Adaptive Page Policy Schemes

This section describes the proposed page-policy schemes. We summarize some architectural aspects, including decisions and trade-offs. The section is divided primarily into two sub-sections: counter and history-based page policies, describing various variations.

3.1   Page-Hit Counter (PHC)

We propose a Page-Hit-Counter (PHC) approach that predicts whether the next access to the page will be a hit or a miss. The predictor is a set of simple saturating counters that count the page hit rate. The counters are provided for each memory channel and are reset periodically to more accurately identify the page hit rates in different phases of the workloads. If the page hit rate is higher than a pre-determined value, then the pages are kept open, and if the page hit rate is lower than the pre-determined value, then the pages are auto-closed.

We explore two variations of the PHC:

1. Global PHC (GPHC) that has a single page hit rate for all the banks in a channel
2. Per Bank PHC (BPHC) that has a page hit rate for each bank.

Figure 2 shows the process to determine whether to auto-close a DRAM page on an access or to keep the page open. The process is the same between GPHC and BPHC, the only difference being the counters used to determine the hit ratio.

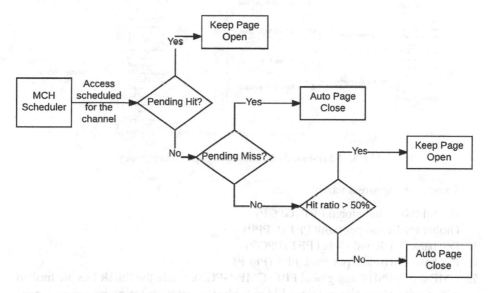

Fig. 2. GPHC and BPHC process flowchart to determine the current page policy

To update the page hit counters accurately, a register is provided for each bank to store the row address of the last access to that bank. When a new access is generated to that bank, the current row address is compared with the last row address. If the row addresses are the same, the page hit counter is incremented, and if the row addresses are different, the page hit counter is decremented. The row address registers are particularly useful in determining the page hits and misses for the cases where the pages have been auto-closed.

3.2   History Based and Thread-Aware Page Predictors

The proposed mechanism predicts whether to keep a DRAM page open or to auto-close the page when the particular page is accessed. The mechanism uses a two-level predictor to predict the policy for each page as shown in Fig. 3. A page history shift register (PSHR) is maintained that records the history of whether a page is kept open or auto-closed on every access. The PSHR is used to index into a page policy table (PPT), where each entry is a 2-bit saturating counter that indicates whether the page should be kept open or auto-closed (00 – strong close; 01 - weak close; 10 - weak open; 11 – strong open). Several variations of this multi-level predictor can be implemented.

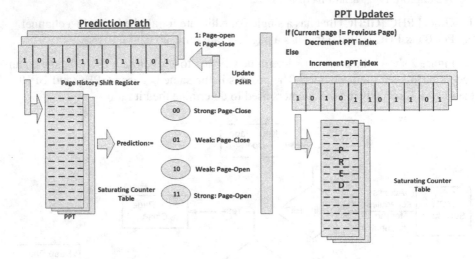

Fig. 3. CMP-based multi-level page prediction policy

Some of the apparent variations are:

1. Global PSHR and global PPT (GPGP)
2. Global PSHR and per-bank PPT (GPPP)
3. Per-bank PSHR and global PPT (PPGP)
4. Per-bank PSHR and per-bank PPT (PPPP)
5. CMP-aware PSHR and global PPT (CMP-GPGP), where the PSHR bits are hashed with some address bits and thread-id to further differentiate the policy for each page

We explain the GPGP mechanism here; the mechanism can be accordingly modified for the other variations. When the memory controller accesses a DRAM page, it uses the PSHR to index into the PPT. If the PPT suggests that the page should be closed, the memory controller generates the command with auto-close enabled. If the PPT suggests that the page should be kept open, the memory controller generates the command with the auto-close disabled. The suggestion from the PPT can be overridden if there is a pending access to the same page or a conflicting access to the same bank. If the prediction is to keep the page open, then the PSHR is left-shifted and a "1" is inserted at the right, and if the prediction is to close the page, then the PSHR is right-shifted and a "0" is inserted at the right.

In parallel to making a prediction, the PPT is also updated based on the previous predictions. If the DRAM access results in a page hit or the page that was last closed on the bank is re-opened, then the PPT index pointed to by the PSHR (or by PSHR hashed with the address bits depending on the implementation) is incremented. It is important to note that the PSHR value for a bank (when using a global PSHR) can change between two consecutive accesses to that bank. Another possible implementation is to record the

PSHR value at the time of prediction and then using that PSHR value, instead of the current PSHR value, to update the PPT. To accurately update the PPT, the address of the DRAM page that was most recently closed is recorded for each bank. On the other hand, if the DRAM access results in a page miss or a page other than the most recently closed page is opened on a bank, the PPT index is decremented.

In addition to GPGP, CMP-aware GPGP scheme variant hashes parts of address-bits and thread-id to distinguish memory streams and avoid polluting saturating counters across threads. This scheme specifically targets multi-core architectures, and includes both, global history of page-predictions and thread specific address isolation needed for large scale CMPs. We also explored thread-based PHSR, however, area cost increases rapidly with growth in number of cores, while CMP-aware GPGP requires no additional hardware in comparison to GPGP.

4   Evaluation Methodology and Results

The proposed page policies were implemented in a cycle-accurate performance simulator for an 8-core processor. The performance simulator models all aspects of server CPUs in comprehensive details, including the CPU cores, interconnect network and snoop traffic, and the memory controller. It is important to note that the precise model details are very important in uncovering and understanding the interplay and contention amongst various threads. Table 2 shows some of the parameters of our model.

Table 2. Performance simulator parameters

CPU	
Cores	8
Out of order/Issue width	3
L2 Size (shared with 2 cores)	2 MB
Interconnect	
Topology	Crossbar/point-to-point
Memory controller	
DDR-speed	DDR3-1600
Memory Channels	2
Pending queue entries	32
Ranks	dual-rank

Our performance model is trace-driven, and we use SPECintrate 2006 traces with 8 copies to measure the performance impact of the proposed policies. It is important to note that only a few components in SPECint2006 exhibit high memory bandwidth, and these workloads are expected to show most performance gains. We use Intel Compiler (IC) version 12.1 compiled binaries.

4.1 Performance Impact of PHC

We measured the performance benefit of the PHC approach, and experimented with a number of counter sizes. In addition to global and bank-aware saturating counters, we updated our schemes to be CMP-aware – maintaining per-thread counters for each scheme. We note that adding per-thread counters increases the overall hardware cost significantly with growing number of cores, however, this hypothetical experiment outlines performance implications of counter contention due to multiple threads.

Figure 4 summarizes the performance benefit obtained for GPHC, BPHC, and CMP-aware variations compared to the intelligent closed-page approach. Although we experimented with several counter-sizes, most optimal performance per additional unit hardware was observed using 5-bit saturating page hit counters. In interest of space, Fig. 4 shows performance using 5-bit saturating counters. It is interesting to note that CMP-aware saturating counter policies show performance advantage on every SPECint component compared to baseline PHC policies – emphasizing on the increase in thread contention. In comparison to the proposed baseline GPHC and BPHC approach which gives an average 0.24% increase in SIR performance, CMP-aware approach improves SIR performance by 0.48% for the tested configuration. In fact, *omnetpp* (high-bandwidth SPECint component) shows performance inversion using baseline GPHC and BPHC policies, primarily due to thread contention not captured by global or per bank saturating counter. However, with CMP-aware saturating counters, pollution due to thread contention is avoided, and all SPECint components show performance improvement. Please note that the overall extent of the performance benefit depends highly on the configuration of the system.

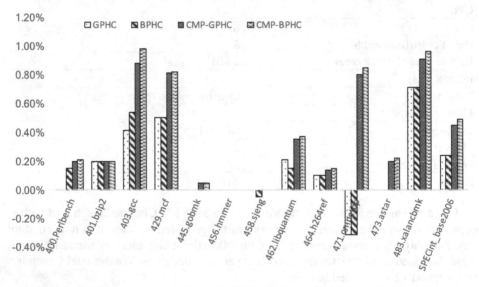

Fig. 4. Performance impact of various PHC policies on SPECintrate2006 over IPC

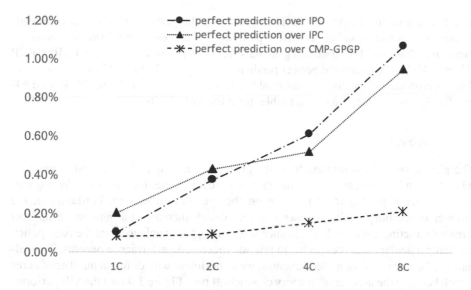

Fig. 5. Performance sensitivity of core-scaling on page-policies

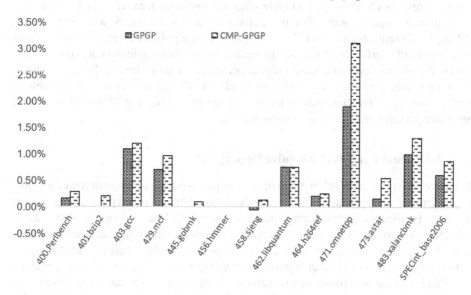

Fig. 6. Performance impact of CMP-based multi-level page prediction policies over IPC

4.2 Performance Impact of History Based and Thread-Aware Schemes

We experimented with several PSHR sizes and Fig. 6 summarizes the performance
benefit obtained with GPGP and CMP-aware GPGP with a 5-bit PSHR, i.e. 32-entry
PPT compared to the intelligent closed-page approaches. GPGP performs an average of
0.6% (>1% for some benchmarks) better than the best performing currently used policy
(IPC for our configuration). In comparison, CMP-GPGP scheme observes SIR

performance improvement of 0.83%, emphasizing the performance impact of thread-awareness. As shown in Fig. 1, perfect prediction achieves 1% performance improvement over baseline IPC translating to 83% relative performance using CMP-GPGP scheme. Unlike hypothetical perfect prediction policy, CMP-GPGP is able to achieve these performance benefits with minimal hardware overhead – 5 bits for PHSR and 64-bits for 32-entry saturating counter table, for a total of 69 bits.

4.3   Core Scaling

The performance improvement from the proposed techniques is expected to increase with the number of cores. As the number of cores increase, the memory BW requirements increase putting more pressure on the memory subsystem. Furthermore, the number of memory banks per core reduces, which increases the number of address streams targeting the same bank. In such a scenario, being able to adapt the page policy for that particular bank is expected to provide increased performance benefits. To evaluate the benefit of the proposed schemes, we experiment with different number of cores which keeping the number of memory channels at two. Figure 5 shows the SIR performance improvements of a perfect page predictor over IPC, IPO and CMP-GPGP (lower point represents closer to perfect policy/higher performance). As can be seen that, performance improvement from the perfect predictor increases with more cores, although difference between IPC/IPO and perfect page policies increases with growing core count. IPO performance is closer to perfect page policies at lower core counts (more banks/thread), however, IPC shows higher performance compared to IPO past 4-cores. In comparison, performance benefits of CMP-GPGP scheme remain comparable to perfect prediction policies with increase core count – achieving 83% of perfect page predictor performance for 8-core configuration.

4.4   Additional Benefits of Adaptive Page-Policies

The benefits of our approach include improved performance because of lower memory access latency (the approach eliminates activations on page hits and pre-charges on page misses). Furthermore, eliminating unnecessary page close and opens also reduces DRAM by eliminating the unnecessary reads and writes in the buffers used in the DRAM to cache the data from the open pages. Our experiments show that our adaptive page policies reduce the total number of page closes and opens by ~5%. Adaptive page policies can also lower the occurrence of row hammer issue compared to any page close policy by reducing the unnecessary row buffer write-backs and re-activations for accesses that would have otherwise hit in the DRAM.

5   Related Work

There are two main categories of mechanisms proposed to improve the page hit rate achieved by the memory controllers. There is a significant body of work on techniques to improve the address mapping in the multi-core systems in order to improve the page hits by reducing bank conflicts [4, 5, 7, 15]. Other page policies proposed to improve the page hit rate are mostly static/look-ahead policies [6–9, 11, 15]. A few adaptive page-policies have been proposed in the past [2–4, 10, 12–14]. The policies in [3, 4] are timer-based controller policies that use an adaptive timer for page closure. Another timer-based approach [13] distinguishes time based on *live* and *dead* timer to keep page open or close. The adaptive policy in [2] uses prediction based on number of accesses to dram row buffer. Some of these approaches use history based techniques [10, 12, 14] with the histories stored in tables or data structures somewhat similar to ours. However, these predictive policies are very expensive to implement and not thread-aware as is required in a many core system. Furthermore, the design focus and evaluation have been limited to single-core systems. In contrast, we propose page-policies that are inexpensive to implement and specifically focused for many core processors. Furthermore, our policies are expected to scale with increasing number of CPU cores [1]. One key aspect for the policies designed for many core systems is that these policies need to handle both the thread contention and traffic mix from the multiple threads while improving the page hit rates.

6 Conclusions

Increasing number of cores in server systems are leading to increased pressure on the memory subsystem due to thread contention and intermix of the memory traffic from the different threads. Static page policies may not be able to perform well in these many core systems and reduce the overall memory controller efficiency. The challenge is to develop adaptive page policies that adapt to the runtime memory traffic characteristics from the different threads in a multi-core system and scale with the number of cores integrated in the CPU. This paper proposes several adaptive DRAM page-policies that predict whether to close a page or keep it open when accessing a DRAM page. The paper also elaborates on the performance implications of these schemes on a representative 8-core server system. Our results show that our proposed policies can achieve 83% performance improvement relative to a perfect page prediction policy with minimal hardware overhead of 69 bits. This also translates to 0.83% absolute performance improvement for SPECintrate2006, with some high bandwidth workloads observing 3% performance gains. We expect the proposed policies to show greater impact with increasing number of CPU cores, leading to increased demand for memory bandwidth.

References

1. Aggarwal, A., Suri, T.: Dynamic Memory Page Policy. US Patent 9,378,127 B2 (2016)
2. Awasthi, M., Nellans, D.W., Balasubramonian, R., Davis, A.: Prediction based dram row-buffer management in the many-core era. In: IEEE International Conference on Parallel Architectures and Compilation Techniques (PACT) (2011)
3. Boughton, K., Gill, R.: Everything you always wanted to know about sdram memory but were afraid to ask (2010). http://www.anandtech.com/show/3851/everything-you-always-wanted-to-know-aboutsdram-memory-but-were-afraid-to-ask
4. Dodd, J.: Adaptive page management. US Patent 7,076,617 (2006)

5. Ghasempour, M., Jaleel, A., Garside, J., Luján, M.: HAPPY: hybrid address-based page policy in DRAMs. In: MEMSYS (2006)
6. Huan, D., Li, Z., Hu, W., Liu, Z.: Processor directed dynamic page policy. In: Jesshope, C., Egan, C. (eds.) ACSAC 2006. LNCS, vol. 4186, pp. 109–122. Springer, Heidelberg (2006). doi:10.1007/11859802_10
7. Jacob, B., Ng, S., Wang, D.: Memory Systems: Cache, DRAM, Disk. Morgan Kaufmann, CA (2010)
8. Kaseridis, D., Stuecheli, J., John, L.K.: Minimalist open-page: a dram page-mode scheduling policy for the many-core era. In: 44th Annual IEEE/ACM International Symposium on Microarchitecture (MICRO) (2011)
9. Ma, C., Chen, S.: A dram precharge policy based on address analysis. In: Digital System Design Architectures, Methods and Tools (DSD) (2007)
10. Miura, S., Ayukawa, K., Watanabe, T.: A dynamic-sdram-mode-control scheme for low-power systems with a 32-bit risc cpu. In: International Symposium on Low Power Electronics and Design (ISLPED) (2001)
11. Park, S.I., Park, I.C.: History-based memory mode prediction for improving memory performance. In: International Symposium on Circuits and Systems (2003)
12. Stankovic, V., Milenkovic, N.: Access latency reduction in contemporary dram memories. Facta universitatis (NIS) (2004)
13. Stankovic, V., Milenkovic, N.: Dram controller with a complete predictor. In: 7th International Conference on Telecommunications in Modern Satellite, Cable and Broadcasting Services (2005)
14. Stankovic, V., Milenkovic, N.: Dram controller with a close-page predictor. In: EUROCON (2005)
15. Xu, Y., Agarwal, Aabhas, S., Davis, Brian, T.: Prediction in dynamic SDRAM controller policies. In: Bertels, K., Dimopoulos, N., Silvano, C., Wong, S. (eds.) SAMOS 2009. LNCS, vol. 5657, pp. 128–138. Springer, Heidelberg (2009). doi:10.1007/978-3-642-03138-0_14
16. Xeon Processor E7 Family. http://www.intel.com/content/www/us/en/processors/xeon/xeon-processor-e7-family.html

A Method for Fast Evaluation
of Sharing Set Management Strategies
in Cache Coherence Protocols

Julie Dumas[1,2](✉), Eric Guthmuller[1,2],
César Fuguet Tortolero[1,2], and Frédéric Pétrot[3]

[1] Univ. Grenoble Alpes, 38000 Grenoble, France
[2] CEA, LETI, MINATEC Campus, 38054 Grenoble, France
{julie.dumas,eric.guthmuller,cesar.fuguettortolero}@cea.fr
[3] CNRS, TIMA Laboratory, Université Grenoble Alpes, 38031 Grenoble, France
frederic.petrot@imag.fr

Abstract. With the emergence of manycore processors with potentially hundreds of processors in the embedded market, the scalability of cache coherence protocols is again at stake. One seemingly simple issue is the management of the set of sharers of a memory block, but with that many processors, it is a major bottleneck in terms of hardware resources. In this paper, we define a high level simulation method to evaluate sharing set management strategies, using memory access traces obtained through cycle accurate simulation (*e.g.* **gem5**). The goal of the method is to rank protocols based on latency, traffic and hardware cost, to help either choose an existing approach for a given application context, or evaluate new approaches. We demonstrate the applicability of our proposal by evaluating three existing scalable cache coherence protocols, obtaining results consistent with previous, low level, evaluations much more rapidly.

1 Introduction

According to [7], we have entered the manycore era for some time now. Even though the scalability of cache coherence protocols has been a problem for long [11], it remains so in the absence of a credible hardware abstraction alternative for software [15].

Cache coherence protocols are often seen as high level Finite State Machines (FSM) governing actions taken for each cache block. These actions may be either local to the cache or be visible by other parts of the system. Many works have been done to compare these FSMs during the 80's, *e.g.* [1], which is representative of the performance analysis that can be done. At that time, most multiprocessors were bus based and thus using something different than the snoop protocol was not appealing. Indeed, as a message sent on a bus is implicitly broadcasted to every connected component, each component can snoop transactions even if it is not the target. With the advent of more sophisticated interconnects, it rapidly

J. Knoop et al. (Eds.): ARCS 2017, LNCS 10172, pp. 111–123, 2017.
DOI: 10.1007/978-3-319-54999-6_9

became clear that the way to identify which cache should be the target of a message was of primary importance, and led to the notion of *sharing set*. The first proposal, due to [6], was to maintain in main memory a presence bit for each processor. The fact of centralizing the information at the memory, called directory, allows to limit the number of messages to the caches that actually need them (multicast). However, it increases linearly the memory cost with the number of processors, which is simply not scalable. Furthermore, the usage of a directory adds one indirection, thus increasing the protocol latency. To cope with these issues, the researchers' imagination was challenged: plenty of solutions have been proposed, many are still under investigation.

Doing a fair comparison between the solutions proposed to manage the sharers set in modern Network-on-Chip (NoC) based multiprocessor architectures is not easy. As snoop protocols broadcast their coherence messages, they potentially generate a lot of traffic, but they have constant latency as long as the NoC is not saturated. Directory-based protocols generate only the necessary traffic and the latency depends on the network topology and application deployment on the CPUs and memory banks. To increase the performance and memory throughput, most existing manycore architectures are NUMA [4], *i.e.* they feature *Non-Uniform Memory Access* times: the memory access time depends on the memory location and the requester CPU location. Still, manycore architects need a way to select the best cache coherence protocol for their application considering performance (*i.e.* latency, bandwidth, power consumption) and hardware related costs. The problem is worsened by the wide number of strategies to manage the sharing set: static ones like bit-vector or snoop protocol [20], or dynamic ones like linked-list protocol [22], Ackwise limited sharers list [12] or the heap sharing set strategy [13]. As many parameters have to be considered (protocol FSM, sharing set management, network topology, traffic shape, etc.), neither analytical models –too complex– nor cycle accurate simulation –too lengthy– are appropriate.

Our goal in this paper is to propose a high level cache coherence protocols simulation method to specifically evaluate sharing set management strategies. This method replays a unique trace captured at the output of the L1 caches on a model that is aware of the topology of the memory hierarchy.

The remainder of the paper is organized as follows. Section 2 presents the related work. Our method to rank sharing set management is described Sect. 3. Section 4 presents the results and compares them to previously published ones. Finally, Sect. 5 summarizes the results and concludes the paper.

2   Related Work

Fully detailed cache coherence protocol evaluation requires CPU, cache and network implementation. As manycore RTL simulations are very slow, there is a need for models at a higher level of abstraction.

An approach advocated for small scale multiprocessors is to use cycle accurate simulation. The work of [14] focuses on the power evaluation of snoop protocols on a single bus based multiprocessor architecture. The evaluations target

L1 cache coherence comparing several high level automata using 5 small kernels, among which 2 are not synthetic ones (FFT and LU from SPLASH2 [25]). Unfortunately, neither the number of processors used in the simulation nor the runtime necessary for these evaluations are reported. In [16], the authors compare the *write policy* impact on NoC based multiprocessors, and report results for up to 64 cores. However, their experiments include only two applications (Ocean and Water from SPLASH2), and do not report the run times of the simulations to obtain their results. The question of the accuracy that can be reached by cycle accurate simulation when simulating memory hierarchy is addressed by [5]. The authors show that the **gem5** simulator [3] can be very accurate, but in order to be so, the cache coherence protocol modeling requires the *ruby* mode. Unfortunately, this mode makes the simulation multiple times slower than the default **gem5** configuration. Finally, we also refer to [17] which targets the simulation of directory protocols for up to 128 cores, in which the authors explicitly state that they limit themselves to three applications because of low simulation speed, despite the fact that they were using a parallel simulator on 32 cores. They also report their results solely in terms of number of invalidation messages, because there is no model of the topology, link capacity, etc. To conclude, even though cycle accuracy is precious, it is hardly usable for running the hundreds or thousands of simulation necessary for design space exploration.

Therefore, other works observed that the actual program behavior is of no importance as long as the memory accesses are well modeled. To that end, they suggest that using traffic generators and modeling only the caches and network can be a solution. These generator can produce either synthetic traffic (random or statistically characterized [21]), or real traffic obtained by accurate CPU/manycore models [24]. This last solution requires clearly at least one lengthy simulation to obtain the cache miss requests, but provides actual benchmarks memory references. By injecting this traffic into a different high level model of the memory hierarchy, it is possible firstly to rapidly evaluate cache coherence protocols performance, and secondly to quantify the error by comparing the results with the one obtained at RTL or cycle accurate level. Indeed, cache coherence protocol implementation is complex, specifically in handling race conditions through transient states, while not required to get an approximation of average access latency and bandwidth usage [1]. These approaches are known as *trace driven simulation* [23], and are still the subject of a large body of research. However, to the best of our knowledge it has never been used specifically to evaluate sharing set management in coherent memory hierarchy.

3   Protocols Ranking Method

The solution we propose requires: (1) traffic extraction, done once for a given benchmark; (2) the replay of these traces through a network on a high-level cache model which includes sharing set management, and gathers statistics during execution. This second step can be done as many times as required with different models, and constitutes the core of this work.

3.1   Traffic Extraction

We produce the traces using a loosely-timed or cycle-accurate simulator (**gem5** in this case). However, to avoid the generation of huge dumps, we store only the events related to L1 misses and L1 evictions (L1 caches are write-back). This has the nice property of filtering out a lot of memory accesses, thanks to the low miss rates of the caches, and thus reduces both the data set size and the simulation time of the high-level cache models. Even though these collected data seem to be exactly the necessary information, this is an approximation because the content of the sharing set will change depending on the strategy under evaluation, and thus future misses would be different. This difference is evaluated in Sect. 4.3 to show that the approximation is acceptable.

The benchmarks producing the traffic (PARSEC [2] and SPLASH2 [25] applications) run under Linux, whose boot phase may disturb the analysis. To focus on the region of interest (ROI), we add simulator specific instructions at the beginning of the ROI to create a checkpoint, and at the end of the ROI to exit the simulator. We choose to restart simulation after the checkpoint to extract traffic that belongs only to the ROI, and to start with cold caches.

3.2   High-Level Cache Modeling

The extracted traffic is injected in a high-level cache model composed of the L1-copy list, L2 caches, L2 meta-data (see Sect. 3.4) and network (see Sect. 3.5). L1 caches are not modeled as we use trace-driven simulation with L1 output traffic. L1-copy list contains identifiers of L1 accessing a given cache block. This list is used to model the response tracking even when the sharing set strategy only offers a limited view of the sharers list (*e.g.* snoop). The L2 caches are set associative and parameters like block size, set number and way number can be configured. The L2 are inclusive but the most updated data is on L1. Although the block replacement policy is configurable, we actually use a pseudo-random policy as it gives good results for big caches [10]. The L2 meta-data has two parts. The first is specific to each sharing set strategy, as described in Sect. 3.3 and the second includes the tag and the MOESI automaton state. The automaton is the high level protocol FSM, and there is no need for modeling transient states, since we focus on the sharing set strategy evaluation. This simplification is possible because we do not care about data values. Cache block states are thus Invalid –copy is not in the L2, Valid –the only copy is in the L2, Shared/Owned –one or several L1 have a copy, Exclusive –a L1 has the copy and can modify the data.

High-level cache models can be instrumented for different metrics such as latency, traffic, power, etc. We focus on latency and traffic, as we will then be able to compare our results to the ones of the literature. We measure latency as the total time taken by the initial read request, the induced coherence requests and the responses to traverse the NoC. In case of a L2 miss, a fixed roundtrip latency of 100 clock cycles is used to model external memory accesses. Purposedly we omit the time taken to process requests in caches as we suppose it constant for all sharing set strategies. The traffic is measured as the number of flits going through each NoC router. In addition to latency and bandwidth, our models track additional metrics: sharing level, cache block lifetime, hit and miss ratio. This last information does not depend on the sharing set strategy but it is useful to characterize benchmarks and specially memory/cache accesses.

3.3 Sharing Set Management Strategies

Among all sharing set management strategies that have been devised, we focus on well known ones for which results are available and cross-checked:

Snoop [20]: Snooping on NoC means broadcasting, *i.e.* each L1 cache request is forwarded to all caches. This solution generates a lot of transactions, but hardware-wise, the meta-data size is small.

Full bit-vector [20]: It uses a directory with a full bit-vector to keep track of all potential sharers of a cache block. This solution allows to multicast the messages only to the caches that need it. From a hardware point of view, it is costly as each block must have one bit per cache in the system.

ACKwise [12]: This protocol uses a limited sharing set organized as a list of k cache identifiers in the directory. When a block has more than k sharers, the coherence messages are broadcasted. In this solution, the hardware overhead due to the directory can be chosen at will, but it generates more messages than the full bit-vector solution when a block is shared by more than k cores. To compare this work with the literature, the threshold is fixed to 5.

3.4 Sharing Set Behavior

In the snoop implementation, the L1 requester sends a message to the L2, which in turn sends a broadcast to all L1s. The L2 waits for the first L1 response and transfers it to the requester. Therefore, the latency corresponds to the latency to the closest L1 that has this copy. If the only valid copy is in the L2, the L2 awaits the responses from all L1s, so the latency is at its maximum. If the cache hierarchy does not hold the data, the L2 sends a refill request to the memory.

In the full bit-vector sharing set approach, a presence bit P exists per cache. It is thus easy to track all sharers, by setting their presence bit to 1. In our implementation, a L1 miss generates a message from the L1 cache requester to the L2. This L2 transfers the message to the exclusive L1 or to the L1 copy which minimizes the latency between L2, L1 copy and requester.

In Ackwise, the sharing list size is a configuration parameter. When this list overflows, a global bit G is set to 1 to indicate that we do not store the exact list of sharers anymore as only a counter of sharers is recorded. Furthermore, a single cache that contains an up to date version of the block (exclusively or shared) is identified as the *keeper*. When there is a L1 read request, this request is forwarded by the L2 to the *keeper* which sends the response to the requester. For an exclusive request, if $G = 0$, the L2 sends a message to all the sharers to invalidate their data. If $G = 1$, the L2 sends a broadcast to invalidate all caches. In this mode, only L1 that have a copy send an acknowledgement because the directory knows the number of copies and waits until this number is reached.

3.5 Network Modeling

We implement a state of the art 2D-mesh network using the X-first routing algorithm. The topology can be easily changed, and so does the routing algorithm, as long as it is deterministic. The L2 memory mapping is configurable: an *interleaving* mode based on select bits of the address; and a *first touch* mode where the cache block is allocated in the nearest L2 at the first access. In the rest of the paper, we use an *interleaving* mapping based on the least significant bits of the address.

In this network, two physical channels are modeled: one for requests, another for responses. The message types on the network are the following: request, response, broadcast waiting for responses from all caches and broadcast waiting for a given number of responses. The broadcast type depends on the evaluated sharing set management strategy. The NoC has hardware support for broadcast messages: the L2 sends a single flit request which is replicated by the network to all L1 caches. All responses are forwarded to the requester and our model takes into account arbitration so that a single response is received at each clock cycle.

Finally, the latency is computed as the number of NoC routers traversed by the message, multiplied by a constant hop latency (fixed to 1 clock cycle in the rest of the paper). This formula heavily relies on the fact that under low traffic load, a NoC presents a constant hop latency. We will verify that we can make this hypothesis in Sect. 4. The NoC also records the traffic, that is the flits number, for each router on 10,000 cycles time windows.

4 Experimentations and Results Analysis

4.1 The gem5 Platform and Benchmarks

To produce traces, **gem5** simulator with classical memory is used, the main parameters used are given Table 1. This simulator comes with the PARSEC [2] and SPLASH2 [25] benchmarks. To keep cycle accurate simulation time under control while still producing a significant number of events, the PARSEC benchmark uses `simmedium` inputs.

Table 1. gem5 parameters

CPU	64 cores Alpha 2 GHz
L1 instructions	32 kB, 2 way set associative
L1 data	64 kB, 2 way set associative
Shared L2	256 kB × 64, 8 way set associative
Block size	64B

We insert monitors between the L1 and the interconnect on which L2 are plugged. There is one monitor per L1-data and one per L1-instruction, thus in this system there is a total of 128 monitors. With the base line memory system available in **gem5**, the L1 and L2 are connected to a crossbar so the architecture is fully SMP (Symmetric multiprocessing) and not NUMA. The cache coherence protocol in this system is MOESI. The simulator is used in its full system version, in which applications are run upon a complete Linux environment.

Our cache modeling differs from **gem5**'s one in several ways. Firstly, **gem5** L2 is not inclusive, while ours is. So we had to modify **gem5** to produce messages in case of L1 cache block eviction to maintain the sharing set coherent. Another difference is the L2 cache replacement policy. **Gem5** L2 can select a different cache block for eviction than ours, or worse the behavior could be completely different in case of differing cache sizes. To check that we do not move away from **gem5** reference behavior, we introduce several sanity checks (see Sect. 4.3). Indeed, we measure the percentage of the L1 read requests for which the L1 is already present in the sharing list, and for a read exclusive when this L1 already exclusively owns this block. We called this *read already present* and this is a first indication that we are moving away from **gem5**. We also measure discrepancies in L1 eviction messages: a L2 receives an eviction on a not cached block, or a L2 receives an eviction from a L1 which is not in its sharing set.

4.2 Measurements

Latency: The main metric to evaluate the quality of a cache coherence protocol is the average latency, because lower average memory access time is expected to lead to reduced execution time.

Figure 1 reports the mean latency for each program. We can see that for all programs, the ranking among the sharing set strategies is the same: snoop has always the highest latency while Ackwise 5 and bit-vector are better and have performances that are close to one another. On average, with respect to bit-vector, Ackwise 5 and snoop have a 2% and 44% higher latency. The higher snoop latency is easily explained by the numerous broadcast messages and the need to wait for all responses. Moreover, the traffic induced by the snoop protocol is so high (see Fig. 1) that it should further increase the latency of coherent requests. So, the snoop protocol latency is underestimated and it should perform much worse than Ackwise and bit-vector. In the case of **dedup** and `freqmine` benchmarks, Ackwise performs better than full bit-vector which is counterintuitive as the bit-vector sharing set is exact. This result can be explained by a read exclusive ratio more important (around 50%) than in other benchmarks as shown Fig. 2. Indeed, in case of read exclusive, Ackwise relies on hardware broadcast (when $G = 1$) for invalidation while full bit-vector uses multicast. Hardware broadcast, while inducing a higher load on the network, is more efficient from a latency point of view, explaining this counterintuitive result.

Irrespectively of the sharing set implementation, the average latency shown Fig. 1 is also strongly coupled to the hit rate shown Fig. 3, due to the high roundtrip latency of 100 clock cycles for L2 refills. Indeed, Fig. 3 shows the hit and miss breakdown for each benchmark. Two benchmarks seem to be apart from the rest. First, `fft` has a hit rate lower than 40%, with around 60% of

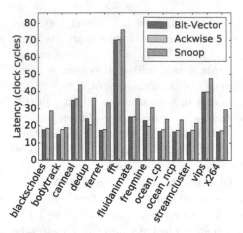
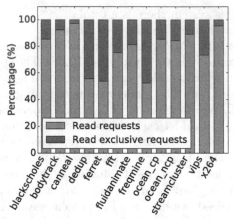

Fig. 1. Mean latency in cycles for each protocol and each program

Fig. 2. Read and read exclusive requests distribution

the requests being capacity or conflict misses. Thus many requests have to go to memory, leading to a higher average latency. On the contrary, `blackscholes` has not many requests, so compulsory miss (first access) are more important than in other programs. The correlation between latency and hit rate is further demonstrated by Fig. 4, which presents the latency distribution averaged over all benchmarks. There are two groups: a first peak is located above 100 clock cycles for read miss requests and another peak is located between 0 and 60 clock cycles depending on the sharing set. We can see that almost 70% of the requests have a round-trip latency under 20 hops for bit-vector and Ackwise. In contrast, snoop latency distribution shows a latency peak shifted toward 25 clock cycles, clearly demonstrating the higher latency induced by broadcast requests. Similarly to Fig. 1, we see that bit-vector has a slightly lower latency than Ackwise. It can be explained by the *home* selection algorithm. Indeed, when the L2 processes a read request, it must choose which L1 will answer the request, as the L2 does not necessarily have the most up-to-date data. In case of the bit-vector, we select the ideal L1 from a latency point of view, while for Ackwise the *keeper* is always selected. Our latency measures are consistent with published results (see Sect. 4.3).

Traffic: Network traffic is an important metric for two reasons: first, it impacts power consumption of the system; second, it helps validating our latency measures, as we do not model contention in the network which is a strong hypothesis. Figure 5 (note the log scale on the y-axis) presents the mean traffic for the request channel, the quartile interval and the maximum values over a 10,000 clock cycles window. Figure 6 does the same for the response channel. One more time, snoop performs worse than Ackwise 5 and full bit-vector. Its traffic is around one order

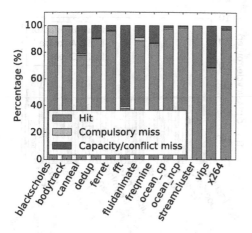

Fig. 3. L2 hit/miss distribution

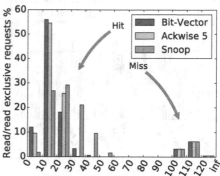

Fig. 4. Latency distribution normalized for all programs

of magnitude higher for request channel and two order of magnitude higher for response channel than the Ackwise and bit-vector traffic. The traffic is asymetric between the two channels for snoop because broadcast messages generates a lot more responses than requests due to the hardware support for broadcast forwarding in the NoC. Moreover, these broadcast messages induces such a high load that our hypothesis of a contention-free network is no longer valid. Indeed, it has been demonstrated in several works, e.g. [9,18], that the load-induced latency can be neglected when the load stays below 10%. While this hypothesis is mostly valid for Ackwise and bit-vector, it is clearly not the case for snoop.

Figures 5 and 6 also show that Ackwise induces a higher load than bit-vector for all benchmarks on both channels: 17% more traffic on request channel and 16% more on response channel. It is coherent with results found in the literature.

Hardware Cost: We have compared performances of 3 sharing set strategies for several benchmarks. To complete the comparison another criterion must be taken into account: hardware cost of these strategies. We define the hardware cost as the number of bits necessary to store the meta-data in the L2. We can easily evaluate this cost analytically in function of the number of L2 entries N and the number of L1 caches n. The bit-vector strategy has to save the state (2-bit) and the sharing set (n-bit). The meta-data for Ackwise are the state (2-bit), multicast or broadcast mode (1-bit), *keeper* ID ($\log_2 n$-bit) and the sharing set ($k \log_2 n$-bit) where k is the sharing list size (threshold). Snoop only needs to save the state (2-bit). Therefore, bit-vector hardware cost is $(2 + n) \times N$-bit, Ackwise cost is $(3 + \log_2 n + k \times log_2 n) \times N$-bit and snoop cost is $2 \times N$-bit. With our example architecture, the full bit-vector entry hardware cost is 66-bit, Ackwise is 39-bit (with $k = 5$) and snoop is 2-bit.

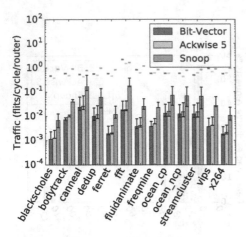

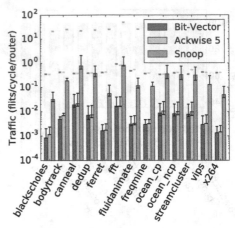

Fig. 5. Mean traffic with 1st, 3rd quartile and max on request channel for each protocol

Fig. 6. Mean traffic with 1st, 3rd quartile and max on response channel for each protocol

4.3   High-Level Cache Modeling Validation

Sanity Checks: As presented in Sect. 4.1, we use several counters to measure the discrepancy between our modeling and **gem5** execution. On average on all programs, our model presents only 0.14% of *read already present* per read/read exclusive request. This value is the same for all our sharing set strategy implementations. Furthermore, we count only 2.08% of evictions where the data was not present in the cache and only 0.51% of evictions where the data was present but the L1 requester was not in the sharing set. This measure is also consistent across all the sharing set strategies. So it shows our modeling does not diverge notably from **gem5** execution flow.

Complexity of Our Approach: Our high-level model has been designed specifically to be fast. To verify this, we compare the execution time of three models on the whole set of programs. First, **gem5** with its classical system memory takes around 4 h per program, but this version does not allow to evaluate different cache coherence protocols. For this evaluation, we have to use **ruby** which takes 2+ days per program execution. Our model, developed in **python**, runs in 6 h for 13 programs with 3 different sharing set strategies with 8 parallel threads. The execution time depends on the number of cache coherence requests, for example, **streamcluster** takes 4 h and **blackscholes** only 30 s. We measure the number of L1 read/read exclusive transactions processed by second for **blackscholes** on an Intel(R) Xeon(R) CPU E3-1241 v3 @ 3.50 GHz, 8 cores (HT) with 32 GB of RAM. Evaluating one protocol, we process in average 110,000 transactions per second for our model with the Pypy JIT Python interpreter [19], versus 290 transactions per second for **gem5** with ruby. Using the classical memory system of **gem5**, we have got 2,750 transactions per second. Therefore, our method is x380 and x40 faster than **gem5** with ruby and classical memory systems, respectively.

We also compare code lines count of this model. In **gem5**, the ruby cache model needs approx. 2,800 lines of c++ and approx. 4,000 lines of slicc for MESI Two level. Our model needs around 150 lines of Python for the cache model itself, 120 lines for the network, plus 150 lines per sharing set strategy.

Comparison to Accurate Models: To assess the validity of the approach, we compare our results to the accurate models of Xu *et al.* [26]. This paper uses Noxim [8], a cycle-accurate simulator based on SystemC. They use the same programs from PARSEC and evaluate network latency, execution time, broadcast overhead and energy consumption. In average, the ranking of the 3 sharing set strategies is the same as what we obtained in Sect. 4.2. However, they observe much higher latency results for protocol than us. It can first be explained by the fact that they simulate 1024 cores instead of 64, thus worsening the impact of broadcasting. Another explanation is our underestimate of load-induced latency for snoop as shown in Sect. 4.2.

We tested different Ackwise threshold and compare our results with Kurian *et al.* [12]. We have one program in common (Ocean C) and the same 2D mesh topology (Emesh in [12]). We get the same results: better performances for higher values of the threshold k and smaller improvements when $k > 5$.

5 Conclusions

In this paper, we propose a method for fast ranking of sharing set management strategies. We use the **gem5** simulator to extract traffic produced by the L1 towards the L2. This traffic is then injected in a high-level model of a distributed L2 cache and its NoC to extract latency and traffic metrics during the execution of multiprocessor benchmarks. We evaluate our method by implementing three sharing set strategies: snoop, full bit-vector and Ackwise. Our method produces results several orders of magnitude faster than cycle-accurate simulation, and the models are much easier to implement than the register transfer level or cycle accurate ones. Even though we do several approximations, the figures of merit we obtain are in line with the one obtained using cycle accurate models. Thus, we believe this method is precious to evaluate new sharing set management approaches before their implementation.

References

1. Archibald, J., Baer, J.L.: Cache coherence protocols: evaluation using a multi-processor simulation model. ACM Trans. Comput. Syst. **4**(4), 273–298 (1986)
2. Bienia, C., Kumar, S., Singh, J.P., Li, K.: The parsec benchmark suite: characterization and architectural implications. In: Proceedings of the 17th International Conference on Parallel Architectures and Compilation Techniques. ACM (2008)

3. Binkert, N., Beckmann, B., Black, G., Reinhardt, S.K., Saidi, A., Basu, A., Hestness, J., Hower, D.R., Krishna, T., Sardashti, S., et al.: The gem5 simulator. ACM SIGARCH Comput. Archit. News **39**(2), 1–7 (2011)
4. Bolosky, W.J., Scott, M.L., Fitzgerald, R.P., Fowler, R.J., Cox, A.L.: NUMA policies and their relation to memory architecture. ACM SIGARCH Comput. Archit. News **19**, 212–221 (1991). ACM
5. Butko, A., Garibotti, R., Ost, L., Sassatelli, G.: Accuracy evaluation of GEM5 simulator system. In: 7th International Workshop on Reconfigurable Communication-Centric Systems-on-Chip, pp. 1–7. IEEE (2012)
6. Censier, L.M., Feautrier, P.: A new solution to coherence problems in multicache systems. IEEE Trans. Comput. **c-20**(12), 1112–1118 (1978)
7. Dally, W.J.: Computer architecture in the many-core era. In: 24th International Conference on Computer Design (2006). Keynote speech
8. Fazzino, F., Palesi, M., Patti, D.: Noxim: network-on-chip simulator (2008). http://sourceforge.net/projects/noxim
9. Foroutan, S., Thonnart, Y., Petrot, F.: An iterative computational technique for performance evaluation of networks-on-chip. IEEE Trans. Comput. **62**(8), 1641–1655 (2013)
10. Hennessy, J.L., Patterson, D.A.: Computer Architecture: A Quantitative Approach. Morgan Kaufmann Publishers Inc., San Francisco (2011)
11. James, D.V., Laundrie, A.T., Gjessing, S., Sohi, G.S.: Distributed-directory scheme: scalable coherent interface. Computer **23**(6), 74–77 (1990)
12. Kurian, G., Miller, J.E., Psota, J., Eastep, J., Liu, J., Michel, J., Kimerling, L.C., Agarwal, A.: ATAC: a 1000-core cache-coherent processor with on-chip optical network. In: Proceedings of the 19th International Conference on Parallel Architectures and Compilation Techniques, pp. 477–488. ACM (2010)
13. Liu, H., Devigne, C., Garcia, L., Meunier, Q., Wajsburt, F., Greiner, A.: RWT: suppressing write-through cost when coherence is not needed. In: IEEE Computer Society Annual Symposium on VLSI, pp. 434–439. IEEE (2015)
14. Loghi, M., Poncino, M., Benini, L.: Cache coherence tradeoffs in shared-memory MPSoCs. ACM Trans. Embedded Comput. Syst. **5**(2), 383–407 (2006)
15. Martin, M.M., Hill, M.D., Sorin, D.J.: Why on-chip cache coherence is here to stay. Commun. ACM **55**(7), 78–89 (2012)
16. Guironnet de Massas, P., Pétrot, F.: Comparison of memory write policies for NoC based multicore cache coherent systems. In: Design, Automation and Test in Europe, pp. 997–1002 (2008)
17. Mukherjee, S.S., Hill, M.D.: An evaluation of directory protocols for medium-scale shared-memory multiprocessors. In: Proceedings of the 8th International Conference on Supercomputing, pp. 64–74 (1994)
18. Ogras, U.Y., Bogdan, P., Marculescu, R.: An analytical approach for network-on-chip performance analysis. IEEE Trans. CAD **29**(12), 2001–2013 (2010)
19. Pypy Team (2016). http://pypy.org/. pypy Python interpreter website
20. Sorin, D., Hill, M., Wood, D.: A Primer on Memory Consistency and Cache Coherence. Synthesis Lectures on Computer Architecture, vol. 16 (2011)
21. Soteriou, V., Wang, H., Peh, L.S.: A statistical traffic model for on-chip interconnection networks. In: 14th IEEE International Symposium on Modeling, Analysis, and Simulation of Computer and Telecommunication Systems. IEEE (2006)
22. Thapar, M., Delagi, B., Flynn, M.J.: Linked list cache coherence for scalable shared memory multiprocessors. In: Proceedings of Seventh International Parallel Processing Symposium, pp. 34–43. IEEE (1993)

23. Uhlig, R.A., Mudge, T.N.: Trace-driven memory simulation: a survey. ACM Comput. Surv. **29**(2), 128–170 (1997)
24. Wilson Jr., A.W.: Multiprocessor cache simulation using hardware collected address traces. In: Proceedings of the Twenty-Third Annual Hawaii International Conference on System Sciences, pp. 252–260 (1990)
25. Woo, S.C., Ohara, M., Torrie, E., Singh, J.P., Gupta, A.: The splash-2 programs: characterization and methodological considerations. ACM SIGARCH Comput. Archit. News **23**, 24–36 (1995). ACM
26. Xu, Y., Du, Y., Zhang, Y., Yang, J.: A composite and scalable cache coherence protocol for large scale CMPs. In: Proceedings of the International Conference on Supercomputing, pp. 285–294. ACM (2011)

HBM-Resident Prefetching for Heterogeneous Memory System

Mahzabeen Islam[1]($\boxtimes$), Krishna M. Kavi[1]($\boxtimes$), Mitesh Meswani[2],
Soumik Banerjee[3], and Nuwan Jayasena[3]

[1] University of North Texas, Denton, USA
mahzabeenislam@my.unt.edu, krishna.kavi@unt.edu
[2] ARM, Austin, USA
mitesh.meswani@gmail.com
[3] Advanced Micro Devices, Inc., Austin, USA
{Soumik.Banerjee,nuwan.jayasena}@amd.com

Abstract. To meet the increasing demands for very large memory capacities, bandwidth and energy efficiency, researchers are exploring the use of heterogeneous memory systems that combine faster 3D-DRAMs, DDRx DRAM and non-volatile memories (NVMs). In this paper we evaluate prefetching in a flat-addressable heterogeneous memory comprising High Bandwidth Memory (HBM) and phase change memory (PCM). We find that large prefetch buffers (64 MB) can outperform smaller buffer sizes (2 MB), however it is not feasible to place such large buffers on the processor die. Hence, in this paper we evaluate an HBM-resident prefetch buffer that provides larger capacity and takes advantage of HBM's higher memory bandwidth. We also present new prefetching policies that accommodate the differences in data path as compared to traditional prefetchers. We show that, reserving a small fraction (1/16th) of HBM memory to host a hardware prefetch buffer can improve IPC for a set of SPEC CPU2006 and HPC benchmarks by an average of 34% and a maximum of 98% over a baseline system with no-prefetching. Prefetching reduces total PCM traffic by 10% on average, which results in more memory traffic to the faster HBM, providing overall performance improvement. We found that such prfetching outperforms CAMEO and Alloy cache schemes on average by 60% and 10%, respectively.

Keywords: Prefetching · Heterogeneous memory · HBM · PCM

1 Introduction

Demand for memory performance has been on the rise, especially for data-intensive applications such as HPC, big data analytics, cloud computing and in-memory databases. These applications need memory systems with very large capacities (100s of GBs to TBs), high bandwidth and energy efficiency. For example, SAP HANA in-memory database system requires 256 GB to 2 TB memory

---

M. Meswani—The author did the work while employed at AMD.

J. Knoop et al. (Eds.): ARCS 2017, LNCS 10172, pp. 124–136, 2017.
DOI: 10.1007/978-3-319-54999-6_10

per host [1]. Conventional DRAM cannot satisfy such capacity and performance demands due power and scaling challenges [2]. Recent 3D-stacked DRAM (3D-DRAM) such as HBM [12] and Hybrid Memory Cube (HMC) [20] provide much higher bandwidth (up to 256 GB/s HBM [12] and up to 320 GB/s HMC [20]) and consume ∼70% [21] less energy than conventional DRAM. There are eight independent channels per HBM stack [12]. However, 3D-DRAM is not likely to meet the capacity requirements of data-intensive applications [3]. Emerging NVM technologies, on the other hand, are much denser, consume low static power and are scalable to provide sufficient capacity [4–8]. PCM is one type of NVM that relies on the state or phase of material to store one bit or multiple bits. Hence it can be much denser than traditional DRAM and provides lower cost-per-bit [22]. Also, PCM consumes less idle state power [13]. PCM may exhibit higher access latency (∼2x for reads and 4x–32x for writes) and higher read (2x) and write energies (4x–140x) than DDRx DRAM [13,22]. It has limited write endurance of 10^6 to 10^9 cycles [4,22]. Addressing PCM limitations is an active research area [4–6,22,23] and it is believed to be one of the most promising NVMs that can be used as main memory in the near future [2,4].

As no single memory technology can provide both large capacity and high bandwidth, it is natural to explore heterogeneous memory systems that employ disparate memory technologies together [3,6,9–11,14,15]. Heterogeneous memory systems introduce their own challenges due to the differences in the characteristics of constituent memory technologies (e.g., storage capacity, access latency, bandwidth, endurance). Recent research has been investigating solutions to these challenges, either employing fast 3D-DRAM memory as a cache for slow memory [6,10,14,15] or employing both fast and slow memories as part of a single physical address space ("flat-address-memory") [3,6,9,11]. Generally, cache-based organizations do not need software changes, but they need to manage large tag space [14,15]. In cache-based organizations the 3D-DRAM capacity is not included as main memory capacity, which may lead to higher numbers of page faults than flat-address-memory organizations which expose the 3D-DRAM capacity as part of main memory [11]. However, flat-address-memory systems need to employ techniques to efficiently place/migrate frequently accessed data into the faster memory.

Since we are interested in designing large memory systems, in this research, we study a flat-address-memory system consisting in faster 3D-DRAM (HBM) and slower NVM (PCM). We propose to use prefetching methods for bridging the performance gap between 3D-DRAM and NVM. Conventional memory-to-processor prefetching brings data from slower memories (farther from core) to an on-chip buffer (nearer to core). Prefetching can continue to improve performance with larger buffer capacities [10,16]. For example, in our study of SPEC and HPC workloads (workload details provided in Sect. 4), we find that prefetch buffer sizes of 32 MB, 64 MB, and 128 MB can improve instruction per cycle (IPC) by 27%, 34% and 40% respectively, whereas a 2 MB buffer can improve IPC by only 19% over no-prefetching. However, placing such large buffers inside a processor is infeasible due to area and power limitations; processor-chip resident prefetch buffer capacity is typically limited to 1 MB to 2 MB of SRAM [17]. Hence, in this paper, we propose "HBM-resident" prefetching by setting aside a portion of faster HBM as a large prefetch buffer and employing customized prefetch policies. The prefetch buffer is split over eight HBM channels, allowing high memory level parallelism (MLP). Conventional DRAM provides only a limited number of channels, therefore we choose HBM to host our prefetch buffer. We prefetch data from slower PCM into a buffer space in faster HBM (by storing a copy) and service last level cache (LLC) misses from the buffer on a hit. In case of write-backs from LLC to PCM, if a hit is found in the prefetch buffer, the write is also buffered there. The advantages are that, it provides faster access to data (than accessing it from PCM) while avoiding costly updates to page tables and TLBs (that is generally required in page migration techniques) and reducing write-backs to PCM. The location changes resulting from prefetching is tracked using a hardware-based address remapping table. Another advantage of prefetching is that it might be able to hide PCM access latency even for "cold" misses, as it can predict unseen future addresses. Neither a straight-forward demand cache nor a hotness-based page migration scheme can avoid cold misses, as they rely on demand or past history of accesses.

We first evaluate a prefetching scheme that relies entirely on predictability, which is generally known as distance prefetching [18]. Next we present a temporal locality based prefetching technique that relies on access counts to data blocks. We also introduce a simple open-page prefetching policy which can be seen as a relaxed caching policy. The main contributions of this paper are:

1. Novel "HBM-resident" prefetching hosted in the faster memory to buffer pages of the slower memory.
2. A buffer architecture that is designed to take advantage of memory-level parallelism afforded by the higher number of channels in HBM.
3. Prefetching policies that are designed to take into account the data transfer path and characteristics of emerging memory technologies.

Our studies show IPC improvements of 33% on average (max. 70%) for a set of SPEC CPU2006 workloads and 40% on average (98% max.) for a set of HPC workloads over a baseline system without prefetching. Stand-alone 3D-DRAM-resident prefetching provides an average performance improvement of 60% over a state of the art page migration policy, CAMEO [11], and 10% over Alloy caching [14], which is one of the leading 3D-DRAM based caching techniques.

2   Motivation for a New Prefetch Architecture

In conventional prefetching, data from lower level memories (farther from core) are fetched into higher levels (nearer to core) before it is requested by the processor. Some basic hardware prefetching techniques are stride prefetching [24], stream buffers [16], Markov prefetching [25], and Distance prefetching [18].

For emerging memory technologies, different hardware prefetching policies have been explored. Ahn et al. [26] proposed to prefetch data from HMC memory layers into a small SRAM buffer residing in the logic layer of HMC using stream prefetching [16] at cache line (64 B) granularity. However workloads with good spatial locality can benefit if more cache lines are fetched. In a study by Oskin et al. [10], HBM is employed as an operating system (OS) page cache for conventional DRAM memory, and they employ stride prefetching at OS page (4 KB) granularity. Yoon et al. [27] proposed caching PCM row buffers with high access and conflict counts into conventional DRAM to avoid repeated opening of the same row in PCM. However, memories with high MLP distribute their cache blocks from the same physical page to a number of channels and, as such, tracking row buffer conflicts may no longer be beneficial since the locality is now spread over channels and they may not conflict. In our evaluation we configure each type of memory with cache-line-level address interleaving to make most of the MLP. Previously we proposed to use a customized distance prefetching policy to prefetch from slower PCM to a processor-chip-resident small SRAM buffer (2 MB) [19]. Here, unlike the processor-resident prefetch buffer, we propose to host a much larger (32x) prefetch buffer in HBM using only 1/16th of the total HBM capacity. This approach not only eliminates the capacity constraints, but also allows high bandwidth utilization through MLP since the prefetch buffer is split over multiple channels of HBM.

3 HBM-Resident Prefetching

3.1 Architecting a HBM-Resident Buffer

Figure 1(a) provides a comparison of high level organizations for processor-resident and HBM-resident prefetch buffers for a flat-address memory system comprising the HBM and PCM used in our evaluations. While designing our prefetch architecture we addressed four design parameters: **(i) prefetch buffer location, (ii) prefetch granularity, (iii) prefetch initiation and (iv) prefetch policies**.

Prefetch buffer location dictates where to host the prefetch buffer and its associated data path for copying data to the buffer, which directly influences the cost/time for completing the prefetch operation. In our design, we

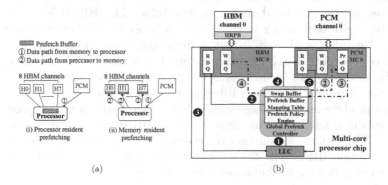

(a)   (b)

Fig. 1. (a) Different prefetching organizations, (b) Proposed system organization.

host the prefetch buffer in the HBM and call it HBM-resident prefetch buffer (HRPB). We compare our design with processor-chip-resident SRAM prefetch buffer, referred to as on-chip prefetch buffer (OCPB), as proposed in [19]. HRPB necessitates a different data path for bringing data to the buffer as shown in Fig. 1(a). For OCPB, data travels one-way from memory to the processor buffer but, for HRPB, data travels first from slower memory to a temporary swap buffer in processor (not shown in the figure) and from there to the memory buffer. This is because there is currently no direct data path from PCM to HBM. **Prefetch granularity** influences the cost for storing and accessing tags for prefetched data. Since the HRPB is large, the tag array size can grow very large when prefetching at finer granularity. Therefore, we use a coarser block (2 KB) granularity. **Prefetch initiation** dictates when to issue a prefetch request; we take an "opportunistic" approach and only prefetch (read) from the PCM when it is not busy serving demand read requests. Finally, we have to design **prefetch policies** to amortize the cost of the longer data path and the difference in buffer storage technology. Details on the polices are described in Sect. 3.3.

3.2   System Organization

Figure 1(b) shows the system organization of our prefetching technique. The multi-core processor chip has a shared LLC and a set of memory controllers (MCs). We use 8 HBM and 2 PCM channels with one MC per channel. Figure 1(b) shows details of one HBM MC and one PCM MC to keep the figure readable. Each MC contains a read queue (RD Q) and write queue (WR Q), and the PCM MC also contains a Prefetch queue (Pref. Q). We reserve a small fraction of the HBM as HRPB (e.g., 64 MB of 1 GB HBM), which is not visible to the OS and hence non-allocable. The hardware-based global prefetch controller is located on the processor chip. The HRPB address range is only visible to the prefetch controller. We have assumed that the OS-visible physical address range is statically partitioned over HBM (excluding the HRPB portion) and PCM.

We prefetch (copy) at 2 KB block granularity from the PCM to the HRPB. The original block is still kept in PCM so no page remapping is required. We store the HRPB tag array inside the global prefetch controller. The tag array also serves as the prefetch buffer mapping table. The HRPB is a 4-way set associative, write-back buffer with least recently used (LRU) eviction policy. In the mapping table, with each 37 bit address tag (which is the original PCM physical address of that 2 KB block) we store 1 valid bit, 1 dirty bit and a 32 bit vector for tracking dirty cache lines in the prefetched block. Hence, for a 64 MB HRPB, the mapping table size will be 288 KB (32,768 entries, each 9 B), which is feasible to place on the processor chip. Since each entry in the mapping table corresponds to a fixed physical address in the HRPB, on a hit in the mapping table, the HRPB physical address can be dynamically generated. While evicting a block from the HRPB, only the dirty cache lines are written back to the PCM. The prefetch policy engine implements the policies.

How to access prefetched data in HRPB: On every LLC miss, the address is redirected to the prefetch controller. The controller first checks the missed address to see if it is a PCM address (we assumed that the physical address range is statically partitioned between HBM and PCM) and, if it is, then the controller looks up the mapping table. If a match found, then the new destination address inside the HRPB is also known, and the request is directed to HRPB. The solid path with numbers 1, 2, and 3 in Fig. 1(b) shows this path. Unlike traditional migration techniques, the missing data is not moved to the OS-visible memory space of the HBM (hence avoiding costly page table remappings), but kept in the prefetch buffer. If no match is found in the mapping table, the LLC miss request is serviced by the PCM (in Fig. 1(b) solid path 4 and 5). The delay overhead for every miss in the mapping table is fairly small: the time to access a 288 KB on-chip SRAM array for a 64 MB HRPB.

How to prefetch data from PCM to HRPB: For every LLC miss to PCM, the policy engine will generate the next address to prefetch depending on the prefetching policy. The prefetch controller first checks if the generated address is already present in the HRPB. Otherwise, it generates prefetch read requests to the PCM and reads that block into a swap buffer located inside the prefetch controller. The swap buffer holds one block of prefetched data (2 KB). The prefetch controller then finds a destination location in the HRPB by checking the mapping table (if needed, write-back of the evicted entry takes place first). After successful writes to HRPB, the mapping table entry is updated with the new block's address tag and the valid bit is set. This flow is shown in Fig. 1(b) by dotted paths numbered 2, 3, and 4.

3.3 Prefetching Policies

Distance prefetching is a generalization of Markov prefetching that relies on correlating deltas (differences) between addresses [18]. Similar to [19], we choose to use the global history buffer (GHB) structure to implement the distance prefetcher as presented by Nesbit et al. [28]. Storage overhead for implementing GHB for distance prefetching is only 8 KB [28]. Distance prefetching width degree determines how many different prefetching paths and depth degree determines how far into the future we want to explore. We found width degree 1 and depth degree 4 as optimal for us.

In **Hotness-based prefetching**, we use the "hotness" metric (a count of the number of accesses to a block) [3,6] in deciding whether to prefetch a block into HRPB. Whenever a block is accessed more than a certain number of times (e.g., 4) we immediately generate a prefetch request for that block. Such temporal locality based prefetching may provide higher confidence that the prefetched data will be useful. We use a hotness count cache with only 16 K (16,384) entries to hold the hotness count of recently accessed blocks, it works in similar manner as filter cache presented in the CHOP study [29]. Each entry of the hotness count cache is 6 B (37b address tag and the rest to keep hotness count), hence the size of the hotness count cache is only 96KB, which can be stored on the processor chip and accessed with small delay overhead in the prefetching path.

In **Open-page prefetching**, to benefit from row buffer locality, we change our physical memory address interleaving from cache line level to memory page (e.g., row with size 2 KB) level granularity so that each 2 KB sized block falls to the same row. To minimize opening the same row in PCM repeatedly, we employ a simple prefetching policy that attempts to prefetch any row buffer that is open. This can be seen as a relaxed caching policy, exploiting spatial locality.

4   Experimental Setup

We assume a 16-core system with main memory comprising 1 GB HBM and 16 GB PCM in a flat-address model. Each of the cores is 4-wide out-of-order issue with 128 entry ROB and operates at 3.2 GHz. Each core has private L1 I (32 KB) and D (16 KB) caches, and all 16 cores share an L2 LLC (16 MB). For HBM and PCM timing parameters we primarily follow [30] and [31] respectively; we list them in Table 1. As a baseline, we used above mentioned memory system without any prefetching or data migration.

We use Ramulator [30] in trace-driven mode with a CPU model to estimate IPC. To generate the traces, we first use PinPlay kit [32] to identify region of interest (ROI) of one billion instructions for each of the benchmarks in Table 2. We have used 17 memory-intensive benchmarks from the SPEC CPU2006 suite [34], and four representative HPC benchmarks from the US Department of Energy: XSBench [35], LULESH [36], CoMD [37] and miniFE [38]. As listed in Table 2, we generate memory access traces for twenty multi-programmed workloads by running 16 copies of ROI traces of one benchmark or ROI traces from different random benchmarks in a 16-core Moola cache simulator [33].

Table 1. Baseline configuration

Parameter	HBM	PCM
Channels, capacity	8, 1 GB (8 × 128 MB)	2, 16 GB (2 × 8 GB)
Memory Controller (MC)	1 per channel	1 per channel
Row buffer size	2 KB	2 KB
Queue size/MC	RD 32, WR 32 entries	RD 64, WR 256, and prefetch 32 entries
Latency	tCAS-tRCD-tRP-tRAS 14ns-14ns-14ns-34ns	Read 80ns (7.5ns tPRE + 62.5ns tSENSE + 10ns tBUS) Write 250ns tCWL
Bus (per channel)	128-bit, 500 MHz	64-bit, 400 MHz

Table 2. Evaluated workloads (WL); footprint (FP) is provided in GB

No.	WL	Benchmarks	MPKI	FP	No.	WL	Benchmarks	MPKI	FP
1	mcf	16x mcf	65.04	16	8	bwav	16x bwaves	6.90	6.82
2	lbm	16x lbm	44.21	6.30	9	cactus	16x cactusADM	3.70	2.31
3	milc	16x milc	23.05	9.05	10	xbmk	16x xalancbmk	4.50	2.89
4	omntp	16x omnetpp	18.96	2.06	11	xsb	16x XSBench	22.01	14.68
5	astar	16x astar	16.80	2.63	12	lul	16x LULESH	13.51	6.80
6	gems	16x GemsFDTD	9.59	10.59	13	mini	16x miniFE	6.72	10.66
7	zmp	16x zeusmp	8.14	3.32	14	comd	16x CoMD	1.41	2.30

No.	WL	Benchmarks	MPKI	FP
15	mix1	3x mcf, sph., 2x ast., 2x lbm, gcc, 2x sop., lib., 2x milc, omn., libq.	29.36	5.64
16	mix2	3x lbm, 2x mcf, 3x deal., 3x sop., bzi., 2x cac., 2x Gem.	20.47	5.08
17	mix3	2x Gem., lib., 2x milc, deal., 2x sph., 2x les., 2x cac., 2x gcc, bzi., ast.	10.99	3.34
18	mix4	mcf, 3x lib., 3x sop., Gems., milc, les., lbm, gcc, 2x bzi., cac., deal.	18.27	3.60
19	mix5	5x mcf, 6x lbm, 5x sop.	42.51	7.61
20	mix6	4x lib., 3x omn., 3x gcc, 3x sph., 2x milc, ast.	19.64	2.11

5 Evaluation

5.1 Performance Analysis

We first present the IPC performance improvements of the three prefetching policies, namely Distance (delta), Hotness-based (hot) and Open-page (open) implemented with HRPB as well as delta with OCPB [19]. The OCPB can be seen as an LLC prefetcher which uses a separate on-chip buffer area for prefetching to avoid the risk of polluting the LLC. Details of the prefetching configurations are provided in Tables 3 and 4. For the Figs. 2, 3 and 4, the positive y-axis shows IPC percentage improvement whereas the negative y-axis shows IPC degradation with respect to a baseline system without any prefetching or migration. We categorize the workloads 1 to 10 as listed in Table 2 as SPEC homogeneous (SPEC_HOM), 11 to 14 as HPC homogeneous (HPC_HOM), and 15 to 20 as SPEC heterogeneous (SPEC_HET).

Figure 2 shows the IPC improvements for different prefetching policies over the baseline. For our basic set of experiments we have chosen the HRPB size as 64 MB and hot policy threshold as 4 after performing capacity and threshold sensitivity analyses (not presented here due to space limitations). The HR_hot

Table 3. Buffer configuration

Legends	Details
HRPB	64 MB, 4-way, write-back, LRU eviction
OCPB	2 MB, 16-way, write-back, LRU eviction

Table 4. Policy configuration

Legends	Details
OC_delta	OCPB with Distance policy, width = 1, depth = 4
HR_delta	HRPB with Distance policy, width = 1, depth = 4
HR_hot	HRPB with Hotness-based policy, threshold 4
HR_open	HRPB with Open-page policy

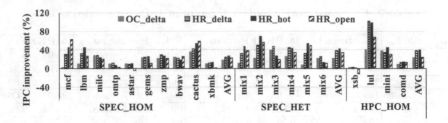

Fig. 2. IPC improvement (%) of different prefetching policies over baseline (negative y-axis shows degradation)

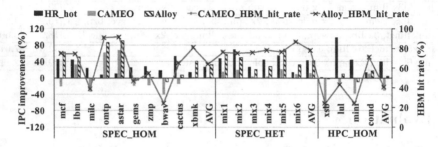

Fig. 3. IPC improvement (%) of HR_hot prefetching, stand-alone CAMEO, and stand-alone Alloy cache over baseline system

scheme provides the best average result over all other policies for all three categories of workloads SPEC_HOM, SPEC_HET and HPC_HOM with average IPC improvements of 27%, 43% and 40% respectively. HR_hot generally works well as usually a block with frequent accesses is a good predictor of that same block being accessed in the future. We find that HR_hot performs the best for 1/2 of the workloads. For most of these cases HR_hot policy's prefetch accuracy and repeated hit to the same block is much higher than the other policies.

The prediction-based delta policy works well when the workloads have predictable sequences which happens when there are repeating sequence of address strides. OC_delta [19] follows a similar trend as HR_delta but since OCPB is much smaller in size (only 1/32th of HRPB), we observe on average smaller improvement for OC_delta. For 1/3rd of the workloads, OC_delta provides performance close to or better than HR_delta. We found that these workloads have diminishing reuse of data with time, hence storing many prefetched blocks for prolonged periods of time does not help improve the performance.

In case of simpler HR_open policy, we have changed the memory address interleaving from cache-line-level to block-level to achieve more row buffer hits. This decreases the MLP and hence we see smaller performance improvement for most of the cases. However, for mcf and cactus our analysis shows that the majority of the blocks have low reuse distance and the HR_open policy is the quickest to initiate a prefetch request since it simply tries to prefetch the most recently accessed row buffer and hence it outperforms the HR_hot policy.

With HBM-resident prefetching, on average, total PCM traffic is decreased by 10%, compared to the no-prefetching baseline. Fewer accesses to PCM leads to better average access latencies and reduced energy consumption.

Comparison with CAMEO and Alloy: Here, we compare our best prefetching policy, HR_hot, with CAMEO page migration technique [11] and Alloy caching [14]. Chou et al. proposed CAMEO (CAche-like MEmory Organization) for a two level memory system comprising 3D-DRAM and DDR DRAM [11]. The 3D-DRAM stores recently accessed data by employing a "cache-like" migration policy, but it is visible to the OS. On a 3D-DRAM demand miss, the requested line (64 B) is filled from DDR DRAM. To make room for the requested line, an older line needs be written back to DDR DRAM (even if it is not dirty) since there is no other copy of this line in memory. We use CAMEO model with HBM and PCM, with a capacity ratio of 1:16. In Alloy cache, faster 3D-DRAM is employed as a large LLC to slower conventional DRAM memory [14]. The 3D-DRAM is employed as a direct-mapped cache with 64 B line granularity. Here both tag and data are kept together. In our implementation we use HBM as Alloy cache to slower PCM memory. In CAMEO, we have total 17 GB of main memory, whereas in Alloy chaching we have 16 GB of main memory. Since each of our workload's memory footprint is below 16 GB, we cannot see the larger capacity benefit of CAMEO over Alloy caching.

In Fig. 3, right y-axis shows the HBM hit rate (%) and the hit_rate lines correspond to it. On average CAMEO degrades IPC by 1%, Alloy cache improves IPC by 29% and HR_hot improves by 34%. In case of CAMEO, every HBM miss results in a write back to PCM and, as a result, HBM hit rate plays an important role in CAMEO's performance. Generally for workloads with HBM hit rate under 74% we see performance degradation with CAMEO. Though writes are not in the critical path of execution, when the write queues are almost full, memory controllers must prioritize write queues over read queues and hence the overall execution time can be slowed down. Here, we have used different memory technology and capacity ratios than proposed in the original CAMEO work [11], and thus due to the high memory pressure in 3D-DRAM and slow writes of PCM, we observe very little performance improvement by CAMEO. In case of Alloy cache, only dirty cache lines are written back to PCM, hence Alloy cache with similar HBM hit rate provides better performance than CAMEO.

5.2 PCM Timing Analysis

Figure 4 shows how sensitive our proposed HBM-resident Hotness-based prefetching is to the PCM timing (due to space limitation we do not include the results for other two prefetching policies; in general they follow a similar trend). In one extreme we have replaced PCM with conventional DRAM (DDR3). Also, we evaluate a 2x faster fast_PCM and a 2x slower slow_PCM taking the PCM timing mentioned in Table 1 as standard. In Fig. 4 the IPC improvements for each timing configuration are compared to the baselines with identical timing.

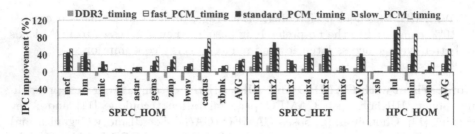

Fig. 4. PCM timing sensitivity for Hotness-based prefetching policy

When we prefetch from DDR DRAM to HBM buffers, we do not see significant benefits because both memories have similar access latencies. However, HBM has more channels and can provide more MLP than conventional DRAM. Hence, in this case we are paying the prefetching cost only to get the higher bandwidth benefit of HBM. From Fig. 4 we can see that for ∼2/3rd of the workloads we achieve negligible IPC improvements or degradations and for the rest we achieve IPC improvements from 8% to 21%. With fast PCM, the amount of time we save on a hit in the HRPB is smaller than the case when we have standard PCM. Hence with fast PCM, we achieve smaller performance improvements. On the other hand, with the slow PCM, we have fewer opportunities to prefetch since PCM is mostly busy responding to demand requests.

6   Conclusion and Future Work

We presented a novel HBM-resident hardware-based prefetching mechanism for heterogeneous flat-address-memory comprising HBM and PCM. We evaluated three different prefetching policies and show that they perform better than a system with no prefetching. In the future, we will explore composite schemes by augmenting such prefetching policies with data migration and caching organizations for heterogeneous memories. Further, HBM-resident prefetch buffer can be employed as a staging area to make the final migration decision of the page to the faster memory. Hence we believe this research opens new opportunities involving prefetching in the context of heterogeneous memory.

AMD, the AMD Arrow logo, and combinations thereof are trademarks of Advanced Micro Devices, Inc. Other product names are used for identification purposes only and may be trademarks of their respective companies.

References

1. HANA Memory Usage. http://saphanatutorial.com/sap-hana-memory-usage-explained/
2. Mutlu, O.: Memory scaling: a systems architecture perspective. In: International Memory Workshop. IEEE (2013)

3. Meswani, M.R., et al.: Heterogeneous memory architectures: a HW/SW approach for mixing die-stacked and off-package memories. In: HPCA, pp. 126–136. IEEE (2015)
4. Qureshi, M.K., et al.: Phase change memory: from devices to systems. Synth. Lect. Comput. Archit. **6**(4), 1–134 (2011)
5. Qureshi, M.K., et al.: Scalable high performance main memory system using phase-change memory technology. ACM SIGARCH Comput. Archit. News **37**(3), 24–33 (2009)
6. Su, C., et al.: HPMC: an energy-aware management system of multi-level memory architectures. In: MEMSYS, pp. 167–178. ACM (2015)
7. Micron NVDIMM. https://www.micron.com/products/dram-modules/nvdimm#/
8. 3D-XPoint. http://www.intel.com/newsroom/kits/nvm/3dxpoint/pdfs/Launch_Keynote.pdf
9. Sim, J., et al.: Transparent hardware management of stacked dram as part of memory. In: MICRO, pp. 13–24. IEEE (2014).
10. Oskin, M., Loh, G.H.: A software-managed approach to die-stacked DRAM. In: PACT, pp. 188–200. IEEE (2015)
11. Chou, C., et al.: CAMEO: a two-level memory organization with capacity of main memory and flexibility of hardware-managed cache. In: MICRO, pp. 1–12. IEEE Computer Society (2014)
12. 3D-ICs. https://www.jedec.org/category/technology-focus-area/3d-ics
13. Numonyx: PCM. http://www.pdl.cmu.edu/SDI/2009/slides/Numonyx.pdf
14. Qureshi, M.K., Loh, G.H.: Fundamental latency trade-off in architecting DRAM caches: outperforming impractical SRAM-Tags with a simple and practical design. In: MICRO, pp. 235–246. IEEE Computer Society (2012)
15. Jevdjic, D., et al.: Unison cache: a scalable and effective die-stacked dram cache. In: MICRO, pp. 25–37. IEEE (2014)
16. Jouppi, N.P.: Improving direct-mapped cache performance by the addition of a small fully-associative cache and prefetch buffers. In: ISCA, pp. 364–373. IEEE (1990)
17. Beckmann, N., Sanchez, D.: Meeting midway: improving CMP performance with memory-side prefetching. In: PACT, pp. 289–298. IEEE (2013)
18. Kandiraju, G.B., Sivasubramaniam, A.: Going the distance for TLB prefetching: an application-driven study. In: IEEE Computer Society, vol. 30 (2002)
19. Islam, M., et al.: Prefetching as a potentially effective technique for hybrid memory optimization. In: MEMSYS. ACM (2016)
20. Hybrid Memory Cube Consortium. http://www.hybridmemorycube.org/
21. Kim, J., Kim, Y.: HBM: memory solution for bandwidth-hungry processors. In: Hot Chips: A Symposium on High Performance Chips (2014)
22. Yoon, H., et al.: Efficient data mapping and buffering techniques for multilevel cell phase-change memories. TACO **11**(4), 40 (2015). ACM
23. Wang, H., et al.: Duang: fast and lightweight page migration in asymmetric memory systems. In: HPCA, pp. 481–493. IEEE (2016)
24. Fu, J.W., et al.: Stride directed prefetching in scalar processors. ACM SIGMICRO Newslett. **23**(1–2), 102–110 (1992)
25. Joseph, D., Grunwald, D.: Prefetching using Markov predictors. In: ACM SIGARCH Computer Architecture News, vol. 25, pp. 252–263. ACM (1997)
26. Ahn, J., et al.: Low-power hybrid memory cubes with link power management and two-level prefetching. Trans. VLSI Syst. **24**(2), 453–464 (2016). IEEE
27. Yoon, H., et al.: Row buffer locality aware caching policies for hybrid memories. In: International Conference on Computer Design, pp. 337–344. IEEE (2012).

28. Nesbit, K.J., Smith, J.E.: Data cache prefetching using a global history buffer. In: IEE Proceedings Software, p. 96. IEEE (2004)
29. Jiang, X., et al.: Chop: adaptive filter-based dram caching for CMP server platforms. In: HPCA, pp. 1–12. IEEE (2010)
30. Kim, Y., et al.: Ramulator: a fast and extensible dram simulator. In: Computer Architecture Letters (2015)
31. Nair, P.J., et al.: Reducing read latency of phase change memory via early read and turbo read. In: HPCA, pp. 309–319. IEEE (2015).
32. Intel PinPlay. https://software.intel.com/en-us/articles/program-recordreplay-toolkit
33. Shelor, C.F., Kavi, K.M.: Moola: multicore cache simulator. In: International Conference on Computers and Their Applications (2015)
34. SPEC CPU 2006. https://www.spec.org/cpu2006/
35. Proxy-Apps for Neutronics. https://cesar.mcs.anl.gov/content/software/neutronics
36. Lawrence Livermore National Laboratory: Hydrodynamics challenge problem. In: Technical report LLNL-TR-490254
37. Mohd-Yusof, J., et al.: Co-design for molecular dynamics: an exascale proxy application (2013)
38. Heroux, M., Hammond, S.: MiniFE: finite element solver. https://portal.nersc.gov/project/CAL/designforward.htm#MiniFE

Parallelism and Many-Core Systems

Reduced Complexity Many-Core:
Timing Predictability Due to Message-Passing

Jörg Mische[(✉)], Martin Frieb, Alexander Stegmeier, and Theo Ungerer

Institute of Computer Science University of Augsburg, 86159 Augsburg, Germany
{mische,martin.frieb,alexander.stegmeier,
ungerer}@informatik.uni-augsburg.de

Abstract. The Reduced Complexity Many-Core architecture (RC/MC) targets to simplify timing analysis by increasing the predictability of all components. Since shared memory interference is a major source of pessimism in many-core systems, fine-grained message passing between small cores with private memories is used instead of a global shared memory.

In this paper, the RC/MC architecture is presented and evaluated by three models: a VHDL model that can be used to synthesise prototypes with up to 6×6 cores on an FPGA; a simulation model written in C that can be used for cycle-accurate simulation of more than 4096 cores; and a timing model for static timing analysis.

1 Introduction

Applications with a computational complexity that only can be satisfied by multicore architectures have reached the embedded systems domain. Computer vision for autonomic driving, physical simulation to optimise combustion or machine learning to improve machine-human interaction are only a few examples. So far these applications do not need to pass a timing analysis. Sooner or later, they will reach safety critical domains and timing analysis will be unavoidable. But timing analysis of recent shared memory multicores is difficult. While single threaded execution on one core is already hard to analyse, the interference of cores via shared memory further complicates the timing model [27].

Speculative features like dynamic branch prediction, out-of-order execution and caches reduce average execution times significantly. However, for timing analysis the (probably extremely exotic) worst case has to be considered and not every detail can be modelled exactly, resulting in pessimistic worst case execution time (WCET) estimates for single threaded execution, possibly far off the average execution time. Additionally, memory accesses from different cores compete for the bus, interconnect, shared cache or memory controller and again, worst case scenarios can be constructed that are very unlikely, but increase the overall WCET of a parallel application.

To overcome the problems of multicore timing analysis, we propose to use a completely different architecture that is optimised for predictability and static timing analysis. It is strongly influenced by the recommendations of Wilhelm

© Springer International Publishing AG 2017
J. Knoop et al. (Eds.): ARCS 2017, LNCS 10172, pp. 139–151, 2017.
DOI: 10.1007/978-3-319-54999-6_11

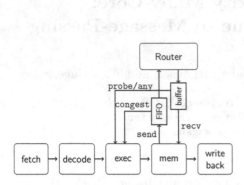

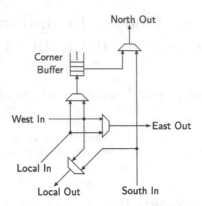

Fig. 1. Core architecture: the message interface is directly integrated into a classic five stage RISC pipeline.

Fig. 2. The PaterNoster router consists of only one FIFO and 4 multiplexers that connect 3 input ports with 3 output ports.

et al. for future architectures in time-critical systems [27], but we go one step further and replace shared memory communication by message passing [17].

Each core consists of a simple in-order pipeline and private memory. A core cannot access any other memory than its own memory, the only way to communicate with other cores is to send messages via the predictable network on chip (NoC) that connects all cores. In contrast to other message passing architectures, solely small messages of 64 bit can be sent, which simplifies router design and increases predictability. Since all components (pipeline, memory hierarchy, network interface, router and message size) are minimised, we call this architecture *Reduced Complexity Many-Core (RC/MC)*.

The basic idea of using message passing and private memories to increase many-core predictability was already presented in [17], but now these recommendations were applied to design the RC/MC architecture. Further contributions of this paper are three concrete models of the RC/MC architecture: a VHDL model to evaluate the hardware costs, a cycle-accurate simulator for performance measurements and a timing model for static timing analysis.

In the next section, the architecture is described in detail, while in Sect. 3 the timing analysis on the RC/MC platform is presented. Section 4 provides guidance, how to deal with the local memory restriction. Related many-core architectures are discussed in Sect. 5, in particular the difference to other message passing architectures that use direct memory accesses to transport messages. Finally, the hardware costs are evaluated and a case study on the WCET computation for RC/MC is presented in Sect. 6. Section 7 concludes the paper.

2   RC/MC Architecture

To avoid shared memory interference, each RC/MC core has its own private memory. The processor core consists of a classic in-order RISC pipeline with five

Table 1. Instruction set extension for fine-grained message passing

Mnemonic	Dest. register	Source register 1	Source register2	Function
send		*coreid*	*message*	send a 64 bit *message* to *core*
recv	*message*	*coreid*		receive a 64 bit *message* from *core*
congest	*flag*			check if send buffer is full
probe	*flag*	*coreid*		check if a message from *core* has arrived
any	*coreid*			check if any message has arrived and return the sender's *coreid*, otherwise -1

stages (see Fig. 1), a pipeline design that is well suited for timing analysis [4]. The instruction set follows the 64 bit RISC-V specification [26]. However, we extended it by some instructions to support message passing at processor word granularity. Table 1 lists the new instructions.

The **send** instruction is used to send a 64 bit message to another core, specified by its unique core id. If the message cannot be sent (due to congestion in the interconnect), the pipeline is stalled. To receive a 64 bit message from a specific core, **recv** is used. Again, the pipeline is stalled if the node has not received a message from the specified core yet.

To support non-blocking communication, the remaining three instructions can be used to check the state of the network interface. **congest** returns 0 if a message can be sent or 1 if sending is blocked. To check if there is a message from a specific core, **probe** is used. The instruction **any** tests if a message from any core has arrived and returns the core id from the sender of the oldest available message.

The **send** instruction puts messages in the send buffer, which is a simple first-in first-out (FIFO) buffer. The network router reads these messages from the FIFO. When messages arrive at the target node, the network router writes the message into the receive buffer, where the **recv** instruction can fetch it. However, the receive buffer is more complex than the send buffer, because the pipeline does not necessarily process the messages in the same order as they arrive at the buffer. The reason for that is that **recv** fetches a message from a specific core, which need not be the oldest message in the receive buffer. This feature increases the hardware costs, but simplifies programming, since disruptive messages that arrive ahead of time from other cores stay in the buffer and can be temporarily ignored by the software.

Via the send and receive buffers, each core is connected to its private router (Fig. 2). The routers are connected to their neighbours and form a NoC that implements PaterNoster [18] routing. The PaterNoster NoC has an unidirectional two-dimensional torus topology (Fig. 3) and is optimised to send small messages of constant length with minimal hardware costs. To avoid the long wrap-around links, a torus can be folded (Fig. 4). There are two routing modes: guaranteed service (GS) [16] and best effort (BE) [18].

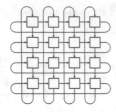   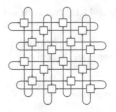

Fig. 3. Torus with wrap-around links.   **Fig. 4.** Folded torus with uniform links.

In GS mode, time division multiplexing (TDM) is used to guarantee a maximum latency and minimum bandwidth for each message transfer. Depending on the core id of the target core, a message is sent only at a specific point of time within a fixed time interval. By fixing the time, when a message can be send, any collisions of messages within the NoC are avoided and the transfer time is not influenced by other messages. If no real-time guarantees are necessary, BE mode can be used to achieve a higher throughput. In BE mode, messages can be injected into the NoC, as long as it is not congested by other messages.

Apart from the injection time, both modes use the same x-y-routing algorithm: it is quite simple, since there are only two input and two output ports in a two dimensional unidirectional torus. During horizontal or vertical transportation, a message is not buffered but constantly forwarded to the next node. Only when the message has to be switched from west to north, it is buffered in the so-called corner buffer. In GS mode, the TDM schedule restricts the message injection and ensures that the corner buffer cannot overflow, but in BE mode messages have to take an extra trip around the horizontal ring if the corner buffer is full. Nevertheless, the order of messages forwarded between two cores is always preserved, providing a simple way to send messages that are longer than 64 bits.

An important feature of the GS mode is that the timing guarantees are independent of the placement within the NoC [16]: the threads of an application can be mapped arbitrarily to any nodes without affecting the worst case traversal time. Additionally, the communication between a group of nodes is not influenced by the communication in another group of nodes, as long as there is no communication between the two groups. Conseqently, several multithreaded applications can be mapped simultaneously to the same NoC and a single application can be stopped and replaced by another multithreaded application while other applications on the remaining nodes continue execution.

All components – pipeline, network interface and router – were designed for maximum timing predictability at minimal hardware costs. The small size of the nodes permits to put a large number of nodes on one chip. Consequently, high performance can be achieved by massive parallelism. Single core performance is only a subordinate design goal, which is not as important as predictability.

3   Timing Analysis of the RC/MC

Because of the isolation of cores in RC/MC, sequential computations on one core can be easily analysed by standard static timing analysis tools for single threaded programs. Additionally, the parallel interaction between sequential code parts must be modelled to get a full timing analysis of a parallel application.

To analyse the timing of a parallel application, we separate sequential parts from parallel operations which connect the sequential parts. In the sequential code parts, a core performs some computation on its own in its local memory, without any interference with other cores. The parallel operations are responsible for communication and synchronisation between cores. From a WCET-centric view, the parallel operations are rules, how the WCETs of sequential code parts have to be combined to get an overall WCET of a parallel program.

To provide a widely accepted programming interface, a subset of the Message Passing Interface (MPI) [15] was ported to the RC/MC architecture. The network traffic generated by these functions and the code of the functions itself is highly predictable to provide tight WCET bounds for the functions that only depend on the number of participating cores and data size [23]. Using this predictable MPI library, parallel applications with a tight WCET can be written [9].

The MPI programming model is ideal for timing analysis: each process executes the same program (single program multiple data, SPMD) and communication between processes is restricted to MPI function calls. As long as only barriers and collective operations (gather, scatter, reduce, broadcast, all-to-all and their variants) are used, timing analysis is straight forward [9], provided that the hardware and the MPI implementation are predictable.

The parallel operations and their dependencies define the structure of the parallel application, in particular which code sequences are executed in parallel. This parallel execution graph given by the parallel operations is complemented by the WCETs of the sequential code sequences and the WCETs of the concrete instantiations of the parallel operations. The latter only depend on the number of participating cores and the transferred data size.

A large number of MPI programs require no more than the afore mentioned predictable MPI subset, but there are also more sophisticated applications that use load balancing between cores to reduce the overall execution time. Dynamic load balancing is good for average performance, but bad for timing analysis. The effects on timing analysis of dynamic load balancing are similar to the effects of out of order execution: both techniques schedule threads/instructions according to their dependencies, for maximum exploitation of thread/instruction level parallelism. Consequently, dynamic load balancing can induce large overestimation or even timing anomalies that inhibit the calculation of an upper timing bound. For a tight timing analysis of applications with load balancing, appropriate WCET-aware load balancing algorithms must be used that provide a tight timing model. The RC/MC architecture provides the hardware platform for such a timing model, but specialists have to develop predictable load balancing algorithms and their timing models.

MPI programs that use send and receive instead of collective operations are another class of MPI programs that cannot be analysed so far. However, pairwise communication can usually be replaced by collective communication and its application has some more advantages apart from predictability [11].

4   Private Memory Restriction

RC/MC is intended to be a minimal starting platform and baseline for further research on predictable many-core architectures with distributed memory and message passing. The main inconvenience when programming RC/MC is the small amount of available memory. More memory can be emulated by using messages to swap memory to another core which exclusively acts as memory controller for its private memory. However, such software memory paging is slow and should be avoided. Programs and algorithms must be adapted to the new constraint instead: computation is cheaper than memory space, thus compact (potentially compressed) data structures should be used and re-computation might be faster than storing an intermediate result.

The memory restriction in combination with the message passing paradigm demands a tremendous change of the programming model. However, the advent of GPGPUs shows, that a completely different and complicated programming model will be accepted, if in return the gain is big enough. This paper presents early hints, that the gains of a distributed memory model in terms of timing predictability might outweigh the costs of changing algorithms and programming models. Compared to the SIMT programming model with instruction set, scheduling and register usage restrictions, the memory and communication restrictions in RC/MC seem acceptable.

Nevertheless, weaker memory restrictions can simplify programming and porting legacy software. To minimise the influence on timing predictability, a partitioned shared memory could be added: Each core gets a distinct part of the shared memory to store its private memory. No two cores are allowed to access the same memory region, therefore the shared memory cannot be used to transfer data between cores. Transfers are still restricted to messages between cores. This way, private, isolated memory accesses are clearly separated from synchronisation or communication that might interfere with other cores. Consequently, the timing analysis of accesses to the partitioned memory is independent from the other cores. Strictly speaking, there is still some interference on the interconnect between core and memory and the arbitration between cores at the memory controller, but for this problem tight timing models do exist [24].

With partitioned memory, caches can replace the local memories, as long as they are not shared between cores. A tight timing analysis is possible, because each core - cache - memory partition triplet is isolated and well-studied cache models from single core processors [20] can be applied. Since the caches and their address ranges are completely separated, no cache coherence is necessary. In other words, cache coherence in a shared memory system is replaced by message passing in a partitioned memory system.

5   Related Work

A widely used many-core architecture is shared memory with multiple memory controllers and individual L1 and L2 caches per core. The timing analysis depends on the predictability of the interconnection network. While the Intel Xeon Phi [12] uses three rings to connect 61 cores, the Tilera TILEPro64 [3] has five meshes and the Godson-T [8] two meshes. All NoCs are very dynamic and highly optimised for maximum throughput and their timing details are confidential.

However, there are some similarities with the RC/MC architecture: all three architectures are based on simple in-order cores and the TILEPro64 uses only three of the meshes for memory data transfers and cache coherence, the other two can be used by the software for explicit message passing. In the Godson-T, the L2 cache is shared between the cores, but the L1 cache can partly be reconfigured to be used as scratchpad memory.

In the parMERASA project [25], a timing predictable shared memory many-core was developed. The memory model is clustered: several cores build a cluster and share one memory that can either be on-chip or off-chip. The processor consists of multiple clusters. Inter-cluster communication is implemented by direct accesses to special regions of the other cluster's memories. Both inter- and intra-cluster connections are real-time capable and provide a predictable latency, but message passing is not supported.

Each of the 48 cores of the Intel Single-chip Cloud Computer (SCC) [14] has exclusive access to a single part of the global memory. These accesses are accelerated by private L1 and L2 caches, but accesses to the memory area of other cores are not allowed. The only way to communicate between cores are small private scratchpad memories called Message Passing Buffers (MPBs). Therefore, the SCC is a message passing many-core with isolated memories like the RC/MC, but its DMA-based message passing is completely different from the fine-grained message passing of RC/MC:

To send a message from core A to core B, the DMA (direct memory access) controller is programmed to copy the message from the private memory of core A to the MPB of core B. The DMA controller uses the NoC to transfer the data from core A to core B. When the transfer is finished, a flag in the MPB of B is set. Core B waits until the flag is set and then copies the message to its private memory to free the MPB for the next message. This message passing variant comprises a lot of overhead, demanding long messages for efficient communication. The pipeline integrated message passing of RC/MC is much more lightweight.

The SCC NoC does not provide any timing guarantees [5], therefore it is not real-time capable. However, the T-CREST architecture [22] uses the same DMA-based message passing in connection with a TDM controlled NoC. A second NoC that connects the cores with the shared memory is also timing predictable due to TDM scheduling. Hence, T-CREST unifies shared memory and message passing in a timing predictable way. The per-core memory architecture is also hybrid: private scratchpad memory is combined with predictable caches for instructions

cores	ALMs	registers	memory bits
2x2	20 586	20 946	2 099 264
3x3	46 776	48 211	4 723 488
4x4	82 945	85 721	8 397 312
5x5	133 034	136 639	13 121 200
6x6	191 009	196 555	18 894 528

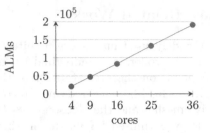

Fig. 5. Synthesis results for RC/MC processors depending on the number of cores

and data. DMA-based message passing is also used by CompSOC [10]. Due to its strong emphasis on predictability and isolating cores it is the architecture with the most similarities with RC/MC.

Anyway, in T-CREST and CompSOC message passing is only an additional feature to the dominating shared memory architecture. Both architectures offer a plethora of mechanisms, paradigms and programming models to enable predictable parallel programming, while RC/MC concentrates on the thorough examination of one alternative programming model.

Scaling down supercomputer architectures inspired the design of the Kalray MPPA-256 processor [6]. 16 compute cores, a resource managing core and 2 MiB of shared memory build a cluster. 16 clusters and 4 I/O subsystems are connected by a rate controlling NoC with torus topology. The shared memory inside the clusters can be partitioned to provide 128 KiB of private memory for every core. However, messages are passed only between clusters, within clusters the shared memory must be used for communication.

The Epiphany architecture [19] is a true distributed memory many-core with up to 1024 cores. Each core has up to 64 KiB of fast local memory, but can access the local memory of every other core via a mesh interconnection. It is designed for high floating point performance and has a timing predictable NoC. Hence, this architecture closely resembles the RC/MC architecture, but there is no possibility for explicit messages.

6   Evaluation

A prototype of the RC/MC architecture was written in VHDL. For design space exploration with a larger number of cores, a cycle-accurate in-house simulator was written in C. Its accuracy was tested against the VHDL model for up to 4×4 cores with several parallel benchmark programs that run up to 5 million cycles. In every single cycle the register contents in the VHDL and the C model were identical.

6.1   FPGA Prototype

We used Altera Quartus Prime 16.0 for an Altera Stratix V E FPGA to synthesise RC/MC prototypes with different numbers of cores. Only the integer ISA

Table 2. Approximate size of the components of a RC/MC core

Component	ALMs	Registers	Memory bits
Pipeline (incl. send buffer)	1800	1600	0
Receive buffer	2500	2300	0
Router	800	1400	0
Memory	100	8	512Ki

subset (RV64I) is supported and every core has 64 KiByte of local memory. As Fig. 5 shows, the architecture scales very well. Area in terms of ALMs[1] scales linearly with the number of cores, hence the size of each core is fixed within the usual statistical fluctuations. Thus it is possible to estimate the sizes of the components, shown in Table 2.

While the send buffer is so small, that it can only hardly be separated from the pipeline logic, the size of the receive buffer is large. The reason for its size is that messages can not only be removed in total temporal order, but also on a per-sender basis (see Sect. 2). Therefore, a FIFO is used for storing incoming messages, but additional hardware is used to search a specific sender core id in the FIFO and remove the message, when the recv instruction is executed.

Since the costs of the receive buffer are so high, we are planning to replace it by a simple FIFO like the send buffer. However, in this case, other instructions must be defined, the MPI interface must be rewritten to buffer messages from other cores and last but not least, the additional branches and loops for buffering messages must undergo a completely new timing analysis.

6.2   Number of Cores

How many RC/MC cores can be put on a chip? To estimate this number, the RC/MC architecture is compared to existing many-cores with published hardware costs.

As mentioned in Sect. 5, the Parallela architecture is very similar to the RC/MC architecture. Local memory, predictable NoC and even the pipeline (64 bit integer and floating point, in-oder issue) are comparable. The tape-out of a processor with 1024 cores was recently announced [19]. Therefore, 1024 cores with 64 KiB memory each seem to be achievable on 117 mm² in 16 nm technology for the RC/MC architecture, too.

Rocket [13] is a RISC-V implementation with a 64 bit single issue in-order pipeline from the University of Berkeley. In 45 nm technology, a core with vector accelerator and 56 KiB of cache fits into 1.46 mm² at a clock rate of 1.3 GHz. Assuming that the vector accelerator of Rocket is not larger than the RC/MC

---

[1] Altera uses the term *Adaptive Logic Module (ALM)* for their elementary logic block, basically a lookup table with 6 inputs and 2 outputs (6-LUT). One ALM is equivalent to approximately 2.5 lookup tables with 4 inputs and 1 output (4-LUT).

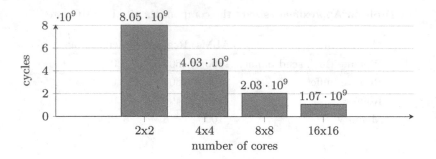

Fig. 6. WCET of CG depending on the number of cores

receive buffer and that 64 KiB local memory are not larger than 56 KiB cache, 100 RC/MC cores with 64 KiB memory each fit into 150 mm². Without the costly receive buffer and only 16 KiB of RAM, the size of one RC/MC core should be around 0.39 mm², the size of a Rocket without accelerator and 16 KiB of cache in 45 nm technology.

The cores of the Kalray MPPA-256 processor [6] consist of a 5-issue VLIW pipeline with 7 stages and 16 KiB of cache. Additionally, the 288 cores have access to 32 MiB of local private memory, about 100 KiB per core. Since the RC/MC pipeline is of comparable complexity, and the Kalray die comprises a lot of other logic, 288 cores with 100 KiB each in 28 nm technology would be realistic for an RC/MC implementation, too.

6.3   Case Study: WCET Estimation

The RC/MC architecture is designed for massively parallel applications. Unfortunately, available real-time benchmarks are still mostly designed for single core systems or multicore systems with only a few cores. If parallel systems are studied, often several independent single threaded applications are executed concurrently to provide a massively parallel workload. However, we believe that in future real-time systems, massively parallel computations will be required, too. For example, the object recognition for autonomous driving or physical simulation of aerodynamics or combustion are scientific applications that might be used in future real-time systems. An application with a close correlation to the typical computation and data access patterns of real scientific applications is the CG (conjugate gradient) method for solving linear equation systems [7]. It is used to benchmark the performance of high performance supercomputers, because its behaviour is less computation bound than the currently used LINPACK benchmark [7].

Therefore we choose the CG implementation of the NAS parallel benchmark suite [1] as typical case study for the WCET estimation of a future scientific real-time application. After porting the program from FORTRAN to C, the custom implemented collective operations had to be replaced by the official MPI collective functions. These functions were implemented in a timing predictable way, using the One-To-One schedule of PaterNoster for a real-time capable communication. WCET estimates for the sequential code parts resulted from a static timing analysis with OTAWA [2]. Details on the WCET estimation methodology can be found in [9].

Figure 6 shows the results for CG with a matrix size of 7000×7000 and 3500 non-zero values. The WCET halves, if $4\times$ the cores are used. Therefore, the scalability is much better than in shared memory systems, where the WCET per core can even increase, when more cores are used [21].

7   Conclusion

The RC/MC architecture is composed of simple, predictable cores that are connected by message passing. Thereby, the cores are isolated and a timing analysis can easily be applied. The programming model is different from shared memory programming, but fits very well to the demands of timing analysis and therefore promises tighter WCET estimates.

So far, the RC/MC architecture is simple, but there are a lot of features that can be added, as long as the predictability is conserved. The FPGA prototype and the corresponding 100% cycle accurate simulator are a strong foundation for future research on predictable many-core architectures. Their source code is available at https://github.com/unia-sik/rcmc/.

References

1. Bailey, D.H., et al.: The NAS parallel benchmarks. Int. J. High Perform. Comput. Appl. **5**(3), 63–73 (1991)
2. Ballabriga, C., Cassé, H., Rochange, C., Sainrat, P.: OTAWA: an open toolbox for adaptive WCET analysis. In: Min, S.L., Pettit, R., Puschner, P., Ungerer, T. (eds.) SEUS 2010. LNCS, vol. 6399, pp. 35–46. Springer, Heidelberg (2010). doi:10.1007/978-3-642-16256-5_6
3. Bell, S., et al.: Tile64-processor: a 64-core soc with mesh interconnect. In: International Solid-State Circuits Conference (ISSCC), pp. 88–598 (2008)
4. Berg, C., Engblom, J., Wilhelm, R.: Requirements for and design of a processor with predictable timing. In: Perspectives Workshop: Design of Systems with Predictable Behaviour. No. 03471 in Dagstuhl Seminar Proceedings (2004)
5. d'Ausbourg, B., Boyer, M., Noulard, E., Pagetti, C.: Deterministic execution on many-core platforms: application to the SCC. In: Many-core Applications Research Community Symposium (MARC), December 2011
6. de Dinechin, B.D., et al.: A distributed run-time environment for the Kalray MPPA-256 integrated manycore processor. Procedia Comput. Sci. **18**, 1654–1663 (2013)
7. Dongarra, J., Heroux, M.A.: Toward a new metric for ranking high performance computing systems. Sandia Report, SAND2013-4744 312 (2013)

8. Fan, D., et al.: Godson-T: an efficient many-core processor exploring thread-level parallelism. IEEE Micro **32**(2), 38–47 (2012)
9. Frieb, M., Stegmeier, A., Mische, J., Ungerer, T.: Employing MPI collectives for timing analysis on embedded multi-cores. In: 16th International Workshop on Worst-Case Execution Time Analysis (2016)
10. Goossens, K., et al.: Virtual execution platforms for mixed-time-criticality systems: the CompSOC architecture and design flow. ACM SIGBED Rev. **10**(3), 23–34 (2013)
11. Gorlatch, S.: Send-receive considered harmful: myths and realities of message passing. ACM Trans. Program. Lang. Syst. (TOPLAS) **26**(1), 47–56 (2004)
12. Corporation, I.: Intel Xeon Phi Coprocessor System Software Developers Guide, 2.03 edn., November 2012
13. Lee, Y., et al.: A 45 nm 1.3 GHz 16.7 double-precision GFLOPS/W RISC-V processor with vector accelerators. In: European Solid State Circuits Conference (ESSCIRC), pp. 199–202. IEEE (2014)
14. Mattson, T.G., et al.: The 48-core SCC processor: the programmer's view. In: International Conference for High Performance Computing, Networking, Storage and Analysis (SC), pp. 1–11 (2010)
15. Message Passing Interface Forum. University of Tennesse: MPI: a Message-Passing Interface Standard. Version 3.1, June 2015
16. Mische, J., Ungerer, T.: Guaranteed service independent of the task placement in NoCs with torus topology. In: Proceedings of the 22nd International Conference on Real-Time Networks and Systems, p. 151. ACM (2014)
17. Mische, J., Metzlaff, S., Ungerer, T.: Distributed memory on chip - bringing together low power and real-time. In: Workshop on Reconciling Performance and Predictability (2014)
18. Mische, J., Ungerer, T.: Low power flitwise routing in an unidirectional torus with minimal buffering. In: International Workshop on Network on Chip Architectures (NoCArc), pp. 63–68 (2012)
19. Olofsson, A.: Epiphany-V: a 1024 processor 64-bit RISC system-on-chip. Technical report, Adapteva Inc. https://www.parallella.org/wp-content/uploads/2016/10/e5_1024core_soc.pdf
20. Reineke, J.: Caches in WCET analysis. Universität des Saarlandes, Saarbrücken, PhD Thesis (2008)
21. Rochange, C., et al.: WCET analysis of a parallel 3D multigrid solver executed on the MERASA multi-core. In: OASIcs-OpenAccess Series in Informatics, vol. 15. Schloss Dagstuhl-Leibniz-Zentrum fuer Informatik (2010)
22. Schoeberl, M., et al.: T-CREST: time-predictable multi-core architecture for embedded systems. J. Syst. Archit. **61**(9), 449–471 (2015)
23. Stegmeier, A., Frieb, M., Mische, J., Ungerer, T.: WCTT bounds for MPI primitives in the PaterNoster NoC. In: 14th International Workshop on Real-Time Networks (2016)
24. Ungerer, T., et al.: MERASA: multicore execution of hard real-time applications supporting analyzability. IEEE Micro **30**(5), 66–75 (2010)
25. Ungerer, T., et al.: Parallelizing industrial hard real-time applications for the parMERASA multicore. ACM Trans. Embed. Comput. Syst. (TECS) **15**(3), 53 (2016)

26. Waterman, A., Lee, Y., Patterson, D.A., Asanovi, K.: The RISC-V instruction set manual, volume I: user-level ISA, version 2.1. Technical report UCB/EECS-2016-118, EECS Department, University of California, Berkeley, May 2016. http://www2.eecs.berkeley.edu/Pubs/TechRpts/2016/EECS-2016-118.html

27. Wilhelm, R., et al.: Memory hierarchies, pipelines, and buses for future architectures in time-critical embedded systems. IEEE Trans. Comput. Aided Des. Integr. Circuits Syst. **28**(7), 966–978 (2009)

Parallel Forwarding for Efficient Bandwidth Utilization in Networks-on-Chip

Elham Momenzadeh[1], Mehdi Modarressi[2([⊠])], Abbas Mazloumi[2],
and Masoud Daneshtalab[3,4]

[1] School of Computer Science, Institute for Research in Fundamental Sciences (IPM),
Tehran, Iran
elham.momenzade@gmail.com
[2] Department of Electrical and Computer Engineering, University of Tehran, Tehran, Iran
{modarressi,a.mazloumi}@ut.ac.ir
[3] Mälardalen University (MDH), Västerås, Sweden
[4] Royal Institute of Technology (KTH), Stockholm, Sweden
masdan@kth.se

Abstract. Networks-on-chip (NoC) provide a scalable and power-efficient communication infrastructure for different computing chips, ranging from fully customized
multi/many-processor systems-on-chip (MPSoCs) to general-purpose chip multiprocessors (CMPs). A common aspect in almost all NoC workloads is the varying size
of data transmitted by each transaction: while large data blocks are transferred as
multiple-flit packets, a part of the traffic consists of short data segment (control data)
that does not even fill a single flit. In conventional NoCs, switch allocator assigns/
grants a switch output (and the link connected to it) to a single flit at each cycle, even
if the flit is shorter than the link bit-width. In this paper, we propose a novel NoC
architecture that enables routers to simultaneously send two short flits on the same
link, effectively utilizing the link bandwidth that otherwise would be wasted. To this
end, new crossbar, virtual channel (VC), and switch allocator architectures are
presented to support parallel short packet forwarding on NoC links. Simulation
results using synthetic and realistic workloads show that the proposed architecture
improves the NoC performance by up to 24%.

Keywords: Network-on-Chip · Heterogeneous packet size · Bandwidth
utilization

1 Introduction

Networks-on-chip (NoC) are widely known as the most promising solution to handle inter-
core communication in multi- and many-core architectures. NoCs provide a power-efficient infrastructure with scalable bandwidth for on-chip communication. As the core count
and workload complexity of chip multiprocessors (CMP) and multi/many-processor
systems-on-chip (MPSoC) increase, the rate and complexity of on-chip communication raise
considerably. Consequently, there is always a growing demand for NoCs with higher
throughput and lower latency.

© Springer International Publishing AG 2017
J. Knoop et al. (Eds.): ARCS 2017, LNCS 10172, pp. 152–163, 2017.
DOI: 10.1007/978-3-319-54999-6_12

NoC bit width (flit size) is a first-order design parameter that highly affects the maximum network bandwidth and packet latency. This parameter determines the bit-width of all NoC datapath components (i.e. link, buffer, and crossbar). As a result, in addition to its impact on performance, bit-width also plays an important role in determining the total NoC implementation cost and power consumption.

Performance metrics always favor enlarging bit-width (as long as the cost constraint allows), because wider links decrease packet serialization overhead, thereby enhance both the speed and throughput of networks.

Recent NoC designs and commercial implementations use links as wide as 128 [1, 2], 144 [3], 160 [4], 256 [5], and 512 bits [6] to maximize performance with respect to area constraints. However, the message size, that is the amount of data transmitted at each network transaction, varies significantly in realistic workloads [7]. For example, in a typical CMP workload, the traffic consists of long data and short control packets. Data packets composed of multiple flits to transfer a cache block, while control packets transfer request and coherency messages that contain a memory/IO address plus a few control bits. Whereas the former benefits from larger bit widths, the latter cannot even fill half of the bit width at each transfer [8].

In some recent studies, it has been shown that a considerable portion of traffic in CMP workload is the short request and coherency packets [7, 9, 10]. For example, it has been shown that more than 78% of the packets in the PARSEC suite programs [11] are short control packets (request or coherency), whereas the remaining packets are long and contain a full 64B cache line [9]. Very different packet sizes (from 8-bit control packets to data packets with kilobits of data) are also reported for multimedia and tele-communication workloads implemented on application-specific NoCs [12]. As mentioned before, NoCs enlarge bit-width to reduce data serialization overhead of time-critical data packets, but this results in considerable bandwidth waste and resource underutilization when sending short packets: A short control flit uses part of the bit-width, leaving the remaining bits idle and the link underutilized. Buffers are also become underutilized in conventional NoCs, because those buffer slots that keep control packets have many bits zero-padded. However, conventional switch allocators allocate the switch output (and the corresponding downstream link) to a single flit, regardless its bit-width usage.

In this paper, we propose a novel architecture that enables routers to transfer and store two short flits through each port in parallel. In this architecture, if two or more short flits request for an output port, the switch allocator grants the port to two flits: the second flit uses the otherwise idle bit-width of the link to go downstream in parallel with the first flit. The input port also supports receiving and buffering two short flits simultaneously.

These scheme decreases the switch allocation failure rate and hence, part of the unnecessary short flit blocking latency is eliminated.

As a quantitative motivation on the potential impact of our proposed parallel forwarding on performance. Table 1 shows the percentage of switch allocations with at least one loser under two representative workloads: a workload with high injection rate from the ISPASS GPU benchmark suite [13] and a workload with light traffic load from the PARSEC CMP suite [14]. The table also shows in what percentage of the total switch allocation failures a short flit is blocked by another short flit.

Table 1. Switch allocation failure analysis

Workload	Total switch allocation failures (%)	Percentage of total failures with two short flits (%)
PARSEC: Ferret (0.08 flit/node/cycle)	16.32	36.12
GPU: BFS (0.3 flit/node/cycle)	38.08	30.93

As the table shows, the proposed parallel short packet forwarding can potentially reduce switch allocation failure rate (which is 16% and 38% in Table 1) by up to 36%. This architecture allows designers to increase bit width in favor of long data packets and mitigate resource underutilization by parallel short packet transfer/storage.

Since control transfers account for a considerable amount of on-chip traffic in CMP workloads, many flits can take advantage of the proposed mechanism and so, the performance and resource utilization of the NoC increases considerably.

Several prior works proposed to use physically separate sub-networks to handle each traffic class (data and control) appropriately [6] or to reduce power [8].

For example, Intel Xeon Phi uses a 512-bit wide ring for data packets and very narrower sub-networks for control and address packets [6]. However, multiple sub-networks have a higher cumulative area than a single network. This can potentially increase the implementation cost and power consumption of the NoC.

Our mechanism implements different sub-networks into the same NoC fabric. It can be considered as a polymorphic NoC: long packets see links and buffers as single n-bit structures, whereas these components act as two n/2-bit parallel structures from the short packets' perspective.

In the next sections, we first explore the related work, introduce the proposed NoC architecture and then show it can reduce NoC latency by up to 24% and throughput by 30%, on average.

2   Related Work

Several hybrid network-on-chip designs can be found in the literature that partition the NoC into multiple parts and optimize each part for a specific traffic class.

Using physically separated NoCs for data and control packets is also proposed in many related work. The authors in [15] show the potential benefits of using multiple physicals sub-networks for control and data packets.

In [16], a NoC is partitioned into two packet-switched and circuit-switched sub-networks using time-division multiplexing (TDM). The packet-switched sub-network carries request packets, whereas the circuit-switched part is used to make shortcut paths for data packets. Each request packet makes circuit for its corresponding data packet while traveling towards the destination. Proactive Resource Allocation (PRA) NoC exploits the distinct characteristics of data and control packet to increase performance [17]. In PRA, most short request packets use conventional packet switching, but multi-flit data packets are provided by pre-allocated paths, on which they are forwarded with low per-hop latency and power consumption.

Cache Coherent NoC (CCNoC) architecture is another hybrid architecture presented in [8]. It uses two different sub-networks for control and data to reduce the power consumption. As cache coherency protocols produce a group of write and read-request messages, managing cache coherency is done more efficiently by using dedicated sub-networks, in terms of both performance and power consumption. As control packets are smaller, lower bit width (64 bits) is applied for the request sub-network. Consequently, power consumption decreases while performance gets no impact. Response packets convey several cache blocks and so, require a higher bit width (112 to 128 bits). They showed that in addition to power-efficiency, using a heterogeneous structure results in a better performance than a unified NoC. As another insightful study in this field, [7] investigates the effect of bit width on performance and scalability of NoCs and concludes that the flit size should be set to the smallest packet type's size.

The above works focus on different aspects of workloads with mixed packet types. To the best of our knowledge, our proposed work is the first method that focuses on the underutilized NoC resources when forwarding short flits and modifies routers to allow parallel transfer of such short flits.

3 The Proposed NoC Architecture

3.1 NoC Packet Size

As our method targets CMP workloads, we consider two different kinds of packets in the network: long data and short control packets. Control packets are either memory and I/O requests or coherency messages that consist of a memory or I/O address along with a few control flags. Data packets are sent in response to a request and transfer a cache or memory block to a remote core. As the payload of these packets is a cache block, which can be as large as 32-128 bytes in a conventional cache (e.g. 64-bytes for Intel Xeon Phi [6] and ARM Cortex A15 [18]), they are long and should be fragmented into multiple flits. Carrying a memory address (which is 40-bit wide in ARM Cortex A15 [18], for example), a control packet would fill half of a 128-bit flit (40 bit memory address as payload, 10 bit destination address for network routing in a 1024-node network, and the remaining 14 bits for control, routing, and error recovery data), while a data packet requires five 128-bit flits (4 payload and one header). As an off-chip example, the HyperTransport protocol, which is implemented in modern AMD processors, also uses 512-bit packet for data and 64-bit packet for control transfer [19]. Therefore, in this paper, we use 128-bit links (flits), 64-bit control messages (that are sent as a single 128-bit flit in a conventional NoC with 64 zero-padded bits) and five-flit data packets.

3.2 Proposed Router Architecture

In a conventional architecture, as mentioned, each datapath element handles a single flit at each cycle. In this work, we propose to transfer and store two short control packet in parallel to use the idle bit width of the links, crossbar switches, and buffers that otherwise would be wasted (filled by zero-padded null data). To this end, several router components must be modified: switch allocator to detect short flits and allocate a 128-bit link to two requesting ones, crossbar switch and links to transfer two short flits in parallel (in addition to the baseline one long flit), and virtual channels to accept and store two short flits simultaneously. This architecture is depicted in Fig. 1.

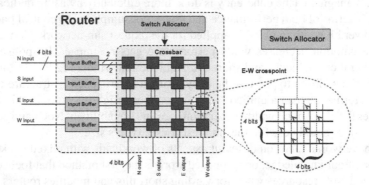

Fig. 1. The proposed router architecture and the internal connections of one crosspoint (East-West crosspoint) of the crossbar. Bit width is set to 4 for the sake of simplicity

Crossbar. In order to send two short flits simultaneously, the crossbar crosspoints should be capable to switch half bit width of inputs and outputs independently. For example, the crossbar should be able to connect the high half (n/2 bit) of input port E to the low half of output port S and the low half of input port E to the high half of output port N. However, if a long data packet is traversing the crossbar, the required connection is established on the full bit-width, just like a conventional NoC.

Figure 1 also shows the internal connections of a crosspoint. The figure shows 4-bit wide links for simplicity. The switches in the orthogonal positions implement the regular connections for full bit-width switching.

The other switches are added in our design to allow half bit width switching. As the figure shows, the new crossbar needs more switches to support half width switching.

Figure 2 shows several sample connections established on the crossbar at a cycle. In this figure, two control flits that come from input port N are connected to output ports S and E. A full width data flit that comes from input port E is connected to output port W. the idle half bit width of output port E is also connected to input port S. The internal connections of two connection points are also depicted in the figure, where the connected switches are identified by a circle.

Links. Two short flits should be able to pass a link at the same cycle. However, there is no need to add any logic to links to manage this parallel transfer, because short flit concatenation is done by crossbar switch. The two short flits will be directed to the right VCs assigned to them at the upstream router through the multiplexer at the downstream input port (Fig. 3). The multiplexers are set by upstream router, just like what a conventional router does.

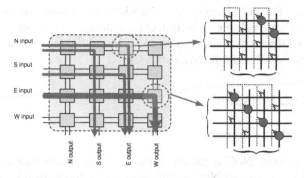

Fig. 2. Several full width and half width connections on the proposed crossbar and the internal connections of two sample switches. The switches identified by a red circle are turned on. (Color figure online)

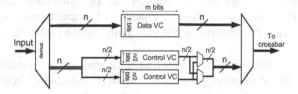

Fig. 3. The structure of the input unit with one data VC and two half width control VCs

Input VCs. NoCs that are used in CMPs often use different VCs for request, data, and coherency messages. The main advantage of using different VCs for each traffic class is that we can assign priority to packets based on packet's VC and order memory transactions to avoid protocol deadlocks. So, we consider two VCs per port and assign them to data and control (coherency or request) packets.

In our design, the data VC has m-entry n-bit wide buffer, as in a baseline router. The control VC consumes the same buffering space, but is horizontally partitioned to get two m-entry n/2-bit buffers (Fig. 3). Each narrow buffer has its own control logic to load/ store flits simultaneously. As Fig. 3 shows, each input port has a single n-bit line to crossbar switch input. Switch allocator configures the multiplexers of this line to connect either one long flit or two short flits to the crossbar based on its allocation decision.

Switch Allocator. This component should distinguish short and long flits and grants each output link to at most one long or two short packets (if any). It should also allow a crossbar input to be shared by two short flits by appropriately setting the select line of the multiplexers between the input units and crossbar (see Fig. 3).

VC Allocator. VC allocator selects one of the control or data VCs for a packet based on its type. If there are more than one control VCs, a VC is selected for a requesting packet in a round robin fashion.

Please note that the VC allocation unit considers each narrow half-width VC as an independent VC. The demultiplexer in front of the input unit is capable to send two half-width flits to two different half-width control VCs in parallel (apart from its basic functionality that sends a full-width flit to a data VC).

4   Experimental Results

4.1   Experimental Environment

We use a cycle-accurate NoC simulator, BookSim [20], to simulate our architecture. We have tested the proposed NoC architecture under the uniform synthetic traffic pattern, as well as several traffic traces from the ISPASS GPU [13] and PARSEC benchmark suites. PARSEC traffic obtained from the Netrace library [14]. The GPU workload is the traffic between shader cores and memory modules extracted by GPGPUSim [13].

We use the mesh topology with wormhole-switched routers and 128-bit links (max flit size = 128). The routers are 3-stage pipelined (look-ahead routing + VC allocation, switch allocation, crossbar traversal + link traversal) and the routing algorithm is deterministic XY.

The network has two message classes that is a common configuration for CMPs to provide different levels of priority for response (data), and control (request and coherency) messages and resolve memory protocol deadlocks. A single virtual channel is considered for each message class. The data virtual channel is 128-bit wide and 8-flit deep. The control virtual channel that keeps short packets is partitioned horizontally and is arranged as two parallel 64-bit 8-flit buffers.

To evaluate our method, we compare each test-case with a conventional packet-switched network (referred to as Conventional in the graphs) that features all the above-mentioned architectural parameters, except that it does not have parallel short packet forwarding and partitioned control VC.

4.2   Performance Evaluation

Synthetic Traffic. First, we use a uniform traffic pattern to evaluate the network performance in different injection rates. The traffic is composed of 50% short (one 64-bit flit) and 50% long (five 128-bit) packets. Figure 4 shows the average packet latency for different injection rates. We consider 4 × 4 and 8 × 8 mesh networks with two half-width VCs for control and one full-width 128-bit VC for data packets.

As illustrated in the figure, our approach outperforms the baseline under most of the traffic injection rates. Furthermore, it pushes the saturation point by 22% for the 4 × 4 and 30% for the 8 × 8 NoCs.

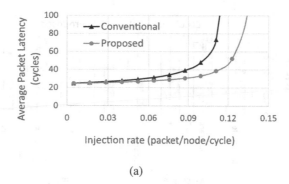

(a)

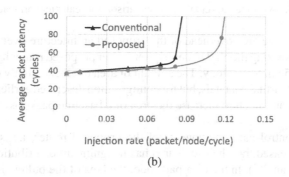

(b)

Fig. 4. Average packet latency of the proposed and conventional NoCs in (a) 4 × 4 mesh and (b) 8 × 8 mesh

Under low traffic, the arbitration failure rate is low, so few flits benefit from parallel packet transfer that is used to resolve arbitration failures. Therefore, the latency approaches to the baseline latency. As the injection rate increases, however, the probability of arbitration failure increase that in turn, provides more opportunity for our proposed parallel packet transfer to improve performance. Consequently, the difference between the performance of the proposed NoC and the baseline increases under higher injection rates.

Realistic Workloads. Next, we evaluate the NoCs under four PARSEC and four GPU workloads. The experiments are done on an 8 × 8 mesh network for PARSEC and 5 × 5 for GPU.

Figure 5 shows the performance comparison results. The request and coherency packets have one 64-bit flit and data (response) packets have five 128-bit flits. In the GPU benchmarks some data packets have two 128-bit flits (together with the 5-flit packets). As the figure shows, performance is improved by 13%, on average for PARSEC and 24% for GPU. Again, the main source of better performance of our method is its ability to effectively use idle link bandwidth to remove many unnecessary control packet blocking situations. The GPU programs have considerably higher traffic loads than PARSEC, which translates to more efficiency of simultaneous packet forwarding.

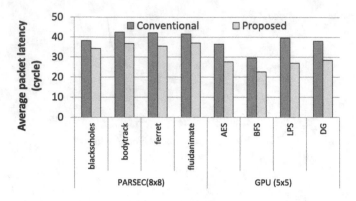

Fig. 5. Average packet latency comparison for realistic workloads

Cost Evaluation. The area overhead of the proposed architecture over the baseline is evaluated by synthesizing the VHDL description of our proposed router by a commercial synthesis tool in 45 nm technology. The amount of area overhead highly depends on the number of depth of virtual channels, but for configuration described earlier in this section the proposed NoC architecture increase the area of a baseline packet-switched NoC by 8%.

The area of control-path components of the proposed router, i.e. switch and VC allocators, are increased, but their total area has insignificant contribution to the entire router area (less than 7%). In the data-path side, the area of the buffers in the proposed router is roughly the same as a baseline conventional router with two VCs. However, the main source of area overhead in our design includes the extra multiplexers at the input port and additional crosspoint switches for the crossbar. Please note that the number of crossbar input and output ports, as well as the bit width of each port, which determines the crossbar layout and has the first-order effect on its area footprint, is the same as the baseline, but the crosspoints are doubled. Our synthesis shows that the modifications increase the crossbar's area from 22,900 um^2 to 24,500 um^2 (the total area of the modified router is 62,000 um^2).

Synthesis results in 45 nm technology also show that in the proposed router, the delay of route computation, switch allocation, VC allocation (two VCs), and crossbar traversal pipeline stages are 63 ps, 380 ps, 435 ps, and 254 ps, respectively. VC allocator has often the longest router pipeline latency, but our simple VC allocation scheme, where the message class determines the VC, leads to a simple and fast VC allocator logic.

As the results show, the latency of all stages is below 500 ps and so, the router can work at 2 Ghz, which is high enough as the working frequency of a high performance NoC.

Comparison with CCNoC. We also compare the proposed method with CCNoC [8]. The network parameters are the same as the previous experiments, but CCNoC has two physically separate sub-networks (128-bit data, 64-bit control) and uses a single VC per sub-network.

Figure 6 compares the average packet latency of the proposed NoC with CCNoC. The figure also compares the performance of CCNoC with a scaled-up version of the proposed NoC that has the same area as CCNoC. Our area analysis shows that by increasing the bit-width of the proposed NoC to 192 bits, it has a close area (within 5%) to an equivalent CCNoC. To simulate this bit-width, three short messages can pass a link simultaneously. Long (5-flit) packets also pass the wider links in four consecutive cycles (1.5 flits per cycle).

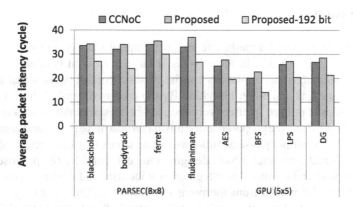

Fig. 6. Average packet latency comparison with CCNoC

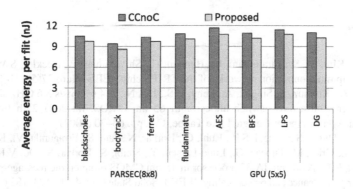

Fig. 7. Energy per flit (J) comparison with CCNoC

This configuration (represented by the bars marked as Proposed 192-bit in Fig. 6) actually shows the performance that the proposed parallel short packet forwarding would offer if the extra area overhead of CCNoC is invested to increase the bit-width of the proposed NoC.

As Fig. 6 shows, although the baseline proposed NoC suffers from an average performance loss of 7.5%, its area-normalized version can improve the performance by up to 21% over CCNoC.

The traffic load of many CMP applications is somewhat light and places between the zero load and saturation points. In CCNoC, this light traffic is further divided into two lighter traffic loads. Consequently, the resources will be left underutilized and the performance is close to our proposal that utilizes the unused bandwidth of a single network to manage both control and data traffic.

Figure 7 compares the energy consumption of CCNoC with the proposed NoC. The results are obtained through the Dsent power library [21] and show that our NoC has 9% less energy usage, on average, mainly due to the less static power it wastes.

5   Conclusion

In this paper, we proposed a method to support parallel transfer and storage of short control flits in modern NoCs. In these NoCs, a large portion of bandwidth is wasted because a considerable part of packets consist of short control packets that are by far narrower than the link and buffer bit width. By the proposed parallel short flit sending the idle bit width is utilized to effectively reduce unnecessary control packet blocking latency. We showed that the proposed mechanism can be a more power and area-efficient alternative of the multiple physical sub-network schemes that has been used in some recent research and commercial NoC designs. One can consider the proposed NoC a polymorphic NoC architecture that integrates a wide data and a narrow control NoCs and has different bit widths from the point of view of different packet classes. The experimental results under a set of realistic and synthetic benchmarks revealed that this architecture can significantly reduce packet latency and improve throughput of NoCs.

References

1. Gratz, P., Kim, C., Sankaralingam, K., Hanson, H., Shivakumar, P., Keckler, S.W., Burger, D.: On-chip interconnection networks of the TRIPS chip. IEEE Micro **27**(5), 41–50 (2007)
2. Kumary, A., Kunduz, p., Singhx, A., Pehy, L.S., Jha, N.: A 4.6 Tbits/s 3.6 GHz single-cycle NoC router with a novel switch allocator in 65 nm CMOS. In: 2007 25th International Conference on Computer Design, Lake Tahoe, CA, pp. 63–70 (2007)
3. Howard, J., Dighe, S., Vangal, S.R., Ruhl, G., Borkar, N., Jain, S., Erraguntla, V., Konow, M., Riepen, M., Gries, M., Droege, G., Lund-Larsen, T., Steibl, S., Borkar, S., De, V.K., Van der Wijngaart, R.F.: A 48-core IA-32 processor in 45 nm CMOS using on-die message-passing and DVFS for performance and power scaling. IEEE J. Solid State Circ. **46**(1), 173–183 (2011)
4. Wentzlaff, D., Griffin, P., Hoffmann, H., Bao, L., Edwards, B., Ramey, C., Mattina, M., Miao, C., Brown III, J.F., Agarwal, A.: On-chip interconnection architecture of the tile processor. IEEE Micro **27**(5), 15–31 (2007)
5. Rotem, E., Naveh, A., Ananthakrishnan, A., Weissmann, E., Rajwan, D.: Power-management architecture of the Intel microarchitecture code-named Sandy Bridge. IEEE Micro **32**(2), 20–27 (2012)
6. Overview of Intel Xeon Phi Coprocessor. https://software.intel.com
7. Lee, J., Nicopoulos, C., Park, S.J., Swaminathan, M., Kim, J.: Do we need wide flits in networks-on-chip? In: ISVLSI, Natal, pp. 2–7 (2013)
8. Volos, S., Seiculescu, C., Grot, B., Pour, N.K., Falsafi, B., De Micheli, G.: CCNoC: specializing on-chip interconnects for energy efficiency in cache-coherent servers. In: Sixth International Symposium on Networks-on-Chip, Copenhagen, pp. 67–74 (2012)

9. Ma, S., Jerger, N.E., Wang, Z.: Whole packet forwarding: efficient design of fully adaptive routing algorithms for networks-on-chip. In: HPCA, New Orleans, pp. 1–12 (2012)
10. Badr, M., Jerger, N.E.: SynFull: synthetic traffic models capturing cache coherent behavior. In: 2014 ACM/IEEE 41st International Symposium on Computer Architecture (ISCA), Minneapolis, MN, pp. 109–120 (2014)
11. Bienia, C., Kumar, S., Singh, J.P., Li, K.: The PARSEC benchmark suite: characterization and architectural implications. In: 17th International Conference on Parallel Architectures and Compilation Techniques, pp. 72–81. ACM, New York (2008)
12. Modarressi, M., Tavakkol, A., Sarbazi-Azad, H.: Application-aware topology reconfiguration for on-chip networks. IEEE Trans. Very Large Scale Integr. Circ. **19**(11), 2010–2022 (2011)
13. Bakhoda, A., Yuan, G.L., Fung, W.W.L., Wong, H., Aamodt T.M.: Analyzing CUDA workloads using a detailed GPU simulator. In: ISPASS, Boston, MA, pp. 163–174 (2009)
14. Hestness, J., Grot, B., Keckler, S.W.: Netrace: dependency-driven trace-based network-on-chip simulation. In: The Third International Workshop on Network on Chip Architectures (NoCArc 2010), pp. 31–36. ACM, New York (2010)
15. Yoon, Y.J., Concer, N., Petracca, M., Carloni, L.P.: Virtual channels and multiple physical networks: two alternatives to improve NoC performance. IEEE Trans. Comput. Aided Des. Integr. Circ. Syst. **32**(12), 1906–1919 (2013)
16. Mazloumi, A., Modarressi, M.: A hybrid packet/circuit-switched router to accelerate memory access in NoC-based chip multiprocessors. In: Design, Automation and Test in Europe Conference (DATE 2015), pp. 908–911 (2015)
17. Lotfi-Kamran, P., Modarressi, M., Sarbazi-Azad, H.: Near ideal network-on-chip for servers. In: 23rd IEEE Symposium on High Performance Computer Architecture (HPCA 2017), TX, USA (2017)
18. Cortex-A15 Technical Reference Manual. https://www.arm.com
19. HyperTransport Technology. https://www.amd.com
20. BookSim 2.0. https://nocs.stanford.edu/cgi-bin/trac.cgi/wiki/Re
21. Sun, C., Chen, C.H.O., Kurian, G., Wei, L., Miller, J., Agarwal, A., Peh, L.S., Stojanovic, V.: DSENT - a tool connecting emerging photonics with electronics for opto-electronic networks-on-chip modeling. In: NOCS, Copenhagen, pp. 201–210 (2012)

PLSS: A Scheduler for Multi-core Embedded Systems

Solomon Abera$^{(\boxtimes)}$, M. Balakrishnan, and Anshul Kumar

Indian Institute of Technology Delhi, New Delhi, India
{solomon,mbala,anshul}@cse.iitd.ac.in

Abstract. In recent years, features and applications of embedded systems have been increasing rapidly. Chip Multi-Processors (CMPs), have been used in these systems to meet the higher demand for performance and energy efficiency. In CMPs, the last level cache (LLC) and the memory bandwidth are usually shared by the cores. Despite the fact that CMPs improve performance of embedded systems, competition for the shared resources makes their performance unpredictable and suboptimal. In this paper, we propose **PLSS**: **P**hase-guided **L**ocality **S**ignature based **S**cheduler for arbitrating LLC requests in multi-core embedded processors. To achieve our goal, we perform phase-wise offline profiling to guide the runtime task scheduling scheme. Our approach can improve performance of dual core system by upto 11% over **IPC** based scheduler (5% on average) and 35% over LLC **number-of-accesses** based approach (6.5% on average).

Keywords: CMP · LLC · Scheduling

1 Introduction

Modern embedded systems run computationally intensive embedded tasks. These tasks require massive computational power. Unlike general processing domain, the demand for high performance comes with power and timing constraints. Therefore, all efforts towards meeting the performance demand should also take these additional issues into account.

Multi-core processors are increasingly being employed in these systems as they offer a good energy-performance trade-off. Examples of embedded multi-core processors include the dual-core Freescale MPC8640D [13], the dual-core Broadcom BCM1255 [14] and the quad-core ARM11 MPcore [15]. High performance multi-core processors allow embedded systems to offer more features and better quality of service. In addition to this, multi-cores can maximize resource utilization by integrating tasks with different requirements on the same system.

On the other hand, it is clear that different cores in a multi-core system are not fully independent in their performance (and other metrics) in relation to a specific task. This is because they share important resources with other cores. In multi-cores, LLC (last level cache) and main memory bandwidth are

© Springer International Publishing AG 2017
J. Knoop et al. (Eds.): ARCS 2017, LNCS 10172, pp. 164–176, 2017.
DOI: 10.1007/978-3-319-54999-6_13

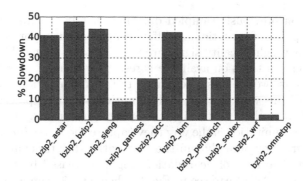

Fig. 1. Performance degradation encountered by bzip2-SPEC2006 benchmark (first 1B instructions) co-running with other tasks on dual-core system sharing 256 KB L2 cache

shared by individual cores. Sharing the LLC enables cooperating tasks to easily share data and instructions. In addition to this, sharing reduces the cost of synchronization and coherency. However, competition for shared cache space creates runtime interferences between tasks running on different cores leading to suboptimal performance. Since the inter-task resource conflicts depend on the behavior of the tasks, it is difficult to predict the potential conflict, making their performance unpredictable. The level of degradation encountered by a task depends on the memory behavior of the co-runners, which is determined by the schedules generated by the scheduler. As we can see in Fig. 1, tasks running on dual-core system, sharing L2 cache can slow down by upto 50%, completely degrading the performance improvement achieved by employing multiple cores. Since embedded systems are designed with size and power constraints, large shared caches are not used in these systems. This makes the impact of contention severe. In addition to this, due to the uncertain nature of inter-task conflicts, it will be difficult to guarantee the worst case execution times for real-time tasks.

In this paper, we propose a cache aware scheduling mechanism for multi-core embedded processors. In embedded domain, tasks which run on a particular system are known apriori. In addition to that, tasks can show wildly different behavior on the course of execution: showing memory bound behavior in one part of the code while being completely compute bound on the other. We perform an offline analysis of the tasks, and generate phase-wise cache access locality signatures for each task. The online task scheduling is guided by these locality signatures.

Most of the previously proposed techniques dealing with contention aware scheduling targeted the general purpose computing domain [2–4]. These techniques are based on online periodic sampling, in which monitoring is done periodically and decisions are based on the sampled data. These approaches have some limitations: the main problem is that the sampled behavior of a task may not reflect its inherent behavior. Rather, it may be a result of the effect of other co-executing tasks. The other problem is the fact that predicting the future behavior based on previously sampled data may not be accurate if the task is having variable phase of execution. A different approach is reported by [6]. They generated a light weight locality signature for each task. Using this, they try to guide the mapping of tasks on available cores. They defined *sensitiveness* and *competitiveness* as two metrics to quantify the task's behavior during sharing. The limitation of this work is that, it does not consider any phase information during profiling. It is clear that a single average signature may not be accurate enough. The other limitation is the way they capture the *sensitivness* parameter of the task, where they actually run the task with other tasks and then record the degradation. The level of degradation might be biased by the behavior of the co-running task. As we can see in Fig. 1, when `bzip2` run with `gamess`, the level of degradation is negligible as compared to its run with `lbm`. In addition to that, repetitive runs with random co-running tasks is time consuming. In order to tackle the problems, we propose phase-guided locality profiling to produce light weight signatures for each phase of a task. We are motivated by the fact that embedded tasks are known in advance and analyzing the memory behavior will be helpful to alleviate the problems faced in previous works. Our system analyzes memory access behavior of the tasks and computes phase-wise locality signatures, rather than average signature, to enhance the accuracy of the runtime performance prediction. In addition to that, we need only a solo-run (without any co-runners) to collect these signatures.

The rest of the paper is organized as follows: Sect. 2 describes previous work in the domain of multi-core task scheduling. Section 3 introduces the PLSS scheduling mechanism, and Sect. 4 discusses the experiment framework and results. Finally, Sect. 5 concludes the paper.

2   Related Work

Less attention has been given to improve the performance of multi-core embedded systems through scheduling compared to the general purpose systems. However, there have been many efforts by the research community that address the shared cache contention issue in general purpose multi-core processors through intelligent scheduling. In cache aware scheduling, the most challenging part of the process is finding a parameter to predict the performance outcome of all potential schedules beforehand. Most of the previous work, one way or another, used Stack Distance Profiles (SDP) and Miss Rate Curves (MRC) to model the possible conflict of cache sharing. Chandra et al. [1] used SDP of each task to accurately predict the additional misses encountered by the sharing tasks. Even though it can predict the extra misses, it is difficult to employ this technique for runtime scheduling process because of two reasons. The first is that, it is very challenging to generate SDP online as it is computationally expensive. The second problem is that their model predicts the extra misses for two sharing tasks. But as the number of tasks increases, the number of possible combinations will be huge. Clearly, such an approach has scalability issues and is not ideal for a runtime use. Other recently proposed schedulers [2–4] approximate the quantification of contention through simple performance metrics such as the LLC miss rate and access frequency. Zhuravlev et al. [2] introduced a task classification scheme based on the *"pain"* parameter of two co-scheduled tasks in order to schedule tasks in a way that minimizes contention. Their *"pain"* parameter is derived from two metrics: the *sensitivity* and *intensity*. They used SDP to characterize the *sensitivity* of a task to sharing and used number of cache requests to characterize the *intensity* of the task. Feliu et al. [3] proposed a scheduling mechanism that aims to distribute shared cache misses in a way that minimizes memory bandwidth requirement of the system. Banikazemi et al. [12] approximate the would-be occupancy ratio of each task from their cache access rate. Based on the predicted occupancy, they predict the miss rate of each.

In the embedded domain, most of the research works target the meeting of worst-case execution times (WCETs), rather than improving the overall performance of the system. Calandrino et al. [5] used cache working set size based scheduling to improve the cache performance and meet the real-time constraints.

3   Overview

In this section, we give an overview of the underlying system model as well as the proposed PLSS task scheduling technique. Figure 2 shows the complete working mechanism of the PLSS technique.

PLSS consists of the following modules: (A) Phase Detection (PD) module (B) Locality Signature Generation (LSG) module and (C) Task Scheduler (TS) module. The PD and LSG modules are offline modules and are used for generating profile signatures while the TS module is an online module and is used for runtime scheduling.

In the offline profiling, the PD module detects the phase transition points and when a phase change is detected, it informs to the LSG module. The LSG module accumulates the values of various parameters (cycles, No. of L2 misses, Modified stack distance, ...) required for generating the locality signatures. When the LSG module gets the phase change signal, it averages the accumulated values and stores the averaged value of each parameter corresponding to the detected phase in a lookup table. The stored average values are used to generate phasewise locality signatures that guide the runtime task scheduling process.

In CMPs, the task scheduling process has two stages. The first stage is selecting (co-scheduling) a group of tasks to run at a particular time slice (time sharing), whereas the second stage is the mapping of tasks to a particular core (setting the affinity). If there is no partially shared cache in the system, and if the cores are symmetrical sharing a single LLC (Fig. 2), the task-to-core mapping phase brings no performance variation. Our proposal only focuses on task-selection phase of the scheduling process. The aim of our scheduling algorithm is to select a set of runnable tasks that have minimum impact on each other. This goal is achieved by evenly distributing the cache aggressive tasks across different time slices (refer Algorithm 1).

In this work, we consider the underlying CMP architecture to be a multi-core architecture consisting of multiple symmetric cores, where all the cores share

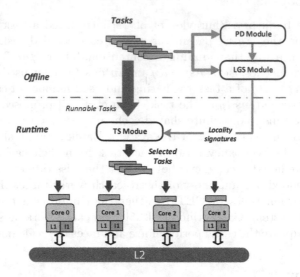

Fig. 2. Overview of PLSS

the LLC. We also consider the tasks to be single threaded, with no data sharing among them.

We prefer phase-wise profiling over average profiling to improve the accuracy of the generated signature. It is often thought that phase-wise analysis adds significant overhead. However, in SPEC2006 benchmark suite which we consider in this work, all the benchmarks have a small number of phases. On an average, the number of detected phases to cover 90% and 80% of the SPEC2006 execution is 8.5 and 5.9 respectively [7]. In addition to this, we only consider long lived phases(in our experiment we considered phases which lasts for a minimum of 50 million instructions, otherwise we average out the statistics for that part of the program).

3.1 Phase Detection Mechanism

As programs run, they exhibit phases of execution where their performance vary significantly from one phase to the other [8]. Within a phase, the program shows stable performance characteristics. The resource requirements of a program vary from one phase to another leading to under- or over-utilization of the system resources. As a result, tracking and detecting program phases is essential to exploit the opportunities for performance optimization and resource management. A lot of prior work have explored different phase detection and classification techniques. Sherwood et al. [8] tried to identify the periodic behavior and representative simulation points in applications using basic block analysis. In an extension to this previous work, Sherwood et al. [9] randomly chose basic blocks to characterize program phases from a pool of static basic blocks existing in a program. Dhodapkar et al. [10] used instruction working set analysis to detect phase changes. In our work, we utilize this instruction working set based phase detection technique to keep track of the task's time varying behavior.

A working set $W(t_i, \tau)$ for $i = 1, 2, 3...$, is a set of distinct segments (of instruction addresses) $s_1, s_2, .., s_\omega$ touched over the ith window of size τ [10]. A working set representing a range of instruction addresses is captured in each interval. A change in the working is observed when a program executes different sections of the code. Once the relative working set distance δ between two consecutive working sets $W(t_i, \tau)$ and $W(t_{i+1}, \tau)$ (see Eq. 1) exceeds a threshold, a phase change is detected.

$$\delta = \frac{|W(t_i, \tau) \cup W(t_{i+1}, \tau)| - |W(t_i, \tau) \cap W(t_{i+1}, \tau)|}{|W(t_i, \tau) \cup W(t_{i+1}, \tau)|}, \tag{1}$$

3.2 Locality Signature Generation Mechanism

The LSG module generates two signatures to guide the online scheduling. These signatures assist the scheduler in predicting the potential performance outcome of the tasks. In this work, we use **Aggressiveness Score** (A_Score) and **Sensitivity Score** (S_Score) metrics as the locality signatures. The A_Score metric models how much a task affects the co-runner task by evicting its cache blocks. The S_Score of a task characterizes the expected degradation it faces when it shares LLC with other tasks.

A_Score. In order to characterize how aggressively a task competes for a cache space, we use the A_Score metric. In prior work, the researchers have tried to measure the competitiveness of a task for the shared cache space with several performance metrics such as miss-rate, number of accesses [2], IPC (memory bound tasks have lower IPC than compute bound tasks and their competitiveness also varies accordingly) [4]. In this work, we are using **miss-frequency** as A_Score. We show that the contention prediction accuracy of this metric is much higher than the others: **IPC** and **L2 number-of-access** (**L2A**) based strategies (Sect. 4.3).

$$\texttt{miss-frequency} = \frac{number\_of\_misses\ (current\ phase)}{number\_of\_cycles} \tag{2}$$

S_Score. In a set-associative cache with LRU replacement policy, the temporal reuse behavior of a task can be captured by its stack distance profile [11]. The stack distance represents the number of distinct addresses referred between two references to the same address. We can capture this reuse behavior of n-way set associative cache using $n + 1$ counters [1] (where n is the associativity of the cache): $C_0, C_1, ..., C_{n-1}$ for the cache hits and counter C_n for the cache misses. The stack distance is the depth of a cache block in the LRU stack from which it is found and accessed. If the access is to the ith position of the LRU stack, C_i will be incremented.

Tasks, with most of their solo-run cache hits occur around the most recently used (MRU) position, do not suffer much during sharing, while tasks with most of their cache hits concentrated around the least recently used (LRU) position suffer more from sharing. Obviously, a stack distance profile captures many aspects of temporal reuse behavior of a task. What is missing in the SDP is a metric that conveys information about the time interval taken to complete a single cache hit by a task. Two instances of cache hits with same stack distance (say 4), may have different time periods (time taken between the previous and current accesses of that block) say 100 cycles and 600 cycles. Hence, the likelihood of a cache hit turning into a miss during a co-run also differs significantly. This phenomena is not captured by the original SDP. Stack distance entries with large duration (*time_period*) have higher chance of turning into a miss during a co-run, than the ones with short period.

In order to solve this problem, we propose a **stack distance profile with time** (SDT). We record not only the stack distance of each cache hit but also the time period between the previous and the current accesses. Let us assume it took 100 cycles between the previous and current access to the cache block which happened at stack distance of 4. Therefore, the stack distance entry is described with its time period as $(stack\_distance(SD), time\_period(TP)) : SDT(4, 100)$. In our work, we try to include this information into the S_Score metric. We accomplish the computation of S_Score using the following steps:

- **Step 1:** First we collect the SDT entries to generate the distribution of $SDT(SD, TP)$. After obtaining the SDT entries, we cluster them into different groups based on the SD values which runs 0 to $n-1$ (associativity): $SDT(0, *), SDT(1, *), ..., SDT(n-1, *)$. Each group will have a range of TP values.
- **Step 2:** Now we sort each group's TP values. Once we sorted it, we represent each group along with its median of TP values as: $SDT(0, \overline{TP}_0)$, $SDT(1, \overline{TP}_1), ..., SDT(n-1, \overline{TP}_{n-1})$.
- **Step 3:** We calculate the S_Score of the task as:

$$Total\_hits = \sum_{i=0}^{i=n-1} |SDT(i, \overline{TP}_i)|, \tag{3}$$

where $|SDT(i, \overline{TP}_i)|$ represents the number of elements (SDT entries) in cluster i, for i in $0, 1, ..., n-1$

$$S\_Score = \sum_{i=0}^{i=n-1} \frac{|SDT(i, \overline{TP}_i)|}{Total\_hits} \times \overline{TP}_i \tag{4}$$

When a cache hit occurs at the MRU position, $SDT(0, *)$ increases by one. The time period, TP, for such kind of hits will be small. When a cache hit occurs at the LRU position $SDT(n-1, *)$ increments by one. The time period, TP, of such hits will be larger. Therefore, if one task has most of its cache hits at the MRU position, and with a small TP, its S_Score will be small and vice versa. The implication is that a task with a lower S_Score will be affected less during sharing than the one with a higher S_Score.

3.3   PLSS: Algorithm

Table 1 lists the notations used in defining the PLSS algorithm, given in Algorithm 1.

Table 1. List of symbols and notations used to describe the PLSS algorithm

m	: number of tasks
$\mathbb{T}$	: set of m runnable tasks $\{T_1, T_2, ..., T_{m-1}\}$
n	: number of cores
A_Score_i	: a vector containing the A_Scores of each phase of T_i
S_Score_i	: a vector containing the S_Scores of each phase of T_i
$A\_Score\_Cur_i$	: the A_Score value of T_i in its current phase of execution
$S\_Score\_Cur_i$	: the S_Score value of T_i in its current phase of execution
[ ]	: operator used to index a sorted list

The main goal of our **PLSS** algorithm is to select co-runner tasks with complementing contention behavior. This is achieved by ensuring that the aggressive tasks are not scheduled together. To implement this, we divide the tasks into high- and low-aggressive task groups and schedule the most aggressive task from high-aggressive group with the least sensitive task from the low-aggressive group and vice-versa. In each iteration of the algorithm, every task gets exactly one quantum of execution time, after which A_Score_Cur and S_Score_Cur for each task are updated.

Algorithm 1. PLSS

Input : m; $\mathbb{T}$; A_Score_i, S_Score_i for $i \in (0, m-1)$; n
Output: schedule of $\mathbb{T}$ on the n cores

1 **repeat**
2 | Update $A\_Score\_Cur_i$, $S\_Score\_Cur_i$ for $i \in (0, m-1)$;
3 | Generate $\mathbb{ST}$ by sorting $\mathbb{T}$ in descending order of $A\_Score\_Cur_i$;
4 | Generate task groups G_0, G_1,..,G_{n-1}, where G_i contains $\mathbb{ST}[(m/n) \times i]$ to $\mathbb{ST}[(m/n) \times (i+1) - 1]$;
5 | Sort the tasks in the last $n/2$ groups (that is, $G_{n/2}, G_{n/2+1}, ..., G_{n-1}$) in ascending order of their $S\_Score\_Cur_i$;
6 | **for** $cur\_quantum \in (0, m/n - 1)$ **do**
7 | | **for** $i \in (0, n-1)$ **do**
8 | | | Assign $G_i[cur\_quantum]$ to the ith core
9 | | **end**
10 | **end**
11 **until** *all tasks finish*;

---

4   Evaluation

In this section, we first briefly describe the experimental setup, and report the results of various experiments (`Phase Detection`, `Contention Metric accuracy` and `Scheduling` experiments).

4.1   Evaluation Setup

We use sniper 6.0 multi-core simulator [16] to validate the proposed methodology. Table 2 shows the processor configuration used for all of our experiments. We modify the simulator to support the offline phase detection and locality signature generation. We also implement a scheduler that checks the S_Score and A_Score values of each task during task selection phase. The scheduler selects tasks based on the contention metrics as shown in Algorithm 1. We use different benchmarks from the SPEC2006 suite in our evaluation. In the scheduling experiments, we compare `PLSS` with `IPC` [4], and `L2A` [2,3] contention metrics based approaches. In order to show the significance of the sensitivity metric, we also evaluate the `PLSS-A` (PLSS with only the A_Score metric and not the S_Score metric). For the `IPC` and `L2A` based scheduling, we schedule high-IPC (high-L2A) tasks with low-IPC (low-L2A) tasks. We achieve this in a manner similar to PLSS. We sort the tasks based on their IPC (L2A), and divide the sorted list into n groups, where n is the number of cores. The scheduler then selects one element from each group iteratively.

Table 2. System configuration

Parameter	Value	Caches				
		Parameter	L1-D	L1-I	L2 (dual-core)	L2 (quad-core)
Cores	2, 4	Size	8 KB	8 KB	256 KB	512 KB
		Block size	64	64	64	64
Frequency	1 GHz	Write policy	WB	WB	WB	WB
		Associativity	4	4	8	8
		Latency (cycles)	3	3	24	24

4.2   Phase Detection Validation

We collect the instruction working set for every epoch of one million instructions, and compare each working set with that of the previous epoch as discussed in Sect. 3.1. In the experiments, we set the threshold δ_{th} to be 0.75. Since we are interested only in long range phases, we average out phases which are less than 50 million instructions. We validate the technique by simulating one Billion instructions of SPEC2006 benchmarks, and correlate the temporal variations in various fundamental metrics of a processor's behavior against the computed phase change points. An example correlation for the `lbm` benchmark is shown in Fig. 3.

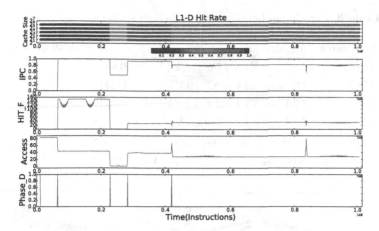

Fig. 3. 1bm, one Billion instruction simulation; top-to-bottom: Cache hit-rate for various cache sizes (1 K to 128 K), IPC, L1-D hit frequency, Number of L1 accesses (10 K) and instruction distance (phase detector)

4.3 Contention Metric Accuracy

This experiment serves to validate the choice of `miss-frequency` as the A_Score metric. Each dual-core experiment takes 13 SPEC benchmarks while the quad-core experiment takes 10 SPEC benchmarks. In the dual-core experiment, all $13C_2 = 78$ pairs are co-run on the aforementioned dual-core processor. For the quad core, all $10C_4 = 210$ combinations are co-run. We run each task for one Billion slice of instructions, if one of the co-runner finishes before the other, we restart and run the fast co-runner till the slow finishes. We study the correlation between the observed slowdown of the benchmarks against different aggressiveness metrics. Let us assume we have two co-running tasks X and Y, and IPC_{solo} and IPC_{co} represent solo-run and co-run instructions per cycle of the tasks respectively. We computed the slowdown as specified in Eq. 5.

$$slowdown = \frac{(IPC_{solo}(X) + IPC_{solo}(Y)) - (IPC_{co}(X) + IPC_{co}(Y))}{IPC_{solo}(X) + IPC_{solo}(Y)} \times 100,$$

(5)

We then studied what parameters of the tasks X and Y present a high correlation with the observed slowdown. We consider three options: the solo-run `IPC`, L2A and `miss-frequency` (misses per 1 K cycles). We also studied two methods of aggregating the parameters of the tasks X and Y: sum and product. Table 3 presents the correlation between the six different candidates for the A_score metric and the actual slowdown.

Both the `IPC` based contention metrics show negative correlation with the slowdown, as high aggregate IPC implies lower contention, resulting in lower slowdown. Aggregated IPC based on summation (IPC_1) shows better correlation (-0.6381) than product based aggregation (IPC_2). The L2A based parameters are the least correlated with correlation indexes of 0.3412 and 0.2788. The

Table 3. Correlation between aggressiveness strategies and slowdown

Parameter	Aggregation	Correl. with slowdown
IPC_1	$IPC_{solo}(X) + IPC_{solo}(Y)$	−0.6381
IPC_2	$IPC_{solo}(X) * IPC_{solo}(Y)$	−0.4315
$L2A_1$	$L2A_{solo}(X) + L2A_{solo}(Y)$	0.3412
$L2A_2$	$L2A_{solo}(X) * L2A_{solo}(X)$	0.2788
$miss\_freq_1$	$miss\_f_{solo}(X) + miss\_f_{solo}(Y)$	0.8518
$miss\_freq_2$	$miss\_f_{solo}(X) * miss\_f_{solo}(Y)$	0.9551

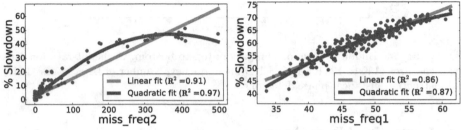

(a) 78 combinations of two SPEC2006 benchmarks on dual-core

(b) 210 combinations of four SPEC2006 benchmarks on quad-core

Fig. 4. Correlation between miss-frequency based A_Scores and Slowdown

best correlation was observed with the `miss-frequency` based metrics, showing correlation indices of 0.8518 and 0.9551. Therefore, in PLSS we use $miss\_freq_2$ as aggressiveness metric as it shows good slowdown prediction.

We also show the correlation between the `miss-frequency` based contention metric and slowdown with scatter plot. Along with the scatter plots, we also include the linear and quadratic regression fit graphs. In the dual-core experiment, we observe high coefficients of determination (R^2) for both linear and quadratic regression: 0.91 and 0.96 respectively (as shown in Fig. 4). In the quad-core experiment, the coefficients of determination are 0.86 and 0.87 for the linear and quadratic regressions respectively.

Our choice of contention metrics, and the proposed technique to compute them, ensure scalability as each application in the workload needs to be profiled only once, in a solo stand-alone fashion.

4.4   Scheduling Experiments

In the experiments, we run ten benchmarks from SPEC 2006 on a dual-core system. The overall simulation time is 2 Billion ns and the context quantum is set to 1000000 ns. If a benchmark finishes within this time, it will be replaced by the next task from same group. We schedule the given bag-of-tasks using the four different schedulers and record the results.

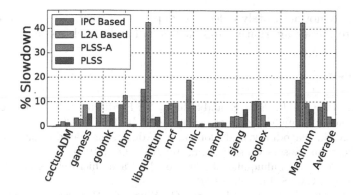

Fig. 5. Slowdown encountered by 10 SPEC2006 benchmarks running on dual-core

As we can see from Fig. 5, PLSS performs the best with an average slowdown of **2.99%**. The maximum slowdown experienced by any task is only **7.02%**. Whereas L2A based approach performs the worst with **42%** maximum and **9.6%** average slowdowns. The IPC based scheduler performs better than the L2A approach with maximum and average slowdowns **18.9%** and **7.94%** respectively. We also observe the PLSS-A performs well with **9.44%** maximum and **3.91%** indicating the scheduling priority should be dispersing aggressive tasks across time slices using A_Score. The S_Score metric further helps to reduce the slowdown, after the aggressive tasks have been distributed.

5   Conclusion and Future Work

Multi-cores are being increasingly used in embedded domain to achieve higher performance with energy efficiency. However, due to shared resources, tasks affect each other and degrade performance. Our proposal PLSS greatly reduces such degradation through intelligent scheduling. The scheduling is based on knowledge gained regarding the tasks through offline analysis. This knowledge is in terms of a novel combination of two metrics: aggressiveness and sensitivity. Unlike previous work, we perform phase-wise profiling and need only a single solo-run to collect these signatures. Through extensive experimentation, we demonstrate that PLSS improves overall system performance and outperforms IPC and L2A based techniques.

Multi-core embedded systems can co-host various embedded tasks with different time constraints. For real-time tasks, the optimization goal is to meet the deadline while for the others the goal is to improve performance. PLSS improves the worst-case performance of tasks, while improving overall system performance. However, it does not guarantee WCETs of real time tasks. In future work, we would like to extend PLSS with dynamic cache partitioning in order to provide isolation for time-constrained tasks while improving the quality of service for others. Additionally, our approach relies on the application's inputs being well known at profile time. If this is not the case, the contention metrics computed may not accurately reflect the application's behavior at run time. We would like to pursue alternative approaches to handle such scenarios.

References

1. Chandra, D., Guo, F., Kim, S. and Solihin, Y.: Predicting inter-thread cache contention on a chip multi-processor architecture. In: HPCA (2005)
2. Zhuravlev, S., Blagodurov, S., Fedorova, A.: Addressing shared resource contention in multicore processors via scheduling. In: ASPLOS (2010)
3. Feliu, J. Petit, S., Sahuquillo, J., Duato, J.: Cache-hierarchy contention aware scheduling in CMPS. In: TPDS (2013)
4. Zhang, X., Dwarkadas, S., Folkmanis, G., Shen, K.: Processor hardware counter statistics as a first-class system resource. In: HotOS (2007)
5. Calandrino, J.M., Anderson, J.H.: Cache-aware real-time scheduling on multicore platforms: heuristics and a case study. In: ECRTS (2008)
6. Jiang, Y., Tian, K., Shen, X.: Combining locality analysis with online proactive job co-scheduling in chip multiprocessors. In: Patt, Y.N., Foglia, P., Duesterwald, E., Faraboschi, P., Martorell, X. (eds.) HiPEAC 2010. LNCS, vol. 5952, pp. 201–215. Springer, Heidelberg (2010). doi:10.1007/978-3-642-11515-8_16
7. Sembrant, A., Black-Schaffer, D., Hagersten, E.: Phase behavior in serial and parallel applications. In: IISWC (2012)
8. Sherwood, T., Perlman, E., Calder, B.: Basic block distribution analysis to find periodic behavior and simulation points in applications. In: PACT (2001)
9. Sherwood, T., Sair, S., Calder, B.: Phase tracking and prediction. In: ISCA (2003)
10. Dhodapkar, A.S., Smith, J.E.: Managing multi-configuration hardware via dynamic working set analysis. In: ISCA (2002)
11. Mattson, R.L., Gecsei, J., Slutz, D., Traiger. I.: Evaluation techniques for storage hierarchies (1970)
12. Banikazemi, M., Poff, D., Abali, B.: PAM: a novel performance/power aware metascheduler for multi-core systems. In: SC (2008)
13. Freescale MPC8640D. http://www.nxp.com/files/32bit/doc/data_sheet/MPC8640DEC.pdf
14. Broadcom. http://www.broadcom.com/products/Enterprise-Networking/Communications-Processors/BCM1255
15. ARM11MPCore. https://www.arm.com/products/processors/classic/arm11/arm11-mpcore.php
16. Sniper Multicore Simulator. http://snipersim.org

Exploring ILP and TLP on a Polymorphic VLIW Processor

Anthony Brandon[✉], Joost Hoozemans,
Jeroen van Straten, and Stephan Wong

Computer Engineering Lab, Delft University of Technology, Delft, The Netherlands
{a.a.c.brandon,j.j.hoozemans,j.vanstraten-1,j.s.s.m.wong}@tudelft.nl

Abstract. In today's computing environments, the concurrent execution of multiple applications/threads is common and multi-cores are very well-suited to handle such workloads. However, they suffer from the fact that any mismatch between the application's inherent instruction-level parallelism (ILP) and the core's parallelism leads to unused resources or loss in performance. An accepted solution is to include several types of cores and match them dynamically depending on the performance needs of the application. This approach becomes less efficient when the number of cores does not match the number of parallel threads. Furthermore, the heterogeneity of (fixed) cores cannot be increased indefinitely as it would result in even higher degrees of mismatching and increased movement of instruction and data streams. In this paper, we are proposing a polymorphic processor, based on VLIW architectures, that can adapt its issue-width during runtime. By design, the processor can be perceived as a single wide core (8-issue VLIW) or two medium-wide cores (4-issue) or four small cores (2-issue) that can run high-ILP/low DLP, medium-ILP/medium DLP, and low-ILP/high-DLP applications, respectively. Furthermore, we are executing one single generic binary while performing these reconfigurations. In order to show the effectiveness of our approach, we synthesized different versions of the core to represent fixed heterogeneous cores and compared them to the dynamic implementation of the core. Our experiments show that the dynamically adaptive solution performs on average 7% faster and uses 5% less area than a platform which consists of fixed cores with 1.5× as many datapaths.

1 Introduction

Modern embedded systems (including smartphone SoCs and other low-power, high-performance systems) are faced with dynamic workloads [1]. Workloads can be dynamic in several characteristics, e.g., performance requirements of tasks, instruction-level parallelism (ILP), data-level parallelism (DLP), or task-level parallelism (TLP). The state-of-the-art in technology in the embedded low-power high-performance domain addresses these workloads using heterogeneous multi-core processing systems, e.g., Exynos that adopts the big.LITTLE approach [2]. These allow different types of tasks to be mapped to a processing unit that most closely matches their characteristics and/or requirements. As the

© Springer International Publishing AG 2017
J. Knoop et al. (Eds.): ARCS 2017, LNCS 10172, pp. 177–189, 2017.
DOI: 10.1007/978-3-319-54999-6_14

processing elements of a heterogeneous system are fixed, the performance of the system depends on the extent to which the workload can be mapped to the hardware (called *performance fragility* by [3]). Previous research [3–8] presented polymorphic architectures as a way to address this problem. A *dynamic* hardware platform, that is able to change its characteristics at runtime, can provide high performance for single-threaded applications by exploiting ILP and high throughput for multi-threaded applications by exploiting TLP [9].

Until now, no-one has quantified the potential benefits of a dynamic hardware platform over fixed platforms. We pose the following question: given the same number of transistors, what is the best possible use of them to provide maximum performance under workloads with varying amounts of ILP and TLP exhibited by modern multi-threaded programs?

In this paper, we introduce and evaluate our proof-of-concept for a dynamic approach to run these dynamic workloads in the high-performance embedded domain. We apply polymorphism, that has been applied previously to high-performance general-purpose designs, to a Very Long Instruction Word (VLIW) processor that is more suitable for low-power systems. The result is a dynamic system that can adapt its processor and cache to the running applications. Note that our "dynamic" approach does not rely on (partial) FPGA reconfiguration. Our designs are written in synthesizable VHDL and prototyped on FPGAs, but are also suitable for implementation on ASIC.

We show that our dynamic approach is able to achieve a more efficient utilization of the available hardware resources. We are able to achieve on average 7% better performance using a dynamically reconfigurable processor when compared to a static system that is roughly 10% larger in area and has 1.5× as many datapaths.

2   Related Work

There are several existing attempts at making reconfigurable processors in order to exploit both TLP and ILP. Some, such as Core Fusion [5], Trips [3], and MorphCore [4] combine multiple small cores into large superscalar (possibly Out-of-Order) cores to exploit the parallelism available at runtime. While these approaches have binary compatibility between the different configurations, they require expensive and power-hungry hardware to extract ILP from the (sequential) code at runtime. Moreover, most of these approaches were only simulated, whereas we have a working prototype on an FPGA.

Other attempts such as Voltron [6] and Smart Memories [7] are based on VLIW architectures, where smaller cores are combined to form a wide issue VLIW. MT-ADRES [10] is a Course Grain Reconfigurable Array (CGRA) which is similar to a VLIW, which can also be configured as either a single wide issue core, or multiple smaller cores. This is similar to our approach, however these do not have binary compatibility between the different configurations. This means that it is determined at compile time which parts of the program will operate in which configuration, giving less flexibility at runtime. Our approach does have this flexibility, which allows the core to be interrupted at any point in time, reconfigure to a different issue-width (in only several clock cycles), and resume execution. Our design also achieves this without any need for state saving and/or context switching.

VLIW processors are an alternative to superscalar processors [11] with the goal of reducing power consumption by moving dependency checking to the compiler, thus simplifying the hardware (and in turn consuming much less power). One downside of fixed issue-width VLIW processors is that resources will go unused if the issue-width is greater than the ILP available in the program. On the other hand, if the issue-width is too low, potential performance gains are lost. Making the issue-width runtime reconfigurable addresses this problem.

The processor we target in this paper is a reconfigurable issue-width VLIW processor [12] based on ρ-VEX [13], a parameterized VLIW processor. The processor can be configured at design time to have an issue-width of 2, 4, or 8 and can be reconfigured at runtime to split into smaller processors with issue-widths of 2 or 4. We explore the platform's performance under different workloads with varying amounts of TLP in order to quantify the benefits of reconfigurability.

3   Approach

Our approach to increase the utilization of execution datapaths in a processor allows for **on-the-fly** composition of cores—the reconfiguration time is expressed in clock cycles as demonstrated in our FPGA prototype (see Sect. 4). Cores can be merged to "construct" wider cores for applications needing performance (with enough available parallelism). When this is not required, multiple applications can be executed in parallel. In addition, (low-priority) applications can be "forced" to execute on a smaller core allowing other applications to execute in parallel. Such a scenario is impossible for fixed processors when a second free processor is not available, or would require costly context-switching, effectively stalling the first application. Our approach is also different from reorganizing datapaths from RISC cores into multiple cores as such approaches would still require (several) power-hungry instruction decoders. Starting from a VLIW architecture, the need for such decoders can be omitted and the reconfiguration can be achieved by simply reassigning the datapaths and register file ports.

The versatility of our core design is achieved by separating the program contexts and the execution datapaths (pipelanes) and controlling their connections via a reconfiguration controller (as depicted in Fig. 1):

- Pipelanes & lane-groups: functional units, instruction fetch and decode, etc.
- Contexts: the register file, and all state related registers, such as program counter, control registers, etc.

The VLIW core comprises multiple execution pipelines, also called pipelanes. For instance, an 8-issue ρ-VEX has 8 pipelanes. Subsequently, we divide these pipelanes into lane-groups. For instance pipelanes 0 and 1 form lane-group 0, and pipelanes 2 and 3 form lane-group 1, and so on. When two lane-groups are joined, the processor functions as a 4-issue VLIW. When they are separate, they function as two independent 2-issue VLIWs.

The contexts contain the state of programs and since we can execute 4 programs in parallel at least 4 contexts are needed. Each lane-group can access each context and which context it accesses depends on the current configuration of the core. In this way, we can reconfigure the core by assigning contexts to lane-groups. The contexts are connected to lane-groups through a switch network which allows each lane to access each context. The register file is described in more detail in [14]. When combining lane-groups, wider-issue VLIW cores can be composed and they benefit from the same flexibility in choosing which context to execute. The added benefit of this approach is that multiple contexts are maintained and context switching among them can be achieved in just a few cycles—basically, flushing the associated pipelanes. In addition, "moving" a context to be executed on a differently-sized core (similar to moving a program from a low-performance core to a high-performance core or vice versa) requires only a reconfiguration of our core. Moreover, the I-caches in our design follow the reconfiguration of the core; therefore, their content is also maintained, thereby removing the need for code movement or a cold start of the I-cache when physically moving a program to another core.

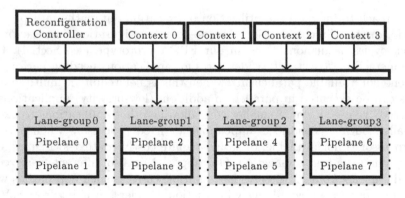

Fig. 1. Interconnect between register contexts and processor pipelines controlled by Reconfiguration Controller.

Because we are dynamically reconfiguring the core, we have to deal in more detail with control flow and interrupts. Each lane-group has its own branch unit and after merging all but one of them is disabled in order to simplify the instruction fetch hardware. When handling interrupts (including exceptions and traps), they must be handled differently depending on the configuration as they are tied to contexts. We designed the core to correctly stall the right context, invalidate any remaining load/store operations in case of a bus-fault, and flush the associated pipelanes before jumping to the trap handler.

Another important aspect of our approach is to maintain binary compatibility of the VLIW instructions when executing them on different issue-width cores. For this purpose, we use generic binaries [15] (reporting a performance hit between 10% and 30%) and employed techniques described in [16] to reduce the performance hit to on average around 5%.

4   Implementation

In Sect. 3, we described the requirements of the reconfigurable processor. In this section we explain how we implemented the reconfigurability in hardware. The design is implemented in VHDL and is completely parameterized using generics, so that it is possible to statically change the number and size of lane-groups that will be available at runtime. For example, instead of having an 8-issue ρ-VEX that can split into four 2-issue, or two 4-issue cores, we could have a 4-issue core that can split into two 2-issue cores. The number of contexts is also parameterized, making it possible to have more contexts than the maximum number of cores.

In Fig. 2, we depict the pipeline stages of a single datapath of the processor. The processor consists of a (design time) configurable number of these datapaths, which are connected through the forwarding logic and the register files as depicted in Fig. 1. Each datapath can be configured to have an ALU, branch unit, load/store unit, and multiplier.

As described in the previous section, the ρ-VEX can be reconfigured at runtime by assigning lane-groups to contexts. This is done by writing to the configuration control register. The control registers are part of a memory mapped address space, so this can be accomplished through a standard store instruction to the right address. Once a new value has been written to the context control register, the reconfiguration controller will check that the requested configuration is valid. For instance, in an 8-issue reconfigurable ρ-VEX, it is not possible for the center two lane-groups to be merged into a single core. Similarly, it is impossible to assign multiple non-adjacent lane-groups to the same context.

Once the requested configuration has been determined to be valid by the reconfiguration controller, the ρ-VEX will stop fetching new instructions and

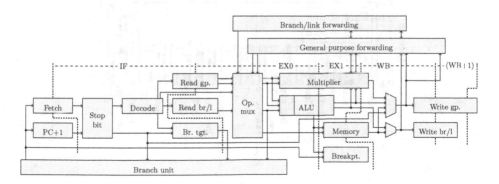

Fig. 2. Schematic of a single datapath of the processor.

will finish executing any in-flight instructions. Once the pipelanes are empty, the actual configuration takes place and each context continues execution where it was last stopped. Note that because all instructions in the pipeline must finish execution before reconfiguration completes, reconfiguration can take a variable number of cycles depending on the exact instructions being executed. The minimum number of cycles for a reconfiguration to take place is five cycles, while the maximum is the same as for a load instruction that causes a cache miss.

5   Experimental Results

In order to demonstrate the benefits of our approach we wanted to show its performance when executing multiple tasks with different performance characteristics on different configurations of the core. By reconfiguring the core at runtime we can adapt to the current workload and in doing so utilize our hardware resources more efficiently.

5.1   Workload Definition

For our experiments we use workloads consisting of Mibench applications [17]. First, we characterized the individual applications in terms of available ILP and execution time. Figure 3 shows the speedup between executions on 2-issue and 4-issue, and between executions on 4-issue and 8-issue. From this figure we can observe that most applications have relatively little ILP, while a handful have high ILP. The reason that FFT can achieve a greater speedup than 2, is because the cache of the 4-issue processor is larger. We also notice that none of the benchmarks have a very large speedup when switching to 8-issue. For this reason, we decided to focus on 4-issue and 2-issue configurations of the ρ-VEX in the remainder of this paper. We do this because implementing a large 8-issue VLIW incurs a large overhead in terms of area, which cannot be justified for these applications.

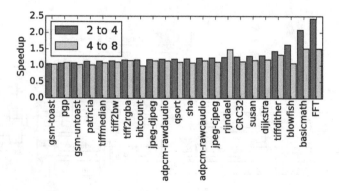

Fig. 3. The speedup for each benchmark from two to four issue, and from four to eight issue.

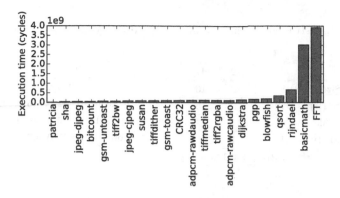

Fig. 4. Execution time for each benchmark.

In Fig. 4, we depict the execution time of each benchmark in cycles. From this figure we can observe that two of the benchmarks are especially long compared to the others. Since we are interested in the performance of multiple threads running on the cores simultaneously, this is undesirable. If we select one of these extremely long benchmarks to run together with shorter benchmarks, the results will be dominated by the performance of a single application running most of the time. In order to mitigate this effect we normalized the execution times for each benchmark to the execution time. This means that we are only comparing the relative improvement from 2-, to 4-, to 8-issue.

In modern embedded devices it is usually not possible to know at design time the exact characteristics of the workload it will be running. For example, a smartphone might be running a single or multiple applications depending on what the user is doing. In order to understand how platforms consisting of various numbers of processor cores will perform under these different conditions we must construct workloads of varying numbers of applications to run simultaneously. Therefore, we randomly choose 1 to 22 different applications from the list of all our Mibench applications and run these simultaneously on all of the platforms. We then measure the time required to finish the entire workload. For each workload size (1 – 22) we created 100 random workloads (2200 total).

In addition to using these real world benchmarks, we also estimated the performance of each platform for a set of idealized synthetic benchmarks which allows us to analyze the performance of the platforms under simplified conditions. These benchmarks exhibit ideal ILP which makes it easier to reason about how the system will perform.

5.2 Resource Utilization

We used Synopsis Design Vision to obtain area results for ρ-VEX on a 65 nm library, and CACTI [18] to obtain area estimates for caches for the different cores. Table 1 shows the parameters used to estimate area for the instruction caches. In this table, we have assumed that for a 4-issue core we will use a cache

Table 1. Instruction cache parameters

	4r	2	4
Cache Size (KiB)	8	8	16
Line Size (B)	16	8	16
Nr. of Banks	1	1	1
Associativity	1	1	1
Size (mm^2)	0.215×2	0.146	0.242

Table 2. Area results on 65 nm (mm^2).

	4r	2	4
Core	0.263	0.114	0.175
I-Cache	0.432	0.146	0.242
D-Cache	0.292	0.146	0.270
Total	0.987	0.407	0.688

twice as large as for a 2-issue core. In order to represent the reconfigurability of the cache for the reconfigurable core we estimate the area as twice the size of a cache with a wider line size. Table 2 shows the area of the 2-, 4- and 4-issue reconfigurable cores, along with instruction and data caches. This table shows that the caches make up a significant amount of the area. Using these numbers we determine several multi-core platforms that fit in similar area.

5.3 Experimental Setup

In order to evaluate our approach, we compared our platform consisting of 2 reconfigurable 4-issue processors to other platforms consisting of multiple static processors of equivalent total area. This resulted in the following platforms:

- 44r (1.974mm^2): The dynamic platform consists of two 4-issue reconfigurable cores. This means that this platform can execute two tasks in parallel on the 4-issue cores, or three tasks in parallel with one on a 4-issue, and two on 2-issue cores, or it can execute four tasks in parallel on 2-issue cores.
- 444 (2.065mm^2): This configuration consisting of three static 4-issue cores is the largest in terms of computational resources that fits in roughly the same area as two 4-issue reconfigurable cores.
- 2222 (1.623mm^2): This platform can achieve the same maximum TLP as the dynamic platform, namely four threads at once, which makes for a more interesting comparison.
- 442 (1.784mm^2): We use this configuration to represent a heterogeneous system similar to big.LITTLE with a mix of cores of different issue-widths. This would allow for efficient mapping of tasks to cores when dealing with a mix of tasks with high and low ILP.

In each of these platforms, the 2-issue cores have an instruction and data cache size of 32 KiB while the 4-issue cores have cache sizes of 64 KiB. The reconfigurable cores have 64 KiB caches each when operating in 4-issue mode, or 32 KiB caches for each core when operating in 2-issue mode.

In order to obtain execution times these platforms were all synthesized for the Xilinx Virtex 6 FPGA running at 37.5 MHz. We use GRLIB [19] for peripherals such as UART output, interfaces to DDR memory, and the interrupt controller.

Listing 1.1. Scheduler for static platforms.

```
# inputs:
# readylist: list of all tasks sorted by
#             descending ILP
# cores: list of processor cores sorted by
#         descending issue-width
while len(readylist) > 0:
    while len(running) < len(cores):
        running.append(readylist.pop())
    running.sort()
    for i in len(running):
        cores[i].task = running[i]
    wait()
```

Listing 1.2. Scheduler for reconfigurable platforms.

```
# inputs:
# readylist: list of all tasks sorted by
#             descending ILP
while len(readylist) > 0:
    while len(running) < 4:
        running.append(readylist.pop())
    running.sort()
    if len(running) == 4:
        cores.config = [2,2,2,2]
    elif len(running) == 3:
        cores.config = [4,2,2]
    elif len(running) == 2:
        cores.config = [4,4]
    else:
        cores.config = [4]
    for i in len(running):
        cores[i].task = running[i]
    wait()
```

In order to run the various workloads as defined in Sect. 5.1 we implemented a simple task scheduler, which runs on the processor. It decides which task to run on which core, and in the case of the dynamic core, in which configuration. The scheduler for the fixed platforms, shown in Listing 1.1, uses a greedy approach to run as many tasks in parallel as possible. The input for this scheduler is the list of tasks which have to be executed, and the issue-width of each available core. The list of tasks is ordered by descending ILP to ensure that tasks with high ILP will be scheduled on the cores with the highest issue-width. If a task is running on a 2-issue core and a 4-issue core becomes available, the scheduler will migrate that task to a larger core. After the tasks are assigned to cores the scheduler waits for one of the tasks to complete, at which point it will run again to schedule any remaining tasks. This continues until all the tasks have finished.

The scheduler for the dynamic platform, shown in Listing 1.2, is slightly different because it not only has to distribute the tasks to the cores, but also determine the desired configuration. The scheduler first selects the maximum number of tasks to run, under the assumption that it is, in most cases, more efficient to run multiple tasks than it is to run a single task on a high issue-with. Next, depending on the number of tasks, the scheduler chooses one of the possible configurations. For example, if there are three tasks to run, it will choose the 422 configuration. It then schedules the task with the highest ILP on the largest core than can be formed.

These two schedulers assume that the average ILP of each task is known beforehand in order to make comparisons in performance assuming the best possible schedules. Techniques for scheduling based on measuring ILP at runtime are out of scope, and are discussed in other work [20].

5.4   Performance of Synthetic Workloads

We will now examine the performance of each of the chosen platforms using artificial workloads tailored to each specific platform. The workloads consist of as many tasks as there are cores in the system, with the ideal ILP for that particular mix of cores. Figure 5 shows how these synthetic workloads could be scheduled on each platforms. Each color represents a task and the height of a block represents execution time, while the width represents the issue-width it is executed on. For a platform with four 2-issue cores we use four tasks, each with an ILP of 2. On the platforms with fewer than four cores the fourth task has to be executed after the other tasks, resulting in longer total execution time. For the *444* platform the workload consists of three tasks with an ILP of 4. As shown in Fig. 5, when this workload is executed on the *44r* platform, the three tasks are executed in parallel, and when one is done, the remaining two are switched to run in 4-issue mode. Our goal in using these synthetic benchmarks was to show that while the reconfigurable platform might not be the best in every single case, it is not bad either, and for the average case performs well.

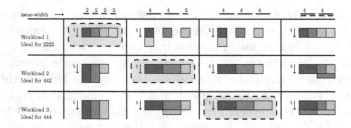

Fig. 5. Three synthetic workloads scheduled onto the four platforms being compared. Each color represents a task, while height represents execution time and width represents the issue-width of the processor executing that task.

The synthetic results in Table 3 show that the average execution time of the *444* platform is the same as for the *44r* platform. The *444* platform performs well for all cases where there are three or less threads, however when there are four or more threads the *44r* platform performs better. The *44r* platform performs worse when there are three high ILP tasks, however, since it can run three tasks in parallel it will only run 50% longer in the worst case. Real world applications do not exhibit this kind of difference between 2- and 4-issue, as depicted in Fig. 3, which means that usually the reconfigurable platform would take less than 50% longer for a workload of three high ILP tasks.

Table 3. Synthetic workload execution times.

	44r	442	444	2222
Workload 1	1	2	2	1
Workload 2	1.5	1	1	2
Workload 3	1.5	1.5	1	2

Table 4. Average execution times and standard deviation of all Mibench workloads.

	44r	442	444	2222
Relative execution time (mean)	1.0	1.11	1.07	1.09
Standard deviation	0.03	0.06	0.06	0.0

5.5   Performance of Mibench Workloads

We also performed experiments with actual applications as explained in Sect. 5.1.
The results, depicted in Fig. 6, show that the reconfigurable platform is always
at least as good as the *2222* platform, as expected. Remember that the *2222*
platform is larger than the reconfigurable platform. When comparing with the
444 platform we can observe that there are some situations where the reconfigurable platform is better, and some cases where it is worse. However, note that
there are fewer cases where the reconfigurable platform is slower, and that the
difference in performance is not as high as in the cases where the *44r* platform is
faster. The *444* platform is also roughly 5% larger than the reconfigurable platform. The average execution times and standard deviation in execution time are
summarized in Table 4. We can observe that the reconfigurable platform is on
average 7% faster than the static *444* platform. Additionally, we notice that the
standard deviation is smaller for the dynamic platform. This means that the difference between workloads that perform well and workloads that perform poorly
are larger on the static platform. We also observe that the *2222* platform has
barely any deviation, however this means it has consistently poor performance.
These results show that although the *444* platform has more total computational
resources, and more available total cache, it cannot always make optimal use of

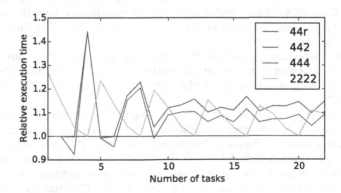

Fig. 6. Results of executing Mibench on different platforms with execution times normalized to 2-issue.

the available hardware, because it cannot make the trade off between thread level parallelism and instruction level parallelism.

6   Conclusion

In this paper, we compared the performance of heterogeneous multi-core platforms to that of a dynamically reconfigurable platform. We did so using ρ-VEX, a reconfigurable VLIW processor with a reconfigurable cache, which is capable of reconfiguring at runtime to exploit either task-level parallelism, or instruction-level parallelism. We demonstrated that, while for a single workload a particular static configuration might be optimal, the reconfigurable platform can adapt to the workload and on average can more efficiently exploit the available hardware. Our results show that the reconfigurable platform is on average 7% faster than a static platform with 1.5× as many datapaths, and 5% larger area. Furthermore, in terms of performance the reconfigurable platform has more stable performance (less deviation) than other platforms for a wide variety of workloads.

References

1. van Berkel, C.H.: Multi-core for mobile phones. In: 2009 Design, Automation Test in Europe Conference Exhibition, pp. 1260–1265, April 2009
2. Greenhalgh, P.: big.LITTLE Processing with ARM Cortex-A15 & Cortex-A7, ARM White paper, pp. 1–8 (2011)
3. Sankaralingam, K., Nagarajan, R., Liu, H., Kim, C., Huh, J., Burger, D., Keckler, S., Moore, C.: Exploiting ILP, TLP, and DLP with the polymorphous trips architecture. IEEE Micro 23, 46–51 (2003)
4. Khubaib, K., Suleman, M.A., Hashemi, M., Wilkerson, C., Patt, Y.N.: Morphcore: an energy-efficient microarchitecture for high performance ILP and high throughput TLP. In: 45th Annual IEEE/ACM International Symposium on Microarchitecture (MICRO), pp. 305–316. IEEE (2012)
5. Ipek, E., Kirman, M., Kirman, N., Martinez, J.F.: Core fusion: accommodating software diversity in chip multiprocessors. In: Proceedings of the 34th Annual International Symposium on Computer Architecture, ISCA 2007, New York, NY, USA, pp. 186–197. ACM (2007)
6. Zhong, H., Lieberman, S., Mahlke, S.: Extending multicore architectures to exploit hybrid parallelism in single-thread applications. In: 13th International Symposium on High Performance Computer Architecture, HPCA 2007, pp. 25–36. IEEE, February 2007
7. Mai, K., Paaske, T., Jayasena, N., Ho, R., Dally, W., Horowitz, M.: Smart memories: a modular reconfigurable architecture. In: Proceedings of the 27th International Symposium on Computer Architecture, pp. 161–171, June 2000
8. Rodrigues, R., Annamalai, A., Koren, I., Kundu, S.: Improving performance per Watt of asymmetric multi-core processors via online program phase classification and adaptive core morphing. ACM Trans. Des. Autom. Electron. Syst. 18, 5:1–5:23 (2013)
9. Balakrishnan, S., Rajwar, R., Upton, M., Lai, K.: The impact of performance asymmetry in emerging multicore architectures. SIGARCH Comput. Archit. News 33, 506–517 (2005)

10. Wu, K., Kanstein, A., Madsen, J., Berekovic, M.: MT-ADRES: multithreading on coarse-grained reconfigurable architecture. In: Diniz, P.C., Marques, E., Bertels, K., Fernandes, M.M., Cardoso, J.M.P. (eds.) ARC 2007. LNCS, vol. 4419, pp. 26–38. Springer, Heidelberg (2007). doi:10.1007/978-3-540-71431-6_3
11. Rau, B.R., Fisher, J.A.: Instruction-level parallel processing: history, overview, and perspective. J. Supercomputing **7**(1), 9–50 (1993)
12. Anjam, F., Nadeem, M., Wong, S.: Targeting code diversity with run-time adjustable issue-slots in a chip multiprocessor. In: Proceeding Design, Automation and Test in Europe, Grenoble, France, March 2011
13. Wong, S., Anjam, F.: The Delft reconfigurable VLIW processor. In: Proceeding 17th International Conference on Advanced Computing and Communications, Bangalore, India, pp. 244–251, December 2009
14. Hoozemans, J., Johansen, J., Straten, J.V., Brandon, A., Wong, S.: Multiple contexts in a multi-ported VLIW register file implementation. In: Proceeding 2015 International Conference on ReConFigurable Computing and FPGAs, Mayan Riviera, Mexico, December 2015
15. Brandon, A., Wong, S.: Support for dynamic issue width in VLIW processors using generic binaries. In: Proceeding Design, Automation & Test in Europe Conference & Exhibition, Grenoble, France, pp. 827–832, March 2013
16. Brandon, A., Hoozemans, J., Straten, J.V., Lorenzon, A.F., Sartor, A.L., Beck, A., Wong, S.: A sparse VLIW instruction encoding scheme compatible with generic binaries. In: Proceeding 2015 International Conference on ReConFigurable Computing and FPGAs, Mayan Riviera, Mexico, December 2015
17. Guthaus, M.R., Ringenberg, J.S., Ernst, D., Austin, T.M., Mudge, T., Brown, R.B.: MiBench: a free, commercially representative embedded benchmark suite. In: IEEE International Workshop on Workload Characterization, WWC-4, pp. 3–14. IEEE (2001)
18. Thoziyoor, S., Muralimanohar, N., Ahn, J.H., Jouppi, N.P.: Cacti 5.1, HP Laboratories (2008)
19. LEON/GRLIB. http://www.gaisler.com/index.php/downloads/leongrlib. Accessed 7 Sept 2016
20. Guo, Q., Sartor, A.L., Brandon, A., Beck, A., Zhou, X., Wong, S.: Run-time phase prediction for a reconfigurable VLIW processor. In: Proceeding Design, Automation and Test in Europe, Dresden, Germany, pp. 1634–1639, March 2016

Scheduling

Scheduling of Datacompression on Distributed Systems with Time- and Event-Triggered Messages

Damian Ludwig$^{(\boxtimes)}$ and Roman Obermaisser

Embedded Systems Group, University of Siegen, Siegen, Germany
{damian.ludwig,roman.obermaisser}@uni-siegen.de

Abstract. The compression of messages can improve schedulability by decreasing network latencies and contention at the cost of computational overhead for compression and decompression. Existing scheduling models do not consider compression as required for the deployment in distributed real-time systems. This paper presents an MILP model with decision variables, constraints and an objective function for selectively compressing messages as required for minimizing the system's makespan, thereby optimizing the trade-off between communication time and computational overhead. We consider multi-hop communication in systems with multiple routers and computational nodes. The algorithm is evaluated using example scenarios and the results are compared to previous work without compression support.

Keywords: Scheduling · Distributed systems · Network on chip · Time-triggered services · Real-time systems · Data compression · MILP · Optimization

1 Introduction

The correctness of distributed embedded real-time systems depends on the completion of computational and communication activities within predictable time. Scheduling and allocation problems must be solved in order to allocate computational jobs to nodes, assign messages to network links, and decide on the ordering and timing of job executions and message transmissions. Scheduling algorithms need to consider the available computational and communication resources, while ensuring the application's deadlines and considering the precedence constraints. Numerous scheduling algorithms are available in the state-of-the-art including mathematical techniques (e.g., bin packing, Mixed-Integer Linear Programming (MILP) [12]), scheduling heuristics (e.g., list scheduling and clustering [10]), meta-heuristics and search algorithms (e.g., tabu search, genetic algorithms [3]).

Scheduling algorithms also need to address complex topologies of today's network infrastructures (e.g., in-vehicle networks, avionics networks [14], factory automations networks) with numerous routers and computational nodes

© Springer International Publishing AG 2017
J. Knoop et al. (Eds.): ARCS 2017, LNCS 10172, pp. 193–204, 2017.
DOI: 10.1007/978-3-319-54999-6_15

interconnected in different topologies. These systems require multiple-hop communication along several routers in order to deliver a message from a producer job to a consumer job. At the same time, different timing models need to be supported such as time-triggered and event-triggered communication [9].

In many of today's systems the trade-off between communication and computational resources is not adequately addressed by the scheduling algorithms. Compressing messages can significantly decrease the amount of data on the networks, thereby decreasing latencies and mitigating network contention. However, the scheduling algorithms need to consider the compression overhead that contributes to the Worst-Case Execution Time (WCET) of jobs.

There are some well known compression techniques and algorithms, like Huffman coding [6], arithmetic coding [11] and the adaptive dictionary methods by Ziv and Lempel [13]. In this paper no specific compression algorithm is used. Instead, compression rates and costs are passed as parameters. In [5] the authors propose methods for optimizing performance and power consumption of NoC, by using storage- and communication-compression [2]. However, they take compression not as a part of an optimization problem but apply it to all data. A model for scheduling of datacompression is presented in [4], where compression costs and total flow time are minimized on unrelated parallel machines.

This paper extends previous work on scheduling time-triggered and event-triggered communication and computations in distributed systems with multiple routers and computational nodes. The decision variables, constraints and the objective function of the MILP model are extended to support the scheduling of data compression. For each message, the decision whether compression shall be enabled becomes part of an optimization problem and significantly influences the other scheduling and allocation decisions.

The remainder of the paper is structured as follows: In Sect. 2 we present an MILP model based on the work done in [7]. Then we illustrate the results by some examples in Sect. 3 and discuss how compression can improve schedulability.

2   Scheduling Model

In [7] the authors present an MILP-based scheduling model for multi-core processors with NoCs supporting time- and event-triggered services. The model handles dependencies between services as well as collision avoidance for time-triggered messages and bandwidth constraints.

The scheduling model consists of a logical model given by a directed acyclic graph and a physical model given by an undirected graph representing a network of compute-nodes and routers. Routers are not capable of running jobs, thus they are marked as non-allocable. The nodes of the DAG are computational jobs with a given WCET. Nodes are connected by edges, where each edge represents a message-based service (Fig. 1). Each service has a maximum hop transmission-time, a minimum interarrival time or period and is either time-triggered or event-triggered. The hop transmission-time is the delay for relaying a message between two routers or for relaying a message between a compute-node and a directly

Table 1. Summary of symbols introduced in underlying work

	Symbol	Meaning
Constants	$m \in \mathbb{N}$	Number of messages
	$n \in \mathbb{N}$	Number of nodes
	$j \in \mathbb{N}$	Number of jobs
	$U \in \mathbb{N}^m$	Hop-time for each message
	$E \in \mathbb{N}^j$	WCET of the jobs
	$S \in \mathbb{N}^m$	s_i is the job sending message i
	$D \in \{0,1\}^{j \times m}$	$d_{i,l} = 1 \Leftrightarrow$ job i receives message l
	$M \in \mathbb{N}^m$	Minimum interarrival time
	$Max_H \in \mathbb{N}$	Maximum possible number of hops
Variables	$O \in \{0,1\}^{m \times n}$	$o_{i,l} = 1 \Leftrightarrow$ message i passes node l
	$H \in \mathbb{N}^m$	Amount of hops per message
	$I \in \mathbb{N}_0^m$	Injection time of the messages
	$AM \in \{0,1\}^{j \times n}$	$am_{i,l} \Leftrightarrow$ job i is allocated to node l
	$P \in \mathbb{N}^{m \times n}$	p_i is the path of message i

connected router. It depends on the size of the message and the bandwidth of the network. When the DAG is fully produced, it will possibly run again. The different runs share a schedule to control job execution and message passing.

We formulated an MILP problem with additional constants, decision variables and constraints for supporting compression and implemented it using the IBM CPLEX optimizer. Table 1 shows the most important constants and variables already introduced in [7]. The constant n is the number of nodes in the physical model, whereas m and j describe the number of messages and jobs in the logical model. The vector U describes the hop transmission-times for all messages and E is the WCET of the jobs. The source and destination of a message can be determined from S and D. The matrix O denotes if a message passes a specific node. The number of hops a message has to take to get from its source node to the destination node is expressed in H. I is the point in time a message is injected into the network. The matrix P is used to describe the path of a message. Each item $p_{i,l} = a$ means message i passes node a at hop l. Further, we define the following sets: MSG $= \{0, \ldots, m-1\}$, NODES $= \{0, \ldots, n-1\}$ and JOBS $= \{0, \ldots, j-1\}$.

2.1   Constants

In addition to the already defined constants, we need a model for the compression itself. As we are dealing with real-time communication, we need to know an upper bound of the compression rate for each message. One could argue that in the worst-case a compression rate is always 1.0, e.g. for random input. Therefore bounds are used that are not exeeded within a given probability. We call such a

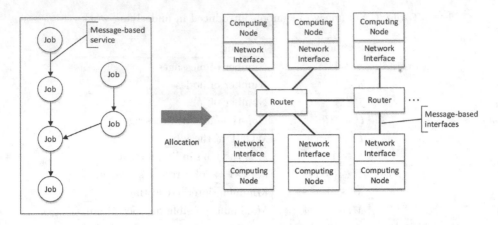

Fig. 1. Allocation of logical model (left) to physical model (right)

bound the *probabilistic Worst Case Compression Rate* (pWCCR), in analogy to the probabilistic worst-case execution time (pWCET), which is a known concept in probabilistic timing analysis (PTA). PTA provides a worst-case execution time with an associated probability of exceedence by deriving the distribution of the execution time and calculating the probabiliy of exceeding a given execution time using a probability distribution [1,8]. Transfered to the pWCCR estimation problem the goal is to obtain pWCCR estimates with given probabilies, so that the estimated pWCCR is exceeded only in very rare cases (e.g. in the region of 10^{-9}). For a message m (edge connecting two jobs) this means that the size of the exchanged data is not larger than the product of the original message-size with its pWCCR by a certain probability. It is beyond the scope of this paper to provide methods for establishing the pWCCR of input data, but in general this could be done by observing actual compression rates in experiments and match them to a probability distribution. In the following, it is assumed that the pWCCR is already available.

Definition 1 (probabilistic Worst-Case Compression Rate). Let $R \in (0,1]^m$ and $i \in$ MSG. Then, r_i is called the *probabilistic Worst Case Compression Rate* (pWCCR) of message i, iff the estimated compression rate is not exceeded by a certain probability.

We also have to consider the costs of compressing messages. Therefore, the WCET of the corresponding operations has to be known. It is assumed that compressing and decompressing both come at equal costs.

Definition 2 (Compression Overhead). Let $W \in \mathbb{N}^m$ and $i \in$ MSG. Then, w_i is called the worst-case execution time (WCET) of the compression operation of message i. The total overhead produced by the compression and decompression of a message i is $2 \cdot w_i$.

2.2   Decision Variables

For each message we have to track its compression status. This is done in a boolean decision variable.

Definition 3. Let $C \in \{0,1\}^m$ and $i \in \text{MSG}$. The item c_i decides whether message i gets compressed and is defined as follows:

$$\forall i \in \text{MSG} : c_i = \begin{cases} 1, & \text{compress message i} \\ 0, & \text{leave uncompressed} \end{cases} \tag{1}$$

As compression reduces the size of a message, the hop-time of the compressed messages is reduced at least by factor of the given pWCCR. The decision vector $\dot{U}$ holds the hop-time of each message. For uncompressed messages the values of U apply.

Definition 4. Let $\dot{U} \in \mathbb{R}^m$ and $i \in \text{MSG}$. Then, $\dot{u}_i$ is the actual hop-time of message i depending on the messages compression status and is defined as:

$$\forall i \in \text{MSG} : \dot{u}_i = r_i \cdot u_i \cdot c_i + u_i \cdot (1 - c_i) \tag{2}$$

Based on the hop transmission-time and the amount of hops H made by a message, the total communication time for each message can be calculated. For this calculation another decision variable is needed, because the product of the two non-binary decision variables $\dot{U}$ and H is not linear and thus cannot be expressed as MILP.

Definition 5. Let $K \in \mathbb{R}_+^m$ and $i \in \text{MSG}$. Then, k_i is the (end-to-end) communication time needed by message i to travel from its source node to the destination node.

$$\forall i \in \text{MSG} : (c_i = 1) \rightarrow (k_i = h_i \cdot r_i \cdot u_i) \wedge (c_i = 0) \rightarrow (k_i = h_i \cdot u_i) \tag{3}$$

Finally, we need to take into account the overhead, which arises on jobs that deal with compressed messages. For each job the overhead is given by the sum of the overhead produced by incoming compressed messages.

Definition 6. Let $\dot{E} \in \mathbb{N}_0^j$ and $i \in \text{JOBS}$. Then, $\dot{e}_i$ is the overhead arising on job i by decompressing incoming messages.

$$\forall i \in \text{JOBS} : \dot{e}_i = \sum_{m \in \text{MSG}} w_m \cdot c_m \cdot d_{i,m} \tag{4}$$

The above variable considers incoming messages needed as dependencies for executing the actual job. The overhead for outgoing compressed messages is handled by a constraint for the injection-time of a message. This enables us to hide latency in case multiple outgoing messages are compressed so we can exploit parallelism on the node.

2.3   Objective Function

The main goal of the scheduling task is to minimize the makespan of the logical model, which is the arrival time of the last message.

Definition 7 (Arrival Time). Let $A \in \mathbb{N}^m$. Then, a_i is the point in time message i arrives at its destination.

In [7] that time was given by $a_i = i_i + h_i \cdot u_i$. Assuming that compression is done before injecting a message (which means i_i is already delayed by w_i), the new arrival time is given by $a_i = i_i + k_i + w_i \cdot c_i$, where i_i is the injection-time and k_i the communication-time. $w_i \cdot c_i$ is the overhead to be applied if the message needs to be decompressed. The objective function is then given by: $\min(\max(a_0, \ldots, a_{m-1}))$.

2.4   Contraints for Compression

In [7], it was allowed for messages to be injected at $t = 0$. This is still fine, but we have to make sure compressed messages will be injected *after* the compression operation finished.

Constraint 8 (Injection Time). Messages should be injected *after* the time needed for compression and *before* the minimum interarrival time is reached.

$$\forall j \in \text{MSG} : i_j \geq w_j \cdot c_j \wedge i_j \leq m_j \tag{5}$$

Incoming messages are dependencies for running a job and thus also for outgoing messages. The injection of a message must be done after the arrival of all incoming messages and the completion of the corresponding job.

Constraint 9 (Dependency Satisfaction). Let m_1 and m_2 be messages and $d_{s_{m_2}, m_1} = 1$, where s_{m_2} is the sender of message m_2. Then, m_2 depends on m_1.

$$\forall m_1, m_2 \in \text{MSG} : d_{s_{m_2}, m_1} \rightarrow i_{m_2} \geq i_{m_1} + k_{m_1} + \dot{e}_{s_{m_2}} + e_{s_{m_2}} + w_{m_2} \cdot c_{m_2} \tag{6}$$

The constraint for the dependency satisfaction enables us to hide latency because m_2 can be injected directly after its compression has finished without having to wait for the completion of other compression operations on job s_{m_2}. Also, time-triggered messages should not collide and must not be at the same link at the same time.

Constraint 10 (Collision Avoidance). Time-triggered messages should not collide on their way. Any two messages must not be at the same router at the same time.

$$\forall m_1, m_2 \in \text{MSG}_{TT}, \forall r_1, r_2 \in \{0, \ldots, \text{Max}_H\} : p_{m_1, r_1} \neq p_{m_2, r_2}$$
$$\vee \, p_{m_1, r_1+1} \neq p_{m_2, r_2+1} \vee r_1 + 1 > h_{m_1} \vee r_2 + 1 > h_{m_2}$$
$$\vee \, i_{m_1} + (r_1 + 1) \cdot \dot{u}_{m_1} < i_{m_2} + r_2 \cdot \dot{u}_{m_2} \tag{7}$$
$$\vee \, i_{m_2} + (r_2 + 1) \cdot \dot{u}_{m_2} < i_{m_1} + r_1 \cdot \dot{u}_{m_1}$$

Since the buffer capacity on the routers and the bandwidth on the links is limited, discarding of messages has to be avoided. As in [7], the ratio of transmission time and minimum interarrival time is used to determine the capacity used by a time-triggered or event-triggered message. The utilization of the bandwidth on a node is then given by summing up the used bandwidth of all messages passing this node. This is the worst-case scenario since the point in time a message passes the node is not taken into account.

Constraint 11 (Bandwidth utilization). The bandwidth at each node is given by summing up the ratio of the transmission time and the minimum interarrival time for messages passing the node.

$$\forall n \in \text{NODES} : \sum_{m \in \text{MSG}} o_{m,n} \cdot \frac{u_m}{m_m} \cdot (c_m \cdot (r_m - 1) + 1) \leq 1 \tag{8}$$

The direct multiplication of $o_{m,n}$ and c_m is possible, because both decision variables are binary. Every part of the sum can only result in three different values $\frac{u_m}{m_m}$, $\frac{r_m \cdot u_m}{m_m}$ and 0.

2.5 Other Constraints

This section describes constraints that do not deal with compression but are important for other parts of the scheduling problem like allocation and finding paths.

Constraint 12 (Connectivity). This constraint considers the path topology of the network. If there is no direct connection between two nodes n_1 and n_2 any message must not travel from n_1 to n_2 within one hop.

Constraint 13 (Progress). Each message must reach the destination node with at most the maximum amount of hops Max_H and must start on the node where its sending job is located at. Since loops should be avoided, a message must not visit a node more than once.

Constraint 14 (Job Assignment). Each job is assigned to exactly one node, therefore the sum of each row in AM must be equal to 1. Additionally, only compute nodes can run jobs. For routers the sum of the corresponding column in AM has to be 0.

Constraint 15 (Visit). Beside P the boolean matrix O indicates if a message m passes a node a.

$$\forall m \in \text{MSG}, \forall a \in \text{NODES} : (\exists r \leq Max_H : p_{m,r} = a) \Leftrightarrow o_{m,a} = 1 \tag{9}$$

3 Results and Examples

We implemented the extended model in IBM CPLEX and ran it on examples used in [7] to compare the compression-aware scheduling with previous results. Table 2 shows the reference values gathered from experiments without compression, using the implementation from [7].

The execution time was measured as the average computation time of 10 runs on one node of the university's high-performance cluster HorUS[1] with 12 cores and 48 GB memory per node and CPLEX using 12 threads. We then compared these results to the ones gathered by the modified model and compression turned off, as shown in Table 3. Although the number of constraints is higher, for most of the examples less time is needed to solve them and CPLEX was able to find a solution for example 1. Generally, the model terminates with an optimal solution for all solvable problems. Nevertheless, CPLEX offers to search for non-optimal solutions, which can provide feasible solutions for problems that could not be solved optimally. If the model terminates without any solution, the most obvious reason is a lack of planned resources (too few compute-nodes, too many messages, etc.) in your physical or logical model.

Table 2. Reference values measured with code from [7]

Example ID	#Jobs	#Message	#Nodes	Solution	#Constraints	Time
1	4	4	8	–	–	3,01 s
2	5	4	7	14	408	2,12 s
3	5	5	7	14	498	4,08 s
4	5	5	8	25	616	6,6 s
5	5	6	7	25	590	6,62 s
6	5	7	7	33	681	9,79 s
7	5	8	7	33	770	12,41 s

Table 3. Compression turned off

Example ID	pWCCR	Overhead	Solution	#Constraints	Time
1	1,0	–	40	854	4,94 s
2	1,0	–	14	425	2,60 s
3	1,0	–	14	518	3,85 s
4	1,0	–	25	636	5,87 s
5	1,0	–	25	613	6,45 s
6	1,0	–	33	707	8,66 s
7	1,0	–	33	799	10,92 s

---

[1] http://www.uni-siegen.de/cluster/hardware.html.

Table 4. Results for different compression rates and overheads

Example ID	pWCCR	Overhead	Solution	#Constraints	Time
1	0,5	1	29	854	22,11 s
2	0,5	1	12	425	4,42 s
3	0,5	1	12	518	5,61 s
4	0,5	1	20,5	636	42,81 s
5	0,5	1	20,5	613	16,26 s
6	0,5	1	28	707	17,88 s
7	0,5	1	28	799	21,92 s
1	0,5	2	34	854	29,20 s
2	0,5	2	13	425	6,09 s
3	0,5	2	13	518	6,34 s
4	0,5	2	22,5	636	25,29 s
5	0,5	2	22,5	613	13,57 s
6	0,5	2	32	707	17,10 s
7	0,5	2	32	799	33,43 s
1	0,5	3	36	854	71,33 s
2	0,5	3	14	425	3,69 s
3	0,5	3	14	518	7,58 s
4	0,5	3	23,5	636	36,46 s
5	0,5	3	23,5	613	15,09 s
6	0,5	3	33	707	21,04 s
7	0,5	3	33	799	16,69 s
1	0,6	1	32,8	854	41,69 s
2	0,6	1	12,6	425	6,34 s
3	0,6	1	12,6	518	5,31 s
4	0,6	1	22,4	636	27,84 s
5	0,6	1	22,4	613	17,96 s
6	0,6	1	30,6	707	25,02 s
7	0,6	1	30,6	799	27,73 s

With compression turned on, CPLEX was able to find better solutions for most of the examples in trade of a higher computation time, depending on the parameters for compression. Table 4 shows the results for different compression rates and different overhead. In comparison with Table 3 the number of additional constraints can be ruled out as a reason for the increased computational time. Instead, the computational time is influenced by the parameters describing the available compression algorithm, as those parameters have an impact on the size of the solution space.

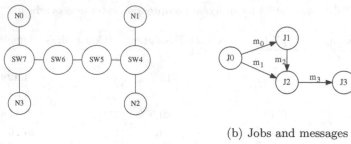

(b) Jobs and messages

(a) Network (physical model)

Fig. 2. Exemplary dependency graph and network

The directed acyclic graph shown in Fig. 2b represents an examplary logical model which should be scheduled to the network shown in Fig. 2a. This physical model consists of 8 nodes from which N0-N3 are compute nodes and SW4-SW7 are routers and thus not able to execute jobs. The logical model consists of four jobs exchanging four messages. All messages but m_2 are time-triggered. In this example we assume a transmission time of 4 clock ticks for each message and a job execution time of 2 ticks. The minimum interarrival time of the event-triggerd messages and the period of time-triggered messages is 40 ticks.

Table 5. Solution for 1st example with compression rate of 0.5 and overhead 1

Job	Node	Message	Compressed?	Hops	Path	Injection	Arrival
j_0	n_0	m_0	Yes	2	n_0, n_7, n_3	1	6
		m_1	Yes	5	$n_0, n_7, n_6, n_5, n_4, n_1$	3	14
j_1	n_3	m_2	Yes	5	$n_3, n_7, n_6, n_5, n_4, n_1$	9	20
j_2	n_1	m_3	Yes	2	n_1, n_4, n_2	24	29
j_3	n_2	–	–	–	–	–	–

Table 5 depicts a solution for the example presented in Figs. 2b and 2a by showing the values of the most important decision variables. Job j_0 is allocated on node n_0 and sends time-triggered messages m_0 and m_1. Message m_0 is compressed and takes two hops, whereas m_1 makes five hops. The arrival time of the last time-triggered message is at tick 29, which is also the solution of the objective function. Arrival times include decompression overhead. The column *Path* shows the nodes a message visits to reach from the producer to the consumer in the sequence of passing.

The Gantt chart presented in Fig. 3 shows allocation and message passing for this example. Message m_0 is injected on node n_0 at tick 1, directly after job j_0 has finished the compression of this message. The compression of message m_1 is started by j_0 at tick 1, but it is injected to the network at tick 3 to avoid a

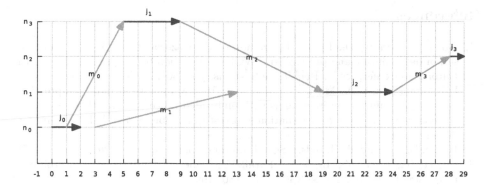

Fig. 3. Gantt chart for example 1

collision with prior sent message m_0. The execution times of jobs j_1 and j_2 are the sum of their WCETs (e.g. two ticks) and the overhead for compressing and decompressing messages (e.g. one tick per operation). Therefore message m_2 can be injected at tick 9, four ticks after the arrival of m_0 at node n_3. Ten ticks later, the message arrives at node n_1 after five hops and can be processed by job j_2. Job j_2 runs five ticks as it has to decompress two incoming messages (two ticks) and one outgoing message (one tick). Note, that waiting for message m_2 cannot be hidden by decompressing message m_1 earlier, as it is not yet supported by the model. The execution time of the task itself is two ticks. Then, message m_3 can be injected to the network at tick 24 and arrives at node n_2 four ticks later. After decompression, this last message is available for normal processing after a total of 29 ticks.

4   Conclusion

The contribution of this paper is an MILP-based scheduling model for time-triggered and event-triggered services with support for data compression while preserving real-time guarantees and avoiding collisions between time-triggered messages. Decreased bandwidth utilization is also considered. Any compression algorithm can be used with the proposed model, as long as you can provide an (probabilistic) upper bound for compression ratio and overhead. The gained results are promising and should lead to further investigation whether compression using known algorithms is useful in real-world applications of distributed embedded systems. Future work may also include new or enhanced compression algorithms to address the needs of real-time systems as well as methods for providing pWCCR estimates for different compression methods based on application-specific input data.

Acknowledgements. This work has been supported by the DFG project DAKODIS under the Grant Agreement No. 275601549 and the European project DREAMS under the Grant Agreement No. 610640.

References

1. Abella, J., Hardy, D., Puaut, I., Quiñones, E., Cazorla, F.J.: On the comparison of deterministic and probabilistic WCET estimation techniques. In: 2014 26th Euromicro Conference on Real-Time Systems, pp. 266–275. IEEE (2014)
2. Benini, L., Bruni, D., Macii, A., Macii, E.: Hardware-assisted data compression for energy minimization in systems with embedded processors. In: Proceedings of the conference on Design, automation and test in Europe, p. 449. IEEE Computer Society (2002)
3. Burke, E.K., Kendall, G. (eds.): Search Methodologies. Springer, New York (2005)
4. Cheng, T., Chen, Z., Li, C.L.: Parallel-machine scheduling with controllable processing times. IIE Trans. **28**(2), 177–180 (1996)
5. Das, R., Mishra, A.K., Nicopoulos, C., Park, D., Narayanan, V., Iyer, R., Yousif, M.S., Das, C.R.: Performance and power optimization through data compression in network-on-chip architectures. In: 2008 IEEE 14th International Symposium on High Performance Computer Architecture, pp. 215–225. IEEE (2008)
6. Huffman, D.A., et al.: A method for the construction of minimum-redundancy codes. Proc. IRE **40**(9), 1098–1101 (1952)
7. Murshed, A., Obermaisser, R., Ahmadian, H., Khalifeh, A.: Scheduling and allocation of time-triggered and event-triggered services for multi-core processors with networks-on-a-chip. In: 2015 IEEE 13th International Conference on Industrial Informatics (INDIN), pp. 1424–1431. IEEE (2015)
8. Nélis, V., Yomsi, P.M., Pinho, L.M., Bernat, G.: Another look at the pWCET estimation problem
9. Obermaisser, R.: Event-Triggered and Time-Triggered Control Paradigms, vol. 22. Springer, New York (2005)
10. Sinnen, O.: Task Scheduling for Parallel Systems, vol. 60. Wiley, Hoboken (2007)
11. Witten, I.H., Neal, R.M., Cleary, J.G.: Arithmetic coding for data compression. Commun. ACM **30**(6), 520–540 (1987)
12. Zeng, H., Zheng, W., Di Natale, M., Ghosal, A., Giusto, P., Sangiovanni-Vincentelli, A.: Scheduling the flexray bus using optimization techniques. In: 46th ACM/IEEE Design Automation Conference, DAC 2009, pp. 874–877. IEEE (2009)
13. Ziv, J., Lempel, A.: A universal algorithm for sequential data compression. IEEE Trans. Inf. Theory **23**(3), 337–343 (1977)
14. Zurawski, R.: Industrial Communication Technology Handbook. CRC Press, Boca Raton (2014)

Semi-partitioned Mixed-Criticality Scheduling

Muhammad Ali Awan[1,2], Konstantinos Bletsas[1,2(✉)], Pedro F. Souto[1,3],
and Eduardo Tovar[1,2]

[1] CISTER/INESC-TEC Research Centre, Porto, Portugal
[2] ISEP/IPP, Porto, Portugal
{muaan,ksbs,emt}@isep.ipp.pt
[3] Faculty of Engineering, University of Porto, Porto, Portugal
pfs@fe.up.pt

Abstract. Scheduling isolation in mixed-criticality systems is challenging without sacrificing performance. In response, we propose a scheduling approach that combines server-based semi-partitioning and deadline-scaling. Semi-partitioning (whereby only some tasks migrate, in a carefully managed manner), hitherto used in single criticality systems, offers good performance with low overheads. Deadline-scaling selectively prioritise high-criticality tasks in parts of the schedule to ensure their deadlines are met even in rares case of execution time overrun. Our new algorithm NPS-F-MC brings semi-partitioning to mixed-criticality scheduling and uses Ekberg and Yi's state-of-the-art deadline scaling approach. It ensures scheduling isolation among different-criticality tasks and only allows low-criticality task migration. We also explore variants that disallow migration entirely or relax the isolation between different criticalities (SP-EKB) in order to evaluate the performance tradeoffs associated with more flexible or rigid safety and isolation requirements.

1 Introduction

Many real-time embedded systems (automotive, avionics, aerospace) host functions of different *criticalities*. A deadline miss by a high-criticality function can be disastrous, but losing a low-criticality function only moderately affects the quality of service. Scalability and cost concerns favor *mixed-criticality* (MC) systems, whereby tasks of different criticalities are scheduled on the same processors but this brings challenges: Lower-criticality tasks interfering unpredictably with higher-criticality tasks can be catastrophic. Conversely, rigidly prioritisation by criticality leads to inefficient processor usage. Therefore, we seek (i) efficient use of processing capacity and (ii) schedulability guarantees for all tasks under typical conditions subject to (iii) ensured schedulability of high-criticality tasks in all cases. Most related works [1] use Vestal's model [2], which views the system operation as different modes (low- and high-criticality) and associates different worst-case task execution times (WCETs) in each mode with a corresponding degree of confidence. This is because the cost of provably safe WCET estimation (and the associated pessimism) is justified only for high-criticality tasks. Other tasks have less rigorous WCET estimates, which *might* be exceeded, very rarely.

© Springer International Publishing AG 2017
J. Knoop et al. (Eds.): ARCS 2017, LNCS 10172, pp. 205–218, 2017.
DOI: 10.1007/978-3-319-54999-6_16

We also adopt Vestal's model, with two criticality levels. Our main contribution is **NPS-F-MC**, an extension of the semi-partitioned scheduling algorithm NPS-F [3] to mixed criticalities. NPS-F is *server-based*, which helps provide both fairness to low-criticality tasks and strict *temporal isolation* between high- and low-criticality tasks. The new algorithm employs the *per-task deadline scaling* scheduling technique by Ekberg and Yi [4], an extension of EDF-VD [5]. NPS-F-MC allows migration among processors only for servers for low-criticality tasks, with less severe safety considerations. However, given the conservative stance of certification authorities [6] towards task migrations, we formulate as another contribution a fully partitioned variant (NPS-F-IMA) and explore the performance gap from disallowing migrations entirely. As third contribution we explore the performance penalty from the strict temporal isolation by NPS-F-MC by formulating new partitioned (P-EKB) and semi-partitioned (SP-EKB) extensions of the (uniprocessor) algorithm of Ekberg and Yi, and comparing with those.

2   Overview

Task Model [2]. The system can be in either low- or high-criticality mode (L-mode or H-mode). A task is of either low or high criticality (L-task or H-task). Each H-task has two different WCET estimates: the one for the L-mode of operation (L-WCET), is *deemed* safe but lacks proof, whereas the one for the H-mode (H-WCET) is provably safe but usually much greater. Each L-task only has an L-WCET. The default system mode is L, but if *any* task exceeds its L-WCET, the system immediately switches into H-mode: all L-tasks are abandoned and only H-tasks remain. In H-mode, all H-tasks (incl. instances present at the time of the mode switch) are pessimistically assumed to execute for up to their H-WCET. Even so, it must be provable that no H-task deadlines can be missed.

MC Scheduling with Scaled Deadlines. Deadline-scaling for mixed-criticality systems originates with EDF-VD ("Earliest Deadline First - with Virtual Deadlines") [5]. EDF-VD uses standard EDF scheduling rules but, instead of reporting the real deadlines to the EDF scheduler for scheduling decisions, it reports shorter deadlines (if needed) for H-tasks during L-mode operation. This helps with the schedulability of H-tasks in the case of a switch to H-mode, because it prioritises H-tasks more than conventional EDF would, over parts of the schedule. This allows them to be sufficiently "ahead of schedule" and catch up with their true deadlines if any task overruns its L-WCET. While in H-mode, the true H-task deadlines are used for scheduling and L-tasks are dropped. EDF-VD proportionately shortens the H-task deadlines according to a single common scale factor and its schedulability test considers the task utilisations in both modes.

Ekberg and Yi [4] improved upon EDF-VD by enabling and calculating distinct scale factors for different H-tasks and using a more precise *demand bound function* (dbf) based schedulability test [7]. This improves performance. The calculation of the scale factors is an iterative task-by-task process. For details, see [4,8]. Recently, Masrur et al. [9] proposed using just two scale factors, to balance scheduling performance and computational complexity. A higher scale factor is used for tasks with an H-WCET/L-WCET ratio above some threshold. Meanwhile, Easwaran developed a test [10] that dominates [4]. In this work we innovatively combine the deadline-scaling technique by Ekberg and Yi [4] with the existing NPS-F semi-partitioned scheduling algorithm.

Semi-partitioning and NPS-F. Under semi-partitioned scheduling, most tasks are partitioned; the rest may migrate, in a carefully managed manner. This allows for efficiently utilising a multicore, without many preemptions, migrations and overheads, under strong schedulability guarantees. Semi-partitioned mixed-criticality scheduling was first proposed in [11]. Here, we conclude that work and adapt the NPS-F algorithm [3] (originally, for single-criticality systems).

Classic NPS-F assigns tasks via bin-packing, not directly to processors but to periodic fixed-budget servers using EDF as their internal scheduling policy. The servers are mapped to the available processors in a form of cyclic executive with a periodicity of S – the "timeslot length". Each server is either implemented as either one periodic "reserve" (fixed-length contiguous time window) on one processor or as multiple periodic reserves on different processors. A given server's tasks can only execute within its reserves, which in turn are exclusively used by those tasks. A server (its reserves) is appropriately sized, to ensure that its tasks meet all their deadlines at run-time. Additionally, the reserves of a server mapped to multiple processors must never overlap in time.

3   System Model

We assume a set of n sporadic tasks $\tau \stackrel{\text{def}}{=} \{\tau_1, \tau_2, \ldots, \tau_n\}$. Each task τ_i has a minimum inter-arrival time T_i, a relative deadline $D_i \leq T_i$, a criticality level $\kappa_i \in \{L, H\}$ (low or high, respectively) and two WCET estimates, C_i^L and C_i^H, one for each mode. The subsets of L-tasks and H-tasks in τ are $\tau(L) \stackrel{\text{def}}{=} \{\tau_i \in \tau | \kappa_i \in L\}$ and $\tau(H) \stackrel{\text{def}}{=} \{\tau_i \in \tau | \kappa_i \in H\}$. It is assumed that $\forall \tau_i \in \tau(H)$, $C_i^L \leq C_i^H$ and $\forall \tau_i \in \tau(L)$, $C_i^H = 0$. Tasks in $\tau(H)$ are not allowed to migrate among processors. The utilisation of τ_i is $U_i^L \stackrel{\text{def}}{=} \frac{C_i^L}{T_i}$ and $U_i^H \stackrel{\text{def}}{=} \frac{C_i^H}{T_i}$ respectively in each mode. The system utilisation in each mode is $U^H \stackrel{\text{def}}{=} \sum_{\tau_i \in \tau(H)} U_i^H$ and $U^L \stackrel{\text{def}}{=} \sum_{\tau_i \in \tau} U_i^L$. Our platform $P \stackrel{\text{def}}{=} \{P_1, P_2, \ldots, P_m\}$ has m identical processors. We assume a set $\widetilde{P}$ of m'' servers, indexed $\widetilde{P}_1$ to $\widetilde{P}_{m''}$, with m'' not a priori defined.

During task assignment, the processing capacity of each server is equivalent to that of a physical processor. The set of tasks assigned to server $\widetilde{P}_k$ is denoted as $\tau(\widetilde{P}_k)$. Each server is only assigned tasks of the same criticality as each other. A server that contains only H-tasks is termed a H-server. Similarly, an L-server contains only L-tasks. The budget of a $\widetilde{P}_k$ is denoted by $X_{\widetilde{P}_k}$.

4 Task Assignment, Scheduling Model and Timing Analysis

Overview. NPS-F-MC partitions the set of H-tasks ($\tau(H)$) over m_H'' non-migrating H-servers. Each H-server will be assigned to a different corresponding processor, so it must hold that $m_H'' \leq m$ or the algorithm will declare failure.

The set of L-tasks ($\tau(L)$) is partitioned over a separate set of L-servers. The "leftover" parts of the timeslots, that remain on the m processors, after the assignment and sizing of the non-migrating H-servers, are reclaimed from the processors for the mapping of the L-servers.

During L-mode operation, all tasks are scheduled within the respective servers under EDF. But if a task τ_i overruns its C_i^L (which triggers a mode switch), then all L-tasks are immediately dropped along with the server arrangement altogether, and the system switches to pure partitioned EDF scheduling of the H-tasks. This raises the question of how to specify the server budgets:

A **naive approach** would (i) partition the H-tasks to the H-servers using a uniprocessor EDF schedulability test that considers the overly conservative estimates C_i^H, to meet deadlines in H-mode, and (ii) assign budgets to the respective servers so that the H-tasks provably meet their deadlines in L-mode, as long as they all execute for up to their respective C_i^L. However, this may lead to missed deadlines during the mode transition.

A **conservative approach** would instead consider the C_i^H estimates, when sizing the H-servers for operation in L-mode. However, this approach decreases the processing capacity available for L-tasks and is inefficient.

Ideally, one should therefore set the server budgets to the optimal intermediate value that minimises the processing capacity used for H-servers (i.e., maximises the capacity available for L-servers) in L-mode without jeopardising the schedulability of the H-tasks at any point in time (even when a mode transition occurs). As part of this work, we identify how to compute these optimal H-server budgets, using the analysis of Ekberg and Yi [4].

In summary, a processor P_p with an H-server assigned to it is equivalently modelled as a separate uniprocessor system, whereupon a transformed task subset runs under EDF with deadline scaling. This consists of all H-tasks assigned to the single H-server $\widetilde{P}_p$ mapped to P_p plus a single "fake" L-task with parameters $(C_{\text{fake}}, D_{\text{fake}}, T_{\text{fake}}) \stackrel{\text{def}}{=} (S - X_{\widetilde{P}_p}, S - X_{\widetilde{P}_p}, S)$, where $X_{\widetilde{P}_p}$ is the budget of $\widetilde{P}_p$. This zero-laxity fake task equivalently represents the periodic unavailability of the processor, for the tasks of $\widetilde{P}_p$ to execute on. The budget $X_{\widetilde{P}_p}$ is then set to the minimum value for which the transformed MC task subset is schedulable on a uniprocessor, using the deadline-scaling by Ekberg and Yi.

In Detail. The proposed approach (outlined in pseudocode as Algorithm 1), is divided into three offline stages, (i) task-to-server assignment, (ii) sizing servers ("inflating", in NPS-F jargon) and (iii) mapping servers to processors.

The first stage assigns H-tasks to servers via First-Fit (FF) bin-packing, subject to an exact uniprocessor EDF schedulability test, from classic (criticality-oblivious) EDF theory [7] that uses the respective H-WCETs as input. The L-tasks are assigned to a different set of servers via First-Fit, using the same test, but using their L-WCETs as inputs.

The "inflated utilisation" $U^{infl.} \stackrel{\text{def}}{=} \frac{X_{\widetilde{P}_p}}{S}$ of each server is computed in the second stage. The sum of inflated utilisations of all servers corresponds to the total processing capacity (informally, the number of processors) required for successfully scheduling the given task set under the proposed approach. Finally, in the third stage, servers are mapped to physical processors and their periodic reserves are arranged to avoid time-overlaps of reserves belonging to same server.

(i) **Task-to-server mapping:** Initially (Algorithm 1, lines 1–5), the H-tasks are assigned to servers (as many as needed) using First-Fit, assuming their C_i^H WCET estimate and according to an exact uniprocessor (single-criticality) EDF schedulability test. The m_H'' servers $\widetilde{P}_1$ to $\widetilde{P}_{m_H''}$ thus formed, are all H-servers.

Algorithm 2 presents the First-Fit bin-packing routine that assigns tasks to servers. The exact uniprocessor EDF schedulability test employed therein makes use of the *demand bound function* [7]. It is an abstraction of the computational requirements of the tasks. The demand of an arbitrary-deadline task τ_i over any possible time interval of length t, denoted by $\text{DBF}(\tau_i, t, \kappa)$, is a tight (i.e., exact and least) upper bound on the maximum cumulative execution requirement of jobs by τ_i over a time interval of length t; the additional argument $\kappa \in L, H$ denotes whether the WCET assumed for those jobs is C_i^L or C_i^H (see Eq. 1). The DBF for a set of tasks and the corresponding schedulability condition are given by Eqs. 2 and 3, respectively.

$$\forall t \geq 0, \quad \text{DBF}(\tau_i, t, \kappa) \stackrel{\text{def}}{=} \max\left(0, \left\lfloor \frac{t - D_i}{T_i} \right\rfloor + 1\right) \cdot C_i^\kappa \qquad (1)$$

$$\text{DBF}(\tau, t, \kappa) = \sum_{\tau_i \in \tau} \text{DBF}(\tau_i, t, \kappa) \qquad (2)$$

$$\forall t \geq 0, \quad \text{DBF}(\tau, t, \kappa) \leq t \qquad (3)$$

Algorithm 1 Semi-partitioned MC algorithm (NPS-F-MC)

Input: τ, P ▷ assuming $U^L \leq 1$ and $U^H \leq 1$ **Output:** Schedulability status

```
 1: for (i := 1; i ≤ n; i + +) do                    14: m'' := Index_Of_Highest_Populated_Server()
 2:    if (κ_i == H) then                                  ▷ m'' is the total number of servers
 3:       Assign_To_Server_FF (τ_i, H)               15: U_tot^{infl} := 0
 4:    end if                                        16: for (q := 1; q ≤ m''; q++) do
 5: end for                                          17:    U_{P̃_q}^{infl} := Mixed_Criticality_Inflate(P̃_q)
 6: m_H'' := Index_Of_Highest_Populated_Server()     18:    U_tot^{infl} := U_tot^{infl} + U_{P̃_q}^{infl}
       ▷ m_H'' is the number of H-servers            19:    if (U_tot^{infl} > m) then return FAILURE
 7: if (m_H'' > m) then return FAILURE               20:    end if
 8: end if                                           21: end for
 9: for (i := 1; i ≤ n; i++) do                      22: Do_Server_To_Processor_Mapping(Inflated Servers)
10:    if (κ_i == L) then                            23: return SUCCESS
11:       Assign_To_Server_FF (τ_i, L)
12:    end if
13: end for
```

The schedulability of a server is tested with the following expression: $\forall t > 0,\ \mathrm{DBF}(\tau(\widetilde{P}_k), t, \kappa) \leq t$. If the test succeeds, a provisional assignment is made permanent. The task-to-server assignment procedure *per se* always succeeds, because we are not *a priori* bounded to any particular number of servers; we can create/populate as many servers as needed (and, at worst, a task will be the first task assigned to a newly populated server). As mentioned, when assigning H-tasks, we assume $\kappa = H$. To speed up the computation, we use the improved Quick Processor Demand analysis (QPA*) by Zhang and Burns [12].

Algorithm 2 Assign_To_Server_FF(τ_i, κ_i)

Input: τ_i, κ_i **Output:** Assignment status
1: **if** $(\kappa_i == H)$ **then**
2: $\quad q := 1$
3: **else**
4: $\quad q := m_H'' + 1$
5: **end if**
6: **while** (true) **do**
7: $\quad$ **if** $(\mathrm{DBF}(\tau(\widetilde{P}_q) \cup \{\tau_i\}, t, \kappa_i) \leq t,\ \forall t > 0)$
8: $\quad\quad$ **then** $\tau(\widetilde{P}_q) := \tau(\widetilde{P}_q) \cup \{\tau_i\}$
9: $\quad\quad$ BREAK
10: $\quad$ **else**
11: $\quad\quad q := q + 1$
12: $\quad$ **end if**
13: **end while**
14: **return** SUCCESS

Algorithm 3 Mixed_Criticality_Inflate$(\widetilde{P}_k)$

Input: $\widetilde{P}_k$ **Output:** $U_{\widetilde{P}_k}^{infl}$
1: $X_{min} := 0;\ X_{max} := S = \dfrac{DT_{min}}{\delta}$;
2: **while** $(X_{max} - X_{min} > \Delta)$ **do**
3: $\quad X := \dfrac{X_{min} + X_{max}}{2}$
4: $\quad$ Create $\tau_{\text{fake}} = \langle T_{\text{fake}} := S, D_{\text{fake}} := S - X,$
$\quad\quad\quad\quad\quad\quad C_{\text{fake}} := S - X, L\rangle$
5: $\quad \tau(\widetilde{P}_k) := \tau(\widetilde{P}_k) \cup \{\tau_{\text{fake}}\}$
6: $\quad$ **if** $(\widetilde{P}_k == H\text{-server \&\&}$
$\quad\quad\quad$ Ekberg_Analysis$(\tau(\widetilde{P}_k)) == $ SUCCESS)
7: $\quad\quad$ **then** $X_{max} := \dfrac{X_{min} + X_{max}}{2}$
8: $\quad$ **else if** $(\widetilde{P}_k == L\text{-server \&\&}$
$\quad\quad\quad (\forall t > 0,\ \mathrm{DBF}(\tau(\widetilde{P}_k), t, L) \leq t))$
9: $\quad\quad$ **then** $X_{max} := \dfrac{X_{min} + X_{max}}{2}$
10: $\quad$ **else**
11: $\quad\quad X_{min} := \dfrac{X_{min} + X_{max}}{2}$
12: $\quad$ **end if**
13: $\quad \tau(\widetilde{P}_k) := \tau(\widetilde{P}_k) \setminus \{\tau_{\text{fake}}\}$
14: **end while**
15: $X_{\widetilde{P}_k} := X_{max}$
16: **return** $U_{\widetilde{P}_k}^{infl} := \dfrac{X_{\widetilde{P}_k}}{S}$

After all H-tasks are assigned to H-servers, if the number of H-servers (m_H'') exceeds the number of processors (m), then NPS-F-MC declares failure (see lines 6-8 in Algorithm 1). This reflects the real-world requirement that each H-server be mapped to only one processor and not allowed to migrate at run-time, because those tasks are critical and their scheduling should be as predictable as possible.

Afterwards, the L-tasks are assigned to the L-servers, indexed $\widetilde{P}_{m_H''+1}$ and upwards, by the same bin-packing procedure, but using their C_i^L WCET estimates for the schedulability test guiding the assignments (Algorithm 1, lines 9-13). Once this is done, m'' servers have been created and populated with tasks: of these, servers $\widetilde{P}_1$ to $\widetilde{P}_{m_H''}$ are H-servers and $\widetilde{P}_{m_H''+1}$ to $\widetilde{P}_{m''}$ are L-servers.

(ii) Sizing servers: The second step of the offline phase performs the server sizing (see Algorithm 1, lines 14-21). The timeslot length S (i.e., the period of all servers) is defined as $S \stackrel{\text{def}}{=} DT_{min}/\delta$ where DT_{min} is the shortest inter-arrival time or relative deadline of all tasks and δ is a positive integer (usually $\delta = 1$)[1]. Let $X_{\widetilde{P}_k}$ denote the fixed time budget of server $\widetilde{P}_k$. Then, the system utilisation consumed by the server (i.e., its "inflated utilisation", in NPS-F jargon) is:

$$U_{\widetilde{P}_k}^{infl} \overset{\text{def}}{=} \frac{X_{\widetilde{P}_k}}{S} \tag{4}$$

The value of $X_{\widetilde{P}_k}$ is computed for each server by the function presented in Algorithm 3. Assume that a contiguous time window $X \leq S$ denotes the time that server $\widetilde{P}_k$ is active within a given timeslot of length S. The remaining fraction of the timeslot, consisting of a time window of length $S - X$ wherein $\widetilde{P}_k$ is inactive, is modelled as an interfering periodic zero-laxity *fake L-task* with the following attributes: $\tau_{\text{fake}} \overset{\text{def}}{=} \langle T_{\text{fake}} = S, D_{\text{fake}} = S - X, C_{\text{fake}} = S - X, L \rangle$. This standard task set transformation technique, for analytical convenience, was first used (for single-criticality workloads) for NSP-F server sizing by Souza et al. and is explained in [13], p. 702. This conceptual fake task along with the real tasks mapped to server $\widetilde{P}_k$, i.e., $\tau(\widetilde{P}_k) \cup \{\tau_{\text{fake}}\}$ are tested with the mixed-criticality schedulability uniprocessor analysis of Ekberg and Yi [4]. This analysis scales the deadlines of H-tasks (if needed) to make the task set schedulable in both H- and L-mode. If the analysis succeeds, the scaled H-task deadlines are output.

Computing $X_{\widetilde{P}_k}$ is an iterative process whose objective is to minimise the value of X (duration of periodic reserve allocated to $\widetilde{P}_k$). This minimum value of X that works corresponds to the optimal value for $X_{\widetilde{P}_k}$. To obtain it we iteratively sample the interval $X \in [0, S]$ using binary search and applying the test of Ekberg and Yi at each iteration, until the desired level of precision. Note that for each feasible value of X, Ekberg and Yi's algorithm could output different task deadline scale factors, in the general case.

Similarly, we compute the server budget $X_{\widetilde{P}_k}$ for each L-server $\widetilde{P}_k$. This is a simpler procedure because L-servers are only active in L-mode. So, there is no need to use the mixed-criticality schedulability test of Ekberg an Yi; the standard (single-criticality) optimal server sizing method for NPS-F is used [13] instead. Again, the attributes of a fake task are computed in a similar way, i.e., $\tau_{\text{fake}} \overset{\text{def}}{=} \langle T_{\text{fake}} = S, D_{\text{fake}} = S - X, C_{\text{fake}} = S - X, L \rangle$. The total demand of an L-server $\widetilde{P}_k$ along with the fake task τ_{fake} is given as follows:

$$\text{DBF}(\tau(\widetilde{P}_k) \cup \{\tau_{\text{fake}}\}, t, L) = \text{DBF}(\tau(\widetilde{P}_k), t, L) + \text{DBF}(\tau_{\text{fake}}, t, L).$$

If $\forall t > 0$, $\text{DBF}(\tau(\widetilde{P}_k) \cup \{\tau_{\text{fake}}\}, t, L) \leq t$, then this server is schedulable with a budget of X. As in the case of H-servers discussed previously, Algorithm 3 minimises the value of X. The process of computing $\forall t > 0$, $\text{DBF}(\tau(\widetilde{P}_k) \cup \{\tau_{\text{fake}}\}, t, L) \leq t$ can be sped up with the QPA* algorithm.

---

[1] Setting S to an integral fraction of DT_{min} was handy for proving a utilisation bound for NPS-F in [3], but in fact the DBF-based server-sizing by Sousa et al. [13] allows for dropping this constraint. In this paper, we just stick to tradition.

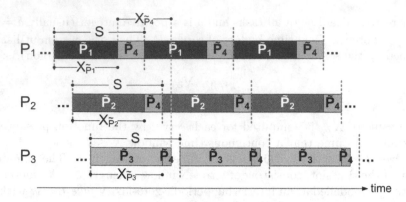

Fig. 1. Mapping of $m'' = 4$ servers to $m = 3$ processors. Three servers ($\widetilde{P}_1$ to $\widetilde{P}_3$) never migrate and the remaining timeslot portions on each processor are re-used for mapping $\widetilde{P}_4$. The timeslot boundaries on different processors are shifted accordingly, such that the reserves of the migrating server never overlap in time. NPS-F-MC assigns H-tasks to non-migrating servers.

If the L-servers are allowed to migrate among different processors then the task set is schedulable if the sum of inflated utilisations of all servers does not exceed m, the number of processors in the platform.

(iii) Server-to-processor mapping: We employ the so-called "semi-partitioned" mapping from the original NPS-F. This ensures that at least m servers never migrate; in our case, it is the H-servers that do not migrate and there can be at most m of those. Figure 1 is an example of this mapping arrangement.

5 Other Derivative Approaches

We now formulate other MC scheduling algorithm variants drawing from NPS-F and the scheduling with deadline-scaling by Ekberg and Yi: NPS-F-IMA, a strictly partitioned variant of NPS-F-MC, and SP-EKB which differs from NPS-F-MC mainly in that tasks of mixed criticalities can be scheduled together in the same server (potentially leading to migration of H-tasks). For comparison, we also formulate cNPS-F, which foregoes deadline scaling but instead sizes H-servers only considering the H-WCETs (i.e., the "conservative approach" of Sect. 4). Finally P-EKB is the partitioned multiprocessor version of Ekberg and Yi's algorithm. Studying these variants helps understand the performance trade-offs of different scheduling arrangements and safety requirements.

IMA-mindful Variant (NPS-F-IMA). The Integrated Modular Avionics (IMA) standard ARINC 653 enforces spatial and temporal partitioning to ensure safety aspects and enable incremental development and certification. However, NPS-F-MC allows L-servers to migrate among different processors.

For a scheduling arrangement more inline with IMA standards, we propose a variant (NPS-F-IMA) that disallows the migration of L-servers and sizes their budgets accordingly.

Algorithm 4 IMA-mindful (NPS-F-IMA)

Additional code to add between lines 8 and 9 in Algorithm 1	Additional code to add between lines 14 to 15 in Algorithm 1
1: **for** $(q := m_H'' + 1; q \leq 2 \cdot m_H''; q++)$ **do**	
2: Create a server $\widetilde{P}_q$ ▷ Note that $S = DT_{min}/\delta$	7: **if** $(m'' - m_H'' > m)$ **then**
3: $X_{\widetilde{P}_{q-m_H''}} := $ Mixed-Criticality-Inflate$(\widetilde{P}_{q-m_H''}) \cdot S$	**return** FAILURE
4: Create $\tau_{\text{fake}} = \langle T_{\text{fake}} := S, D_{\text{fake}} := C_{\text{fake}} := X_{\widetilde{P}_{q-m_H''}}, L \rangle$	8: **end if**
	9: **for** $(q := m_H'' + 1; q \leq 2 \cdot m_H''; q++)$ **do**
5: $\tau(\widetilde{P}_q) := \tau(\widetilde{P}_q) \cup \{\tau_{\text{fake}}\}$	10: $\tau(\widetilde{P}_q) := \tau(\widetilde{P}_q) \setminus \{\tau_{\text{fake}} \in \tau(\widetilde{P}_q)\}$
6: **end for**	11: **end for**

The pseudocode for NPS-F-IMA is derived by adding a few lines of pseudocode to Algorithm 1, as described in Algorithm 3. As we know, each H-server is mapped to one processor. The leftover portion of the timeslot on such a processor can be turned into an L-server. Assume that m_H'' is the number of H-servers. Then up to m_H'' L-servers each share a processor with an H-server. Assume that H-server $\widetilde{P}_q$ and L-server $\widetilde{P}_r$ share a processor P_m. Let $X_{\widetilde{P}_q}$ be the size of periodic reserve allocated to $\widetilde{P}_q$. Then $\widetilde{P}_r$ should be filled with L-tasks such that its periodic reserve size never exceeds $S - X_{\widetilde{P}_r}$. In order to ensure this requirement, we add to $\widetilde{P}_r$ a fake task $\tau_{\text{fake}} = \langle T_{\text{fake}} = S, D_{\text{fake}} = X_{\widetilde{P}_q}, C_{\text{fake}} = X_{\widetilde{P}_q}, L \rangle$, that corresponds to the workload of $\widetilde{P}_q$, before adding any real task into it. The method ensures that, after the task-to-server assignment completes, the size of the periodic reserve for $\widetilde{P}_r$ (which is computed based on the computational requirements of the *real* tasks assigned to it), never exceeds $S - X_{\widetilde{P}_q}$.

This procedure is repeated for all servers indexed $m_H'' + 1$ to $2 \cdot m_H''$. The pseudocode of this additional code that adds fake tasks to L-servers is presented in Algorithm 4 (lines 1 to 6). An L-server that does not share the processor with an H-server is not subject to this and can therefore use the full timeslot if needed. The NPS-F-IMA algorithm declares failure, if the number of L-servers exceeds the number of processors (see lines 7 to 8 in Algorithm 4). Once, L-servers are instantiated, these "placeholder" fake tasks are removed (see lines 9 to 11 in Algorithm 4). The inflated utilisation of all the servers is then computed. In the server-to-processor mapping phase, each H-server $\widetilde{P}_k$ is mapped to processor P_k with the same index. An L-server $\widetilde{P}_k$, whose index lies in the range $m_H'' + 1$ to m'' is mapped to processor $P_{k-m_H''}$.

Non-deadline-scaled cNPS-F. To assess the benefits from deadline-scaling in semi-partitioned scheduling, we define cNPS-F, a variant not using deadline-scaling. It uses the same bin-packing but (i) bases scheduling decisions on the real deadlines also in L-mode and (ii) uses only the H-WCETs for H-server sizing.

P-EKB and SP-EKB. Ekberg and Yi's approach, formulated for uniprocessors, can be used for multiprocessor scheduling with processor partitioning. We call this approach P-EKB. Tasks are assigned to the m processors via bin-packing (we assume First-Fit). On each processor, to test the feasibility of each assignment, the deadline scaling algorithm is used, as a schedulability test. Each time that a new task is assigned, the deadline scale factors of already assigned tasks are computed anew. This arrangement is migration-free but L-tasks and H-tasks are scheduled together on each processor, without strict isolation.

Similarly, for a semi-partitioned approach that borrows from NPS-F but without the server-level isolation of H-tasks and L-tasks, one could perform this bin-packing over m'' bins (as many as needed; not necessarily bound to m) and then create mixed-criticality servers out of those, which are mapped to the m processors as in NPS-F. We call this arrangement SP-EKB. One thing to note is that, for the purpose of sizing servers under SP-EKB, the "fake task" modelling the periodic unavaibility of the processor to the server has to be modelled as an H-task – unlike what was the case for MC-NPS-F. The reason for this is that, in the general case, neighboring servers may have both H-tasks and L-tasks meaning that it would not be possible in the H-mode to drop the server arrangement and collapse to pure partitioning/use of an entire processor's full capacity for a server's H-tasks. This means that, all other things being equal, a server would have greater inflated utilisation under SP-EKB than under MC-NPS-F.

Although SP-EKB dominates P-EKB (*if* the same task ordering is used for both algorithms), it allows the migration of high-criticality tasks, which may be undesirable for in practice. Table 1 summarises the different design aspects.

Table 1. Comparison of scheduling approaches

Algorithm	Scheduling class	Deadline scaling	Server-based	H-task/L-task isol.	H-task migration
NPS-F-MC	semi-part.	YES	YES	YES	NO
NPS-F-IMA	part.	YES	YES	YES	NO
cNPS-F	semi-part.	NO	YES	YES	NO
P-EKB	part.	YES	NO	NO	NO
SP-EKB	semi-part.	YES	NO	NO	YES

6   Evaluation

Experimental Setup. To evaluate the theoretical scheduling effectiveness of the approaches presented, we apply the respective offline schedulability tests to synthetic task sets, whose generation is controlled with the following parameters:

- L-mode utilisations (U_i^L): Generated using the UUnifast-discard algorithm [14] for unbiased distribution. C_i^L is derived as $U_i^L \cdot T_i$.

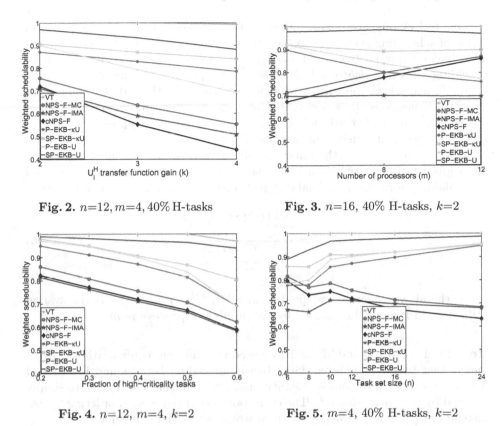

Fig. 2. $n{=}12, m{=}4, 40\%$ H-tasks

Fig. 3. $n{=}16,\ 40\%$ H-tasks, $k{=}2$

Fig. 4. $n{=}12,\ m{=}4,\ k{=}2$

Fig. 5. $m{=}4,\ 40\%$ H-tasks, $k{=}2$

- Task period (T_i): Generated with a log-uniform distribution, in the range of 10 ms to 100 ms, i.e., $T_i = 10^x : x \in [log_{10}10, log_{10}100]$.
- Task deadline (D_i): The scheduling approaches discussed work for constrained deadlines ($D_i{\leq}T_i$) but this evaluation assumes implicit deadlines ($D_i{=}T_i$).
- Distribution of high and low criticality tasks: The fraction of H-tasks in the task set is configurable. (For an integer number of H-tasks, we round up.)
- H-mode utilisation (U_i^H): Derived from U_i^L via a transfer function $f(U_i^L, k)$ with a parameter k. For small values of U_i^L, $f(U_i^L, k) \approx k \cdot U_i^L$ but for greater values the gain is progressively smaller, so that $U_i^L \leq f(U_i^L, k) \leq 1, \forall\ U_i^L \in [0,\ 1]$. For details, see the Appendix of our TR [15]. C_i^H is computed as $T_i {\cdot} U_i^H$.

The resolution is microsecond. Each task set is generated for a given target utilisation $U^* = x * m : x \in (0, 1]$, where m is the number of processors. For each combination of input parameters explored we generate 1000 task sets.

We compare the scheduling approaches listed in Table 1. To keep the number of plots in check, in each experiment we vary one parameter with the others fixed. We also plot a "validity test" (VT), namely: $(U^L \leq m) \wedge (U^H \leq m)$. This test (a necessary but not sufficient condition for schedulability) rejects trivially infeasible tasks sets. Its curve over-approximates the feasible task sets.

Due to lack of space instead of providing plots comparing the algorithms in terms of scheduling success ratio (i.e., the fraction of task sets deemed schedulable under the respective schedulability test), we condense this information by providing plots of *weighted schedulability*.[2] This performance metric is adopted from [16] and allows condensing what would have been three-dimensional plots into two dimensions. It is a weighted average, in which more weight is given to task-sets with higher utilisation, i.e., task-sets that are supposedly harder to schedule. Specifically, using the notation from [17]:

Let $S_y(\tau, p)$ represent the binary result (0 or 1) of the schedulability test y for a given task-set τ with an input parameter p. Then $W_y(p)$, the weighted schedulability for some schedulability test y as a function of parameter p, is:

$$W_y(p) = \frac{\sum_{\forall \tau} \left(\bar{U}^L(\tau) \cdot S_y(\tau, p) \right)}{\sum_{\forall \tau} \bar{U}^L(\tau)} \tag{5}$$

In the above equation (adapted from [17]), $\bar{U}^L(\tau) \overset{\text{def}}{=} \frac{U^L(\tau)}{m}$ is the system utilisation in L-mode, normalised by the number of processors m.

Results. For P-EKB and SP-EKB, we used two different configurations: "-κU" means that tasks are indexed with H-tasks preceding L-tasks and in order of non-increasing U_i^L, for same-criticality tasks. "-U" means that tasks are simply indexed by non-increasing U_i^L. The corresponding variants with ordering by D_i, instead of U_i^L, almost always performed worse, so we don't include them.

For all four parameters varied (transfer function gain k, number of processors m, fraction of H-tasks, number of tasks n), most of the time[3] SP-EKB outperforms P-EKB. In turn, P-EKB usually outperforms NPS-F-MC and, by a larger margin, cNPS-F. Figure 3 is an exception, with P-EKB dropping in performance, as m rises, contrary to the other algorithms, and being overtaken by NPS-F-MC and NPS-F-IMA. This is because, when both the system utilisation (normalised by m) and the number of processors are kept the same during task generation but m increases, the average U_i^L also increases. This implies increased bin-packing fragmentation for non-server-based partitioned approaches.

Some conclusions drawn from these experiments:

- Semi-partitioning helps moderately but noticeably with performance. (Compare NPS-F-MC to NPS-F-IMA and SP-EKB to P-EKB).
- For SP-EKB and P-EKB, the choice of task ordering for the bin-packing matters a lot.

---

[2] The plots of (non-weighted) schedulability can still be found in the Appendix of our TR [15].

[3] Recall that, for the same configuration, SP-EKB strictly dominates P-EKB. However, some task sets schedulable by SP-EKB-κU are unschedulable by P-EKB-U (and vice versa) and some tasks schedulable by SP-EKB-U are unschedulable by P-EKB-κU (and vice versa).

– The isolation of H-tasks from L-tasks, through separate servers for the two task categories, sharply penalises performance. (Compare NPS-F-MC to SP-EKB.) By comparison, the performance hit from disallowing L-server migration is smaller. (Compare NPS-F-MC with NPS-F-IMA.)

Ultimately, the choice of scheme will depend on the kind of scheduling guarantees and isolation the particular application scenario requires, but our experiments explore the performance ceilings associated with each arrangement.

7   Conclusions and Future Work

This work brought together server-based semi-partitioning and deadline-scaling techniques for mixed-criticality scheduling. Our main contribution, the scheduling algorithm NPS-F-MC, offers isolation between tasks of different criticalities but allows low-criticality tasks to migration, for better system utilisation. Our experiments show that deadline scaling also works well in a semi-partitioned context. However, enforcing complete scheduling isolation, can be expensive. In practice, different application requirements might mean that any task migration is to be avoided or, conversely, that complete scheduling isolation between task of different criticalities is not a requirement, as long as schedulability is ensured even in the case of mode change. For these cases, we therefore formulate the related scheduling algorithms NPS-F-IMA and SP-EKB, respectively. Our experimental results of theoretical schedulability offer some preliminary exploration of the performance tradeoffs when considering different scheduling arrangements: partitioning vs semi-partitioning, scheduling isolation for tasks of different criticalities by use of separate servers vs mixed-criticality scheduling within the same server, use of deadline scaling in the context of a semi-partitioned approach.

As future work, we intend to also incorporate the effects of task contention over cache and memory into the schedulability tests.

Acknowledgments. We would like to thank Pontus Ekberg for clarifying to us some aspects of his algorithm.

This work was partially supported by National Funds through FCT/MEC (Portuguese Foundation for Science and Technology) and co-financed by ERDF (European Regional Development Fund) under the PT2020 Partnership, within the CISTER Research Unit (CEC/04234); also by FCT/MEC and the EU ARTEMIS JU within project ARTEMIS/0001/2013- JU grant nr. 621429 (EMC2).

References

1. Burns, A., Davis, R.: Mixed criticality systems: A review, TR. Computer Science, U. of York, UK (2013)
2. Vestal, S.: Preemptive scheduling of multi-criticality systems with varying degrees of execution time assurance. In: Proceedings of the RTSS, pp. 239–243 (2007)
3. Bletsas, K., Andersson, B.: Preemption-light multiprocessor scheduling of sporadic tasks with high utilisation bound. In: Proceedings of the RTSS (2009)

218 M.A. Awan et al.

4. Ekberg, P., Yi, W.: Bounding and shaping the demand of mixed-criticality sporadic tasks. In: Proceedings of the ECRTS, pp. 135–144 (2012)
5. Baruah, S., Bonifaci, V., D'Angelo, G., Li, H., Marchetti-Spaccamela, A., van der Ster, S., Stougie, L.: The preemptive uniprocessor scheduling of mixed-criticality implicit-deadline sporadic task systems. In: Proceedings of the ECRTS, pp. 145–154 (2012)
6. Federal Aviation Authority, CAST-32: Multi-core Processors (2014). https://www.faa.gov/
7. Baruah, S., Mok, A., Rosier, L.: Preemptively scheduling hard-real-time sporadic tasks on one processor. In: Proceedings of the RTSS, pp. 182–190 (1990)
8. Ekberg, P., Yi, W.: Bounding and shaping the demand of generalized mixed-criticality sporadic task systems. Real-Time Syst. **50**(1), 48–86 (2014)
9. Masrur, A., Müller, D., Werner, M.: Bi-level deadline scaling for admission control in mixed- criticality systems. In: RTCSA, pp. 100–109 (2015)
10. Easwaran, A.: Demand-based scheduling of mixed-criticality sporadic tasks on one processor. In: Proceedings of the RTSS (2013)
11. Bletsas, K., Petters, S.M.: Using NPS-F for mixed-criticality multicore systems. In: Proceedings of the RTSS WiP (2012)
12. Zhang, F., Burns, A.: Improvement to quick processor-demand analysis for EDF-scheduled real-time systems. In: Proceedings of the ECRTS, pp. 76–86 (2009)
13. Sousa, P.B., Bletsas, K., Tovar, E., Souto, P.F., Åkesson, B.: Unified overhead-aware schedulability analysis for slot-based task-splitting. Real-Time Syst. **50**(5–6), 680–735 (2014)
14. Bini, E., Buttazzo, G.: Measuring the performance of schedulability tests. Real-Time Syst. **30**(1–2), 129–154 (2009)
15. Awan, M.A., Bletsas, K., Souto, P.F., Tovar, E.: Semi-partitioned mixed-criticality scheduling, TR. CISTER/ISEP (2016). http://www.cister.isep.ipp.pt/docs/CISTER-TR-161102
16. Bastoni, A., Brandenburg, B., Anderson, J.: Cache-related preemption and migration delays: empirical approximation and impact on schedulability. In: Proceedings of the OSPERT, pp. 33–44 (2010)
17. Burns, A., Davis, R.: Adaptive mixed criticality scheduling with deferred preemption. In: Proceedings of the RTSS, pp. 21–30 (2014)

Power and Energy

DVFS Space Exploration in Power Constrained Processing-in-Memory Systems

Marko Scrbak[1(✉)], Joseph L. Greathouse[2], Nuwan Jayasena[2], and Krishna Kavi[1]

[1] University of North Texas, Denton, TX, USA
markoscrbak@my.unt.edu, krishna.kavi@unt.edu
[2] Advanced Micro Devices, Inc. (AMD), Sunnyvale, CA, USA
{joseph.greathouse,nuwan.jayasena}@amd.com

Abstract. In order to deliver high performance under stringent power constraints, future systems may include die-stacked memories with processing-in-memory (PIM) cores. Because of their proximity to the memory, PIMs are expected to target applications which require high bandwidth, implying that PIMs do not need the same computational capabilities as traditional host processor and can therefore be implemented using slower, low-leakage transistors to increase energy efficiency. Such systems must carefully balance design-time choices, such as the circuits used to build the devices, and run-time choices, such as DVFS states and the preferred hardware platform on which to run the application. This paper explores these parameters in a GPGPU PIM system with a large compute-optimized host and a collection of bandwidth-optimized PIMs. We develop high-level performance and power models and use them to find optimal DVFS and kernel placement decisions for a series of GPGPU applications targeting maximum energy efficiency. We find, for instance, that the energy efficiency of PIM systems is greatly affected by DVFS; simply selecting the optimum hardware (host/PIM) results in $7\times$ higher ED^2 than migrating work in conjunction with DVFS.

Keywords: Processing-in-Memory · DVFS · GPGPU · High performance computing · Energy efficiency · Computer architecture · 3D-DRAM

1 Introduction

With the breakdown of Dennard scaling, architects rely on increasingly sophisticated dynamic voltage and frequency scaling (DVFS) controls to optimize performance while meeting stringent power, energy, and thermal targets [2,5,15,19]. For related reasons, modern processors are increasingly adding heterogeneous accelerators, most commonly GPUs [10,20]. As techniques such as DVFS and heterogeneous processing increase the computational efficiency of processors, the memory system is becoming a growing performance and energy bottleneck [4]. Recent stacked memory technologies, such as Hybrid Memory Cube (HMC) [16]

© Springer International Publishing AG 2017
J. Knoop et al. (Eds.): ARCS 2017, LNCS 10172, pp. 221–233, 2017.
DOI: 10.1007/978-3-319-54999-6_17

and High Bandwidth Memory (HBM) [9], can provide higher bandwidth and reduced access energy compared to traditional technologies such as DDR4. Some researchers propose to use 3D die stacking to place cores in a logic layer under the memory dies and migrate some computation closer to memory, a configuration referred to as processing-in-memory (PIM) [1,7,13,17,21,23]. In these studies, a collection of PIM devices are used along with a traditional "host" processor [17,18,21,23]. The host can be optimized for traditional compute-heavy workloads and can be implemented using high-performance transistors. In contrast, PIMs can be optimized for bandwidth-intensive workloads, can be implemented using lower-power circuits, and can be smaller and run at lower frequencies. This can significantly increase energy efficiency and reduce difficulties from tight PIM thermal constraints [6].

In this paper, we evaluate the effects of DVFS on the power and performance of a PIM-enabled system while taking into account the architectural and process differences between a compute-focused host and PIMs optimized for memory bandwidth. We develop power and performance models which capture the key differences between these devices and use them to study the design space. Our findings show that running some compute-intensive kernels on low-frequency host cores decreases ED^2 by 2×, while others see up to 4.5× benefit from the lower-powered PIMs. Memory-intensive applications can reduce ED^2 10× compared to the host when the PIMs can run at lower frequencies. Compared to simply migrating workloads, making DVFS decisions in conjunction with migration decisions can result in a 7× reduction in ED^2. In addition, a mix of DVFS and workload migration can allow applications to achieve higher performance under tight power caps. To the best of our knowledge, we are the first to explore the impact of DVFS on power and performance of GPU-based PIM systems. The key contributions of this paper are:

- An analytical power model which captures the differences in leakage and dynamic power of host and PIM devices.
- An evaluation of optimal hardware platform (host vs. PIM) for OpenCL™ kernels in order to achieve maximum energy efficiency.
- Evaluation of maximum achievable performance under different power constraints.

The rest of the paper is organized as follows. In Sect. 2, we explain the system organization. Section 3 describes the performance and power models. Section 4 describes the details of our methodology and experimental setup. In Sect. 5, we present our results and discuss the findings. Section 6 covers the related work and Sect. 7 concludes the paper.

2   Baseline System Organization

Figure 1(a) shows an illustration of the system we study. At the heart of the node is a heterogeneous chip containing both a CPU and GPU. This design is also equipped with 3D-stacked DRAM [9,16], which can deliver the high bandwidth

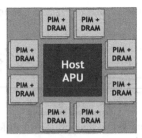

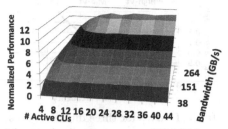

(a) A heterogeneous processor consisting of a host APU and multiple 3D DRAM stacks with PIMs. PIMs are low-power GPGPU cores and as such can utilize the high in-stack memory bandwidth

(b)   *DeviceMemory.readGlobalMemoryCoalesced* scaling curve. Performance scales with bandwidth and stagnates with increase in compute power. Such a kernel is classified as memory bound.

Fig. 1. Baseline system (a) and kernel performance scaling on GPUs (b)

necessary for the on-chip GPU. 3D die stacking allows for tight integration of optimized DRAM and logic dies. As such, it allows near-data computing in the form of PIM, where computation devices embedded on the logic layer can utilize the high in-stack bandwidth to improve the performance of memory-intensive applications [1,17,21,23]. A multitude of PIM designs have been explored, such as PIMs built from low-power CPU cores [17,21], GPGPUs [23], and reconfigurable logic [7]. While low-power CPU PIMs were shown to be very energy efficient, they were able to utilize only a fraction of the available in-stack memory bandwidth [8]. A multitude of CPU cores could push more bandwidth but would exceed the power and thermal envelope of the memory stack. Zhang et al. proposed a PIM architecture based on GPU accelerators (GPGPUs) [23]. These highly multi-threaded vector processors are suitable for running highly-parallel application kernels and provide high computational and memory throughput. At the same time, the GPU compute units are simple in-order cores, which makes the architecture energy efficient and provides opportunity for embedding them in the logic layer of 3D-stacked DRAM. Furthermore, mature programming models (e.g., OpenCL^{TM}) ease the programmability of such devices. In this study, we focus on GPUs as PIMs and compare their power and performance to the host on-chip GPUs. In a heterogeneous PIM system, GPU PIM compute units will be aimed at improving the energy efficiency and performance of memory-intensive code. The host GPU will primarily be used for compute-intensive code, since it has less memory bandwidth and more compute resources than the PIMs.

3   Performance and Power Models

3.1   Performance Model

In order to assess the performance for our target hardware configurations, we rely on an analytical GPU performance modeling framework [22]. Such models

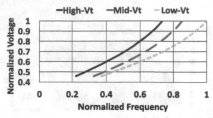
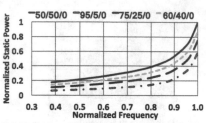
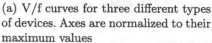

(a) V/f curves for three different types of devices. Axes are normalized to their maximum values

(b) Relative leakage values for different Vt distributions.

Fig. 2. V/f characteristics and relative leakage power for different types of devices.

are more effective for large design space explorations than cycle-level simulators, and they capture enough detail to reasonably estimate future hardware performance [14].

The model described in [22] has between 10% and 30% error, which is comparable to state-of-the-art system simulators [3]. The idea is to run a series of GPU kernels on native hardware and collect performance statistics for each kernel invocation for different hardware configurations. This allows us to obtain knowledge about how each kernel's performance scales with hardware resources such as frequency, memory bandwidth and compute units. An example of kernel scaling characteristic is shown in Fig. 1(b).

Our model was built from over 200 kernels at 720 different hardware configurations across various frequencies, memory bandwidths and number of active compute units on an AMD FirePro™ W9100 GPU. The gathered scaling statistics are clustered into groups with similar scaling characteristics. A machine learning model is then trained which is later used to classify previously unseen kernels into one of the scaling groups. We finally use the kernel scaling characteristic to extrapolate kernel performance from a native hardware configuration to a desired target hardware configuration (host/PIM).

3.2 Power Model

The total power for host/PIM devices is calculated as the sum of chip dynamic power and leakage power. We modeled dynamic and leakage power in a way that they capture host and PIM architectural differences (number of CUs, frequency) and differences in process technology (host - high performance process, PIM - low power process). The difference in process technology affects the voltage/frequency (V/f) characteristics of the devices which, in turn, affects dynamic and leakage power. Our models assume a feature size of 14 nm.

DVFS Characteristics. Modern computer chips are designed using multiple types of transistors, i.e. a mixture of low-, medium-, and high-threshold transistors, to target different design tradeoffs, e.g. high-performance vs. low power.

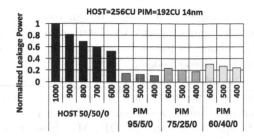

Fig. 3. Leakage power values for host and PIM with different Vt distributions. A low-power PIM with minimal leakage power (such as PIM-95/5) would be desirable in order to minimize total PIM power consumption.

Low-threshold voltage (Low-Vt) devices are used in timing-critical paths, but have high leakage power. High-threshold voltage (High-Vt) devices have low leakage power but are slower, and are typically used in circuits that are off the timing-critical paths. Medium-threshold voltage (Mid-Vt) devices offer a tradeoff between High-Vt and Low-Vt devices by having medium power requirements and medium delay. In general, low power chips are designed using a larger percentage of High-Vt devices and high-performance chips with a larger percentage of Mid-Vt and Low-Vt devices. The host processor is assumed to execute compute-intensive code and will therefore be a high-performance device. PIMs are assumed to be an equivalent of a low-power device, and will have significantly lower leakage power than the host and run on lower frequencies and consume less dynamic power.

Figure 2(a) shows V/f characteristics of three different types of devices for a 14 nm process. Instead of modelling a V/f characteristic of a design with a specific Vt distribution, we chose the V/f characteristics of both the host and the PIMs to be equivalent to that of Mid-Vt devices and limit the operating frequency ranges for host and PIM. We used this method because the Vt ratios change based on the process maturity and process variation and thus it would be impractical to model specific V/f curves for host/PIM. We choose the operating frequency range for host to be 600 MHz–1000 Mhz and that of PIM 400 MHz–600 MHz. We also study the impact on leakage power if the frequency ranges require a different mix than the nominal one we picked.

Leakage Power. Leakage power depends on operating voltage, temperature, and the ratios of devices used in a chip design. We pick the ratios for host to be representative of a high performance GPU with a 50/50 High-Vt/Mid-Vt distribution. We performed a parameter sweep of three different device ratios for the PIMs and observed their impact on leakage power. High-Vt/Mid-Vt ratios included in the model are 60/40, 75/25, and 95/5 respectively. We model the leakage power by estimating the leakage power value of host at the highest voltage-frequency (V/f) point and then scale it to other V/f points using relative leakage values between host and PIM. The relative leakage values between different ratios are obtained from a circuit design tool. Figure 2(b) shows the relative leakage values for four different Vt distributions studied. Derived leakage power numbers are shown in Fig. 3. At identical frequencies (600 MHz) PIM devices will have up to 3× lower leakage than the host.

It is important to target low-leakage PIM designs for several reasons. First, the power dissipation needs to be minimal so as to not exceed the 3d memory stacks' power and thermal limitations. Second, a higher power dissipation would increase the stack temperature and the DRAM refresh rate. Third, most of the applications executed on PIM will have lower dynamic power and therefore leakage power will take up a significant portion in PIM total power. For the rest of the paper we assume a 95/5 High-Vt/Mid-Vt distribution for the PIMs.

Dynamic Power. The dynamic power of the host and PIM devices is a function of the target hardware configuration (frequency, voltage, number of CUs) as well as the running kernels switching activity. We calculate the dynamic power of host/PIM devices by scaling the dynamic power of a base hardware configuration such as an AMD FirePro™ W9100 GPU to a desired target hardware configuration (host/PIM - Table 1) using the following equation:

$$P_{dynamic} = MAXDP * \frac{CU_{target}}{CU_{base}} * \frac{f_{target}}{f_{base}} * \frac{V_{target}^2}{V_{base}^2} * C_{AC} * C_{scaled} \quad (1)$$

The idea is to scale a known *maximum dynamic power (MAXDP)* consumed by a high-end GPU (such as the AMD FirePro W9100 GPU) at a given frequency, voltage, and number of compute units, to a target hardware configuration *(f, V, CUs)*. The assumption is that the PIM and host CUs will be architecturally similar to present high-end GPUs, and therefore the maximum dynamic power consumed per each CU will be roughly the same for the same feature size, frequency and voltage. This way we can estimate the maximum dynamic power consumed by the target hardware, i.e. at 100% switching activity. The actual dynamic power consumed by a GPU kernel will depend on the chip switching activity (shown as C_{AC} in Eq. 1) during kernel execution. The total dynamic power will therefore be a fraction of the target maximum dynamic power. Target capacitance (as compared to the base GPU capacitance) will also be lower and ultimately will lower the target dynamic power. We factor this in as the last element of the equation C_{scaled}.

4   Methodology and Experimental Setup

4.1   Target Hardware Baseline

We assume the target node, as depicted in Fig. 1, will have a high-performance host APU and eight 3D DRAM stacks with low-power GPU PIM cores. Details of the target system are listed in Table 1. We set the PIMs' aggregate memory bandwidth to be 2× higher than the host's, assuming that only 50% of the

Table 1. Target system parameters

	host	PIM
# of CUs	256	192 (8 × 24)
Mem. bandwidth	1 TB/s	2 TB/s
Frequency (MHz)	600–1000	400–600
Tech. node	14 nm FinFET	14 nm FinFET
Process	High-performance	Low-power

possible in-stack bandwidth will be available to the host due to the high power consumption of the active links needed to support high off-chip memory bandwidth. Each of the eight PIM stacks is assumed to have 24 embedded low-power GPU CUs, for a total of 192 PIMs. The host APU is assumed to have 256 GPU Compute Units (CUs) and has more compute power than the eight PIM stacks. Such a high number of CUs is an optimistic assumption, however it will be achievable with future technology scaling.

4.2 Benchmark Selection

We selected 15 applications from a wide range of publicly available GPU benchmark suites. These benchmarks tend to exhibit enough parallelism to utilize, and are expected to scale to, the target hardware configurations. In addition, the benchmarks selected rely on algorithms for which we can easily split data and tasks such that the PIMs primarily access their local DRAM stacks. The 15 selected applications are categorized based on their performance scaling characteristics [12]. Compute bound benchmarks - *lavaMD, NBody, MonteCarloAsian, MaxFlops, CoMD* - contain mostly kernels which scale with compute resources. Memory bound benchmarks - *kmeans, MatrixTranspose, miniFE, DeviceMemory* - contain mostly kernels which scale with memory bandwidth. Balanced benchmarks - *b+tree, MatrixMultiplication* exhibit different scaling behavior for different compute/bandwidth ratios. We also select benchmarks which have a mix of compute/memory/balanced kernels - *backprop, GEMM, BoxFilter, XSbench* to show the impact of kernel placement on total runtime/power consumption when kernels have different scaling characteristics.

4.3 Experiments

We collected performance counters for each kernel invocation of the 15 benchmarks and estimate their power/performance using previously described power and performance models. We also include the energy spent on memory accesses. We evaluated the optimal hardware choices to run the kernels when using DVFS and compared them to cases where all benchmark kernels run on either the host or PIM devices, while targeting maximum energy efficiency (minimum ED^2). Figure 4 shows the motivation of the potential tradeoffs. We also evaluated the

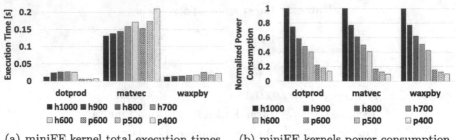

(a) miniFE kernel total execution times   (b) miniFE kernels power consumption

Fig. 4. miniFE kernels runtime (a) and power consumption (b) for host 600 MHz–1000 MHz and PIM 400 MHz–600 MHz

maximum performance under power constraints and show how optimal hardware choice shifts to PIMs, which consume significantly less power. It is assumed that once a kernel is running on the host/PIM it will remain there (i.e., it will not migrate between devices) for all invocations of that kernel.

5   Results and Analysis

For the purpose of analyzing the energy efficiency we evaluated the energy-delay^2 metric because it represents a tradeoff between energy and performance. Figure 5 compares the ED^2 value for ED^2 optimal placement with ED^2 of host-only and PIM-only placement. We observe that for highly compute intensive benchmarks like *MaxFlops* and *NBody*, the host has significantly better ED^2 and is the optimal choice. Interestingly, these two applications achieve minimum ED^2 when running at the highest DVFS points. This implies that PIMs aren't necessarily the most energy-efficient choice for computation. Other benchmarks have better ED^2 when all kernels run on the PIMs, except *CoMD* where 2 kernels have better ED^2 when running on the PIMs while the others are best on the host. Figure 5 shows how PIMs are an optimal choice in many cases when targeting

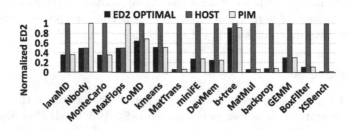

Fig. 5. ED^2 comparison when trying to optimize for minimum ED^2. Very high compute intensive applications achieve minimum ED^2 while running on host. This means that host will be more energy efficient for such applications than PIM regardless of the higher power consumption.

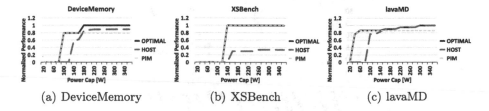

(a) DeviceMemory   (b) XSBench   (c) lavaMD

Fig. 6. Maximum performance under power constraints

energy efficiency. This shows that the addition of PIMs to a heterogeneous node architecture can yield high throughput and high energy efficiency even when compared to host running at lower DVFS states. In many cases, including applications that are somewhat compute-bound, the work would move to PIM, which significantly reduces power at the expense of small performance loss. Exceptions are highly compute intensive applications like *b+tree, MaxFlops, and NBody*.

5.1 Maximum Performance Under Power Constraints

The host can deliver higher performance for applications that are very compute intensive. The question remains whether this will remain true under power constraints, and at which point the PIMs will deliver better performance than the host. To confirm that PIMs are in many cases indeed a better choice, even when host is running at a lower DVFS state, we evaluated what is the maximum performance we can get from a benchmark when each kernel consumes less power than a specified power constraint. There will be a performance optimal hardware choice for each kernel, and this will change depending on the power limit. Figure 6 compares the maximum performance under different power caps for 3 benchmarks. We show a subset of all benchmarks because others show similar behavior and same conclusions can be made. We see that the host always consumes at least 100 W (at the lowest DVFS state) and cannot perform under power constraints lower than 100 W. PIMs can on the other hand deliver good performance even under tight power budgets due to their low power consumption. In cases of memory bound benchmarks like *XSBench*, PIMs always deliver significantly higher performance due to higher memory bandwidth. An interesting case is *lavaMD*, where the PIM outperforms the host at some intermediate DVFS state. This is because the application can compensate the lower performance of lower DVFS state by exploiting higher memory bandwidth.

5.2 Discussion

When optimizing applications for maximum energy efficiency, benchmarks which consist of heavily compute intensive kernels achieve $2\times$ lower ED^2 when running on host at highest DVFS states (1000 MHz). However, other compute intensive kernels achieve lower ED^2 when running on PIM ($1.5\times - 4.5\times$ lower than on host), while suffering minimum performance losses (20%–50%) over performance

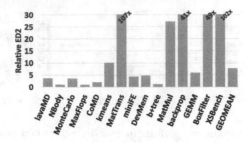

Fig. 7. Comparison of ED^2 values when host and PIM employ DVFS with a case where host and PIM run only at highest DVFS states (host-1000 MHz, PIM-600 MHz). By using DVFS in conjunction with PIMs we can on average improve the minimum achievable ED^2 by 7x, and in cases of memory intensive benchmarks by 40x – 100x.

optimal case. While optimal hardware choices play a significant role, the addition of DVFS to the system proves to be crucial in maximizing the energy efficiency. Figure 7 compares the minimum achievable ED^2 value of a host/PIM system with DVFS to a host/PIM system without DVFS (running on highest DVFS state). We can see that by using DVFS to complement the already energy-efficient system design we can on average improve the energy efficiency by 7×, and in some cases between 40× – 100×. When optimizing applications for maximum performance for systems with lower power budgets we can achieve 1.2× – 2.5× better performance if we pick the right hardware (host/ PIM) and allow for DVFS. For small power budgets, PIMs can achieve better performance than the host at a lower DVFS state, while for power budgets lower than 100 W, the host would exceed the power limit while PIMs would be able to remain operational and deliver performance comparable to host for a fraction of power consumed. Our findings strengthen the hypothesis of PIMs being a useful heterogeneous platform and show the importance of DVFS as a mean to maximize performance and energy efficiency in HPC systems with PIM. Additionally, our study allows for future exploration of optimizations when multiple applications are executing in the system by trading off power and performance of different applications to achieve combined optimum performance gains.

6   Related Work

Zhang et al. [23] proposed a PIM architecture based on GPGPUs and evaluated the performance and power benefits of such systems. However, this work only considered a single operating point for the host and PIMs, and evaluated host and PIM execution in isolation. We extend this work to include the characterization of the impact of DVFS and co-optimization of both host and PIM. In addition, we created power models which can capture the differences between host and PIM and evaluate the system on application level and not just kernel level.

Schulte et al. [11] investigated the effect of varying engine frequency/voltage, memory bandwidth and number of compute units on GPU performance and power. The authors explored DVFS for standalone GPUs. We instead consider the presence and co-optimization of heterogeneous execution engines (i.e., high-performance host and low-power PIM).

Ščrbak et al. [21] explored a variety of design choices in ARM-based PIM systems, including caches, frequency/voltage and their effect on the overall energy efficiency of the system. The research remained focused on ARM-based PIM architectures and doesn't explore GPUs as an alternative.

7 Conclusion

In this paper we explored the effects of DVFS on energy efficiency of a GPU PIM system while accounting for architectural and process differences of the host and PIM devices. We developed analytical power and performance models to capture these differences and use them to explore the PIM DVFS design space. Our findings show that a PIM system with DVFS is more energy-efficient than a PIM system without DVFS, and results in 7× lower ED^2 values on average. By utilizing DVFS for host we can additionally decrease ED^2 by 2× for compute-intensive applications and by 4.5× when using DVFS with PIMs. Furthermore, when using DVFS and low-power PIMs and optimizing performance for systems with tight power budgets, we can achieve 1.2×–2.5× better performance if we pick the right hardware (host/PIM) and DVFS point. Our study allows for future exploration of optimizations when multiple applications are simultaneously executing in the system. We will evaluate such optimizations in future work.

AMD, the AMD Arrow logo, AMD FirePro, and combinations thereof are trademarks of Advanced Micro Devices, Inc. OpenCL is a trademark of Apple Inc. used by permission by Khronos. Other names used herein are for identification purposes only and may be trademarks of their respective companies.

References

1. Ahn, J., Hong, S., Yoo, S., Mutlu, O., Choi, K.: A scalable processing-in-memory accelerator for parallel graph processing. In: Proceedings of the International Symposium on Computer Architecture (ISCA) (2015)
2. Akram, S., Sartor, J.B., Eeckhout, L.: DVFS performance prediction for managed multithreaded applications. In: International Symposium on Performance Analysis of Systems and Software (ISPASS) (2016)
3. Binkert, N., Beckmann, B., Black, G., Reinhardt, S.K., Saidi, A., Basu, A., Hestness, J., Hower, D.R., Krishna, T., Sardashti, S., Sen, R., Sewell, K., Shoaib, M., Vaish, N., Hill, M.D., Wood, D.A.: The gem5 simulator. ACM SIGARCH Comput. Archit. News 39(2), 1–7 (2011)
4. Black, B.: Die stacking is happening. Presented at MICRO (2013)
5. Cochran, R., Hankendi, C., Coskun, A.K., Reda, S.: Pack & Cap: adaptive DVFS and thread packing under power caps. In: Proceedings of the International Symposiyum on Microarchitecture (MICRO) (2011)

6. Eckert, Y., Jayasena, N., Loh, G.H.: Thermal feasibility of die-stacked processing in memory. In: Workshop on Near-Data Processing (WoNDP) (2014)
7. Farmahini-Farahani, A., Ahn, J.H., Morrow, K., Kim, N.S.: NDA: Near-DRAM acceleration architecture leveraging commodity DRAM devices and standard memory modules. In: Proceedings of the International Symposium on High Performance Computer Architecture (HPCA) (2015)
8. Islam, M., Ščrbak, M., Kavi, K.M., Ignatowski, M., Jayasena, N.: Improving node-level mapreduce performance using processing-in-memory technologies. In: Proceedings of the International European Conference on Parallel Processing (EuroPar) (2014)
9. Joint Electron Devices Engineering Council: High Bandwidth Memory (HBM) DRAM. JEDEC Document JESD235A (2015)
10. Krishnan, G., Bouvier, D., Zhang, L., Dongara, P.: Energy efficient graphics and multimedia in 28 nm Carrizo APU. Presented at Hot Chips (2015)
11. Lee, J., Sathisha, V., Schulte, M., Compton, K., Kim, N.S.: Improving throughput of power-constrained GPUs using dynamic voltage/frequency and core scaling. In: Proceedings of the International Conference on Parallel Architectures and Compilation Techniques (PACT) (2011)
12. Majumdar, A., Wu, G., Dev, K., Greathouse, J.L., Paul, I., Huang, W., Venugopal, A.K., Piga, L., Freitag, C., Puthoor, S.: A taxonomy of GPGPU performance scaling. In: Proceedings of the IEEE International Symposium on Workload Characterization (IISWC) (2015)
13. Nair, R., Antao, S.F., Bertolli, C., Bose, P., Brunheroto, J.R.: Active memory cube: a processing-in-memory architecture for exascale systems. IBM J. Res. Dev. **59**(2/3), 17:1–17:14 (2015)
14. Nowatzki, T., Menon, J., Ho, C.H., Sankaralingam, K.: gem5, GPGPUSim, McPAT, GPUWattch, "Your favorite simulator here" considered harmful. In: Workshop on Duplicating, Deconstructing, and Debunking (2014)
15. Paul, I., Manne, S., Arora, M., Bircher, W.L., Yalamanchili, S.: Cooperative boosting: needy versus greedy power management. In: Proceedings of the International Symposium on Computer Architecture (ISCA) (2013)
16. Pawlowski, J.T.: Hybrid Memory Cube (HMC). Presented at Hot Chips (2011)
17. Pugsley, S.H., Jestes, J., Zhang, H., Balasubramonian, R., Srinivasan, V., Buyuktosunoglu, A., Davis, A., Li, F.: NDC: analyzing the impact of 3D-stacked memory+logic devices on mapreduce workloads. In: Proceedings of the International Symposium on Performance Analysis of Systems and Software (ISPASS) (2014)
18. Schulte, M.J., Ignatowski, M., Loh, G.H., Beckmann, B.M., Brantley, W.C., Gurumurthi, S., Jayasena, N., Paul, I., Reinhardt, S.K., Rodgers, G.: Achieving exascale capabilities through heterogeneous computing. IEEE Micro **35**(4), 26–36 (2015)
19. Su, B., Gu, J., Shen, L., Huang, W., Greathouse, J.L., Wang, Z.: PPEP: online performance, power, and energy prediction framework and DVFS space exploration. In: Proceedings of the International Symposium on Microarchitecture (MICRO) (2014)
20. TOP 500 List: Titan - Cray XK7. https://www.top500.org/system/177975 (2012). Accessed 31 July 2016
21. Scrbak, M., Islam, M., Kavi, K.M., Ignatowski, M., Jayasena, N.: Processing-in-memory: exploring the design space. In: Pinho, L.M.P., Karl, W., Cohen, A., Brinkschulte, U. (eds.) ARCS 2015. LNCS, vol. 9017, pp. 43–54. Springer, Cham (2015). doi:10.1007/978-3-319-16086-3_4

22. Wu, G., Greathouse, J.L., Lyashevsky, A., Jayasena, N., Chiou, D.: GPGPU performance and power estimation using machine learning. In: Proceedings of the International Symposium on High Performance Computer Architecture (HPCA) (2015)
23. Zhang, D., Jayasena, N., Lyashevsky, A., Greathouse, J.L., Xu, L., Ignatowski, M.: TOP-PIM: throughput-oriented programmable processing in memory. In: Proceedings of the International Symposium on High-performance Parallel and Distributed Computing (HPDC) (2014)

Reducing Data Center Resource Over-Provisioning Through Dynamic Load Management for Virtualized Network Functions

Andreas Oeldemann[✉], Thomas Wild, and Andreas Herkersdorf

Chair for Integrated Systems, Technical University of Munich,
Arcisstr. 21, 80333 Munich, Germany
{andreas.oeldemann,thomas.wild,herkersdorf}@tum.de

Abstract. Network Function Virtualization aims at replacing specialized hardware network appliances by commodity servers. In this paper, we address sub-second variations in data center network workloads, which place highly volatile processing demands on the servers. This makes an efficient dimensioning of the hardware resources dedicated to network function execution challenging. Based on the observation that short-term peak workloads typically do not hit all machines at exactly the same time, we propose to enable the servers to reuse under-utilized resources of their peers by selectively redirecting packets when local resources are exhausted. To satisfy line rate performance demands, we present a hardware load management layer, which is located in the ingress path of each server. Our simulative evaluation shows that the load management layer can reduce the hardware resources required for network function execution by up to 24% while maintaining network throughput and latency performance. Especially in large data centers, these resource savings can significantly reduce network expenses.

1 Introduction

Today's telco and data center networks provide many services, which go far beyond offering connectivity among end-hosts. Intrusion detection systems scan traffic for security threats, firewalls filter packets based on access rules, and virtual private networks establish encrypted connections between remote networks. Due to compute-intense operations and stringent performance requirements, these *network functions* (NFs) are traditionally executed by specialized hardware appliances, so-called *middleboxes*. In the presence of volatile network workloads, dimensioning the capacity of these middleboxes is challenging. Typically, operators *over-provision* network resources to prevent performance degradation when peak workloads hit [6]. Due to their custom-tailored hardware design, middleboxes cannot be reused for other data center services in off-peak times [11] and thus leave valuable processing resources idle. With the introduction of *Network Function Virtualization* (NFV) to the data center, operators aim to reduce network costs through an increased deployment flexibility of network functions. By decoupling the NF functionality from the underlying hardware

© Springer International Publishing AG 2017
J. Knoop et al. (Eds.): ARCS 2017, LNCS 10172, pp. 234–247, 2017.
DOI: 10.1007/978-3-319-54999-6_18

platform and multiplexing multiple NFs on a single commodity server (further referred to as *network node*), operators obtain the flexibility to reassign consolidated infrastructure resources among NFs and other data center services as workload demands vary [11]. Centralized NFV *orchestrators* monitor network node utilization and adapt the allocation of resources in response to changes in processing demand. However, due to control latencies resulting from the spatial separation between the network nodes and the centralized control instance, as well as the time it takes to reassign resources and adapt network routing, reassignment of resources is primarily applied to workload fluctuations, which occur sufficiently slow (i.e. on timescales of hours, days and larger) and are well-predictable [15].

In this paper, we address resource dimensioning inefficiencies arising due to the fact that network workloads also vary on smaller, sub-second timescales, where centralized network control is unable to respond by reassigning processing resources in time. These fluctuations are partly caused by volatile network data rates [1], and partly by diverse per-packet processing demands among different NFs sharing the virtualized hardware resources of the same network node. Dimensioning the resources dedicated to processing such dynamic network workloads comes with a trade-off between utilization efficiency and *Quality-of-Service* (QoS). At one extreme, an over-provisioned dimensioning for maximum link load and the pessimistic assumption that all packets require the most compute-intensive processing guarantees that all packets are handled on the fly, but yields low hardware utilization and thus is not cost-efficient. At the other extreme, dimensioning for average link load and average computational complexity requires fewer hardware resources, but can lead to long packet queues, excess latency and eventually packet loss. Depending on the amount of tolerable queuing delays, operators typically opt for an economical over-provisioning sweet-spot between average and worst-case dimensioning.

We propose to increase the resource dimensioning efficiency by enabling network nodes to offload excess workloads by selectively redirecting packets to peers within their neighborhood. We exploit the fact that when multiple network nodes executing the same set of NFs are grouped in clusters, the probability that all network nodes are fully utilized at the same time is decreasing with a growing cluster size. By enabling network nodes to reuse under-utilized resources of their peers, we are able to reduce resource over-provisioning without incurring QoS drawbacks. To implement the offload of excess workloads, we extend each network node by a load management layer. In contrast to conventional load balancers, our load management layer is distributed to the ingress paths of the network nodes. This has the advantage that it can closely monitor the local resource utilization at high time-resolution and take offload decisions as soon as they become necessary. Since determining whether data should be processed locally or forwarded to another network node must occur on a packet-by-packet basis at line rate without negatively impacting network function performance, we propose and outline a hardware implementation of our load management layer to be integrated into the network interface card.

The paper is structured as follows: After surveying related work in Sect. 2, Sect. 3 will motivate our work by providing background information on network workload fluctuations. We will detail the key design ideas of the load management layer in Sect. 4, before evaluating its effectiveness in Sect. 5. Section 6 will conclude the paper.

2   Related Work

Efficient dimensioning and utilization of network resources has been the goal of many research endeavors in the past. In the field of traffic engineering, dynamic load balancing aims at distributing an incoming packet stream to a set of network links, such that the maximum utilization of the network is minimized under varying load conditions [8,17]. However, these approaches focus on the lowest level of the network infrastructure (i.e. the links and routers), where all packets come with equal transmission and routing cost. In contrast, our load management layer aims at distributing the processing load placed on the hardware resources executing higher layer network functions, where the processing actions and resource demands vary significantly among packets.

In-network load balancing does not balance the utilization of the network infrastructure itself, but rather aims at balancing incoming application requests to the application servers attached to the network. Google's Maglev [4] and Microsoft's Ananta [12] are examples for software-based in-network load balancers applied in large scale data centers. Both approaches rely on a multitier implementation hierarchy for scalability, but eventually distribute incoming requests to back-end servers by simply hashing the packet header without taking application processing demands into consideration. In contrast, our work does not aim at evenly distributing the number of packets processed by each network node, but rather targets a distribution of workload caused by diverse per-packet processing demands.

The authors of [2] aim at a resource-efficient execution of softwarized network monitoring systems that rely on deep-packet-inspection. Rather than scaling the amount of hardware resources dedicated to network function processing in response to varying workloads, the proposed system dynamically controls the processing requirements by adaptively changing the number of packets that are inspected for each network flow. Unfortunately, the approach is limited to network monitoring and fails to generalize for other network functions.

NFV-Vital [3] addresses the problem that the performance of network functions is strongly influenced by the network node configuration (e.g. different IO technologies, CPU pinning, power saving states), as well as the configuration parameters of the network functions. NFV-Vital presents a profiling framework that enables operators to characterize NF resource demands in different environments. Although the results potentially enable network operators to better understand the amount of resources required to achieve momentary performance goals, they do not provide a mechanism to actively react on volatile workloads.

3   Short-Term Processing Demand Variations

Data center network workloads fluctuate on a wide range of timescales. Our work targets variations on short, sub-second timescales. These fluctuations are caused by highly volatile network data rates [1] and diverse per-packet processing demands among network functions executed on the same network node.

For general-purpose platforms, the *processing complexity* of a network function is often expressed as the number of CPU instructions required to process each arriving packet. Table 1 [13] quantifies the number of *instructions per packet* (IPP) for a set of different network functions. While the IPP for NFs that solely operate on the packet header does not depend on the packet length, the processing complexity of NFs operating on the packet payload typically increases with larger packet length. Considering average data center packet lengths around 850 bytes [1], it is evident that the processing complexity of different NFs varies by multiple orders of magnitude.

In order to quantify real-world variations in processing demand caused by both volatile data rates and different per-packet processing requirements, we analyzed a set of network packet traces captured on a 10 Gbps data center backbone link. These traces are available in the *CAIDA Anonymized Internet Traces 2015* data set [14]. Unfortunately, network traces alone do not allow us to draw conclusions on the processing demand, because they lack information about which NFs are executed on the trace data. To exemplify the impact of varying per-packet processing requirements, we therefore randomly assign each packet of a chosen trace excerpt[1] to one of three NFs under the following assumption: 30% of all processing should be allotted to an NF executing Fingerprinting, 30% to String matching and 40% to IPSec-AES encryption (we will elaborate our mapping methodology in Sect. 5). For such a mapping, Fig. 1 shows the resulting processing demand on a 10 millisecond timescale. It is clearly visible that peak processing demands significantly exceed the long-term 10 second average. Although packet buffering can absorb the processing peaks to a certain extent,

Table 1. Number of CPU instructions per packet and payload byte for different network functions [13]

Network function	Type	Instructions per	
		packet	payl. byte
IPv4 radix	Header	4,493	0
Flow classification	Header	153	0
IPSec-AES	Payload	1,272	61
String matching	Payload	433	11
Fingerprinting	Payload	52	78

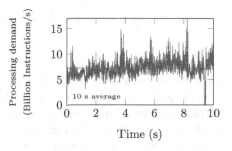

Fig. 1. Varying processing demand based on arrival pattern of packets bound for different NFs

---

[1] CAIDA trace: Equinix Chicago data center (dirA), 15/02/19 13:00:00-13:00:10 UTC.

we will show in Sect. 5 that a significant amount of resource over-provisioning is required to limit queuing latencies to reasonable ranges.

4   Load Management Layer

In order to allow network operators to dimension the processing resources dedicated to network function execution more cost-efficiently, we propose to enable network nodes to offload short-term excess workloads to peers within their neighborhood. Our proposal is motivated by an intuitive observation: we consider a cluster of multiple network nodes, where each node is serving incoming network traffic with short-term processing demand variations. When reducing the amount of over-provisioned resources required to fulfill a given latency requirement, the probability of each individual network node violating this requirement when excess loads hit increases. However, with growing cluster size it becomes less likely that all network nodes of the cluster fully utilize their processing resources at exactly the same time. Thus, instead of queuing packets until resources become available, we allow network nodes to offload processing by redirecting excess traffic to those nodes in the cluster that currently have under-utilized resources.

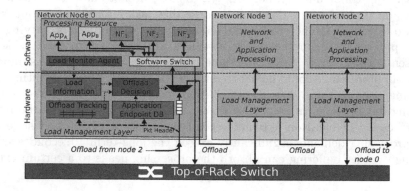

Fig. 2. Three network nodes equipped with the Load Management Layer

To enable the offload of excess workloads, we place a *Load Management Layer* (LML) in the ingress path of each network node. Figure 2 shows a cluster of three network nodes, all equipped with the LML. Typically, the NFV infrastructure's commodity servers are mounted in server racks and receive incoming data from so-called *Top-of-Rack* (ToR) switches. In our current design, each network node is additionally connected to two of its cluster peers to form a ring topology. When packets arrive at the network node, the load management layer acts as an ingress *bouncer*. If sufficient CPU capacity is available for local processing, packets are admitted to continue through the standard NFV processing chain: they are passed to a software switch for classification and then forwarded to the target network function. If the LML becomes aware of a local processing bottleneck, it instead redirects the packets to its neighbor peer where the next LML repeats the process. Packets continue to traverse the ring until the LML of one network node decides that sufficient resource capacity is available for local processing. To prevent packets from looping the ring multiple times when all nodes are temporarily overloaded, the network node that initially received a packet from the ToR switch must admit it for local processing when an entire circulation has been completed. A circulation is detected when the destination MAC address of the unaltered Ethernet frame arriving from a ring neighbor matches the MAC address of the network interface connected to the ToR switch.

In some cases, operators may decide to share a server's processing resources among network functions and other applications. To ensure that packets bound for the applications can always reach their destination, we exclude these packets from being offloaded. The LML maintains an *application endpoint database*, which contains a list of IP addresses assigned to the executed applications, and always delivers packets bound for one of these addresses locally.

Since all incoming network traffic traverses the LML before network function execution takes over (possibly multiple times in different network nodes after offloading), the latency induced by the LML must be kept to a minimum. Also, the goal of an increased resource provisioning efficiency can only be achieved if the LML does not put a significant processing load on the CPU of the network nodes. Transferring every packet from the network interface card to main memory and taking the offload decision in software would neither satisfy latency, nor CPU load demands. However, these issues can be overcome by implementing the load management layer in hardware and directly integrating it into the network interface card (NIC). Such a hardware implementation has two major advantages: it guarantees that the latency added to each packet is kept small and the packets chosen to be offloaded never reach the CPU of the local network node.

4.1 Offload Granularity

In the initial design phase, we identified three primary requirements, which the hardware load management layer must fulfill:

1. **Agility:** The time it takes to resolve overload situations must be on a par with the timescales on which fluctuations in processing demand occur. To allow for the reduction of over-provisioned resources, it is crucial that the time, which passes from overload detection until a sufficiently large number of packets is redirected to other network nodes, is minimal.
2. **Avoid packet reordering:** The LML must not negatively impact end-to-end network performance. We identified packet reordering as a possible performance issue when the path that packets traverse through the network dynamically changes during run-time.
3. **Performance:** The LML inspects every packet arriving at the network node to determine whether it shall be offloaded or processed locally. The LML shall operate at line rates of at least 10 Gbps.

We found that fulfilling these requirements reduces to the question: at which data granularity should the LML take decisions on whether to process an arriving packet locally or offload it to another network node? Initially we considered two options: decisions on a per-packet and on a per-flow basis. In terms of offload agility, per-packet decisions are ideal, because arriving packets can be redirected immediately when a local bottleneck is detected. However, since choosing the path through the network for each packet individually can cause packet reordering, we considered this approach to be unsuitable. Offload decisions on the flow-level avoid packet reordering, because all packets belonging to the same flow follow the same path through the network. Unfortunately, keeping track of the offload decisions taken for all active flows requires large lookup tables. To achieve low-latency and line rate performance, such lookup tables are typically implemented by *Content Addressable Memories* (CAMs) with high power consumption. Furthermore, offload agility is decreased, because active, long-lasting flows cannot be redirected and thus prevent in-time overload resolution.

To overcome these issues, we opted for an intermediate offload granularity level: *flowlets*. Flowlets are bursts of packets belonging to the same network flow. Each flowlet groups a set of subsequent packets, whose inter-arrival-gap does not exceed a flowlet timeout $\delta_{flowlet}$. Originally, Kandula et al. [9] propose *flowlet switching* as a technique to balance network traffic on a set of network paths with different transfer delays. By ensuring that $\delta_{flowlet}$ is set to a value larger than the worst-case difference of transfer delays, flowlets may be individually forwarded on different network paths without packet reordering to occur.

Taking offloading decisions on the granularity level of flowlets allows the LML to satisfy all three design requirements: (1) Splitting network flows, which often last multiple seconds or minutes, into smaller flowlets increases offload agility. With decreasing values of $\delta_{flowlet}$, flows are split into an increasing number of flowlets allowing more frequent offload decisions. Our evaluation in Sect. 5 shows that the response time of the LML to imminent overload situations is sufficiently small to allow for the reduction of the provisioned processing resources dedicated to NF execution by up to 24%. (2) Packet order of all network flows can be fully ensured by conservatively setting the flowlet timeout $\delta_{flowlet}$ to the sum of the worst-case time it takes the network nodes to serve a single packet and the time it takes a packet to complete one full LML ring circulation. Even though we choose $\delta_{flowlet}$ marginally smaller to benefit offload agility, we found that in all our experiments less than 0.035% of all packets may cause reordering. (3) Finally, we show in the next section that keeping track of flowlet offloading decisions does not rely on expensive CAM. Instead, offload decisions are stored in a hash table located in random access memory. Although we are not in possession of a full LML hardware implementation at the time of writing, literature documents that hash calculation in hardware, as well as table lookups and updates, take only a couple of clock cycles [5] allowing offload decision tracking at data rates beyond 10 Gbps.

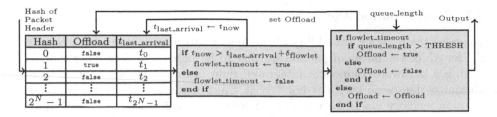

Fig. 3. Load management layer offload decision and tracking logic

4.2   Offload Decision and Tracking

Figure 3 illustrates the offload decision and tracking logic of the hardware load management layer. The hash-based tracking of flowlet paths and the identification of new flowlets has originally been proposed in [9]: For each arriving packet, a CRC16 hash is calculated based on the packet header five-tuple. By hashing the header five-tuple, it is ensured that all packets belonging to the same network flow are always mapped to the same hash value. The calculated hash serves as an index to a hash table, where each entry stores two pieces of information: (1) the arrival time $t_{last\_arrival}$ of the last packet hitting the entry and (2) whether the packet was offloaded or not. After both values have been extracted from the hash table, it is determined if the arriving packet starts a new flowlet and thus is a candidate for offloading. If a period larger than the flowlet timeout $\delta_{flowlet}$ has passed between the hash entry's last packet arrival time $t_{last\_arrival}$ and the current time t_{now}, the packet starts a new flowlet and may be offloaded. If the time difference does not exceed the timeout period, we must assume that the packet belongs to an active flowlet. Thus, it is no offload candidate and must follow the output path stored in the hash table entry. After the information has been evaluated, the hash table entry's $t_{last\_arrival}$ value is updated to the current time.

To decide whether a new flowlet should be offloaded or not, the load management layer must assess if a sufficient amount of processing resources is available at the local network node. A clear indicator for a CPU bottleneck is an increasing length of the queue holding packets waiting to be processed. Thus, once a packet has been identified as an offload candidate, the current queue length is compared to a pre-defined threshold value. If the threshold is exceeded, the packet is offloaded to the neighbor node in the ring, otherwise it is dispatched to the standard NFV processing chain of the local network node. In both cases, the hash table entry is updated with the outcome of the offload decision.

Due to multiple flows hitting the same hash table entry (i.e. *hash collisions*), the stored timeout and output information cannot be uniquely associated with a single flowlet. As a result, the start of a new flowlet may be masked when a packet belonging to another flowlet resets the $t_{last\_arrival}$ value. Therefore, a new flowlet can only be offloaded when *no* flowlet hit the hash table entry for a period larger than $\delta_{flowlet}$.

4.3   Load Monitor Agent

To assess the resource availability at the local network node, the LML evaluates the length of the queue of packets waiting to be processed. Assuming that the LML is a hardware component integrated right into the network interface card, obtaining the queue length is not trivial. Since modern NICs transfer packets to main memory via DMA transfers at line rate (typically over a PCIExpress interconnect), queues build up on the host-side, not on the NIC. In order to enable the load management layer to decide whether to offload packets or not, we rely on a software component (running on the host), which monitors the queue length. Once a pre-configured upper threshold is reached, the software notifies the hardware LML by sending a control message via the PCIExpress interconnect. In an analogous manner, a control message is sent when a lower threshold is passed and hence an imminent overload situation is resolved.

4.4   Relation to Centralized Network Control

Similar to NFV's centralized orchestration of network function instantiation, *Software Defined Networking* (SDN) promotes centralized control of network forwarding via protocols such as *OpenFlow* [10]. A centralized SDN *controller* configures the forwarding rules of the physical data center switches, as well as the software switches responsible for dispatching packets within the network nodes (see Fig. 2). Although our proposal to enable network nodes to decide at which location in a cluster a flowlet is processed may appear to oppose the trend of control centralization, we point out that the LML in no way aims at replacing it. The LML rather acts as a *delegate* optimizing short-term network operation on timescales where an external control instance is unable to react in time (i.e. milli- and microseconds). On larger timescales, centralized network control remains responsible for assigning an initial amount of processing resources to NF execution, setting up the forwarding rules of the hard- and software switches, monitoring the utilization of processing resources and optimizing resource assignment in response to long-term shifts in processing demand.

The LML is designed in such a way that it operates independently of the forwarding rules configured in the software switch of the network nodes. All new flowlets are equally considered for offloading. It remains the job of the SDN controller to configure the forwarding rules of the software switches in each network node of a cluster in such a way that an arriving packet is always forwarded to the same type of network function, no matter at which location in the LML ring it is admitted for local processing. Our proposal does not require modifications of the software network stack or the SDN and NFV control protocols.

4.5   Limitations

Although the proposed load management layer allows network operators to increase the resource dimensioning efficiency for a wide set of network functions, its applicability is limited in some scenarios. Due to the design decision to allow network nodes to offload traffic at the granularity of flowlets, it can occur that packets belonging to the same flow are processed at two different network nodes. Although sufficiently large flowlet timeouts ensure that directly succeeding packets are always directed to the same network node, some *stateful* NFs require to see all packets belonging to a flow for correct operation. In some cases, the network function must not only see the inbound traffic, but also the return traffic. Currently, our load management layer is unable to ensure this persistence.

5   Evaluation

We assess the effectiveness of our load management layer based on a simulation model created on top of the *OMNeT++* [16] discrete event simulator. Our model consists of two components: a trace replay engine, which generates simulation stimuli based on a prerecorded network trace, and a network node, which includes a processing resource and the LML. The processing resource is modeled as a Single-Server Queue, where incoming packets are processed in FIFO order. Its capacity, given in *instructions per seconds*, is parameterizable. NFs are executed in the same process space; we assume no context switching overheads. This is in line with recent proposals such as [7]. NF execution is abstracted by annotating the processing time of each packet based on the NF-specific *instructions per packet* (IPP) and the resource capacity configuration. Although we are aware that the model of the processing resource makes several simplifying assumptions (e.g. we do not consider load balancing across multiple CPU cores), we believe that the obtained results are a first indicator for the effectiveness of our concept.

Our simulated network consists of eight network nodes executing the same set of NFs. Unless noted otherwise, LML-enabled network nodes are grouped in two clusters, each consisting of four network nodes connected by the ring topology. Network nodes cannot offload processing load across cluster boundaries. As pointed out in Sect. 4.1, the flowlet timeout $\delta_{flowlet}$ affects both the amount of packet reordering to occur and the response time to imminent overloads. To balance between minimizing packet reordering and maximizing offload agility, we set $\delta_{flowlet}$ to 5 ms after performing an extensive parameter exploration. We will elaborate the impact of our choice at the end of the evaluation.

5.1   Simulation Stimuli

To allow for reproducibility of our results, the simulation is driven by a set of publicly available network traces captured on a 10 Gbps data center backbone link (*CAIDA Anonymized Internet Traces 2015* data set [14]). We selected several 80 s long trace excerpts[2] and cut them into eight 10 s sections; each section serves as stimulus for one of the network nodes. Based on the observation that

---

[2] CAIDA traces: Equinix Chicago data center (dirA), 15/02/19 (Trace 0), 15/05/21 (Trace 1), 15/09/17 (Trace 2), 15/12/17 (Trace 3) 13:00:00-13:01:20 UTC.

variations in processing demand occur on milli- and microsecond timescales, we consider a simulation time of 10 seconds sufficient. Although the enormous amount of trace data available in the CAIDA trace set prevented us from exhaustively performing and analyzing simulations for all trace stimuli, we explicitly selected a subset of trace excerpts that have been recorded in different months throughout the entire year 2015 to cope for seasonal changes in traffic characteristics. Network traces unfortunately lack information about which network functions are executed on the recorded packets. The precise assignment of NFs to network nodes and traffic depends on the use case and, to the best of our knowledge, no reference model is documented in literature. We thus randomly assigned each packet of the individual 10 s trace sections to a set of NFs with the constraint that all packets bound for the same /24 IPv4 or /64 IPv6 subnet must be assigned to the same NF. We further constrained the assignment by defining the percentage of processing allotted to each NF in relation to the total number of instructions required to process the entire trace section. For this evaluation, we made the following assumption: 30% of the total number of processing instructions shall be allotted to an NF executing Fingerprinting, 30% to String matching and 40% to IPSec-AES encryption (see Table 1 for IPP values). We repeated the mapping 20 times for statistical significance.

5.2   Resource Over-Provisioning

For each packet-to-NF mapping, we determine the long-term average capacity required to handle all packets of the trace (i.e. sum of the total number of packet instructions divided by trace duration). Although this *baseline capacity dimensioning* allows the network nodes to process all packet eventually (if no buffer overflows occur), queuing delays are introduced when workloads exceed the average. Our simulations aim at determining by how much the baseline capacity needs to be over-provisioned such that a specified percentage of packets (*target latency probability*) does not exceed a specified *target latency*. We evaluate the effectiveness of the LML by comparing the amount of over-provisioned resources obtained from simulation runs where the LML is once enabled and once disabled. To enable a fair comparison between network nodes equipped with and without the LML, we start the latency measurement when a packet enters the first network node and stop the measurement when the packet has been completely processed (i.e. we include packet forwarding latencies in the LML ring).

Figure 4a shows the average multiplier, by which baseline capacity must be over-provisioned to reach a latency target in the range of 100 us and 1 ms for 99.5% of all the processed packets for four different trace sets. Results are averaged over 20 runs with different packet-to-NF mappings (we refrain from displaying the standard deviation for better readability, but include it when quantifying the resource savings). As expected, the amount of required processing resources decreases when target latencies are increased, because packet queuing becomes increasingly tolerable. It is clearly visible that the LML allows for a reduction of over-provisioning for all trace sets and target latencies. For the sake of brevity

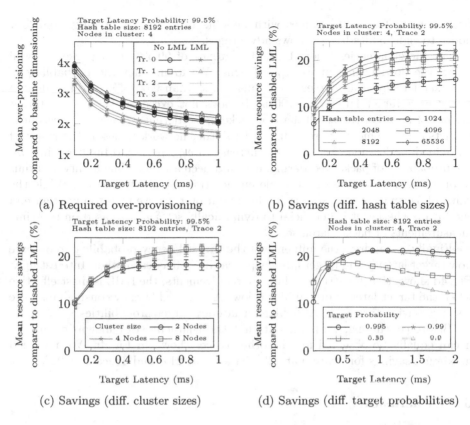

(a) Required over-provisioning

(b) Savings (diff. hash table sizes)

(c) Savings (diff. cluster sizes)

(d) Savings (diff. target probabilities)

Fig. 4. Over-provisioning demands and savings for several traces and parameters

and visibility, we picked Trace 2 to further evaluate the benefits of the LML in detail (we will present a summary of the results for the other traces later).

Figure 4b quantifies the average resource savings of the runs where the LML was enabled compared to the ones where it was disabled. Error bars show the standard deviation of the runs performed for 20 packet-to-NF mappings. Savings are plotted for a number of offload tracking hash table sizes. Due to the stringent target latency probability of 99.5%, we observe the LML to perform particular well with increasing target latencies. If latencies in the range of a few hundred microseconds are tolerable, resource dimensioning can be reduced by as much as 21%. Even at stringent latency constraints of 100 us, 10% of resources are saved. We further observe that resource savings increase with a growing hash table size, where the probability of multiple active flowlets mapping to the same hash entry decreases and therefore offload decisions can be taken more frequently.

We next evaluate the impact of the number of network nodes in each LML cluster. Although Fig. 4c shows that cluster size has no impact on resource savings at very low target latencies, an increasing cluster size affects resource savings when target latencies are increased. While doubling the cluster size from two nodes to four nodes comes with benefits in savings, switching from four nodes to eight nodes barely shows advantages.

For target latencies below 1 ms, the latency of 99.5% of all packets is well below the flowlet timeout $\delta_{flowlet}$ of 5 ms. We found that the probability of a packet latency being larger than 5 ms is less than 0.0018% for all evaluated traces at a target latency of 100 us. It does not exceed 0.035% for a target latency of 1 ms. For this small share of packets, reordering can occur if subsequent flowlets of the same flow are redirected to other network nodes as the result of an offloading decision. Although an increase of $\delta_{flowlet}$ would further minimize the probability of packet reordering, it would decrease offloading agility and thus resource savings, because hash table entries timeout less frequently. While the value of 5 ms yields good results in all simulation runs, we plan to investigate in the future whether it is beneficial to dynamically set $\delta_{flowlet}$ based on run-time measurements of packet latencies.

Finally, we address the influence of the target latency probability to observe how target latency and target latency probability affect each other. Interestingly, Fig. 4d shows that for stringent latency requirements, the LML is most effective when the target latency probability is low. At reduced latency constraints, more resource savings are achieved for higher latency target probabilities.

Before concluding, we point out that the characteristics shown in Fig. 4b–d can equally be observed for the other traces shown in Fig. 4a. We recorded maximum savings for Trace 0 at 14%, Trace 1 at 21% and Trace 3 at 24%.

6   Conclusion

We presented the concept and simulative evaluation of a hardware load management layer, which allows network nodes to dynamically offload excess workloads to peers within their neighborhood when peak workloads hit. Our results show that the amount of resources dedicated to NF execution can be reduced by up to 24%. Especially in large data centers, where tens of thousands of servers are housed, these resource savings can significantly reduce capital (i.e. device acquisition) expenses. Although the abstraction level of our simulation model hides several low-level effects, the obtained results show the range in which resource savings can be expected. After implementing the load management layer in hardware and verifying its applicability in practice, we plan to investigate energy savings originating from the increased resource dimensioning efficiency.

References

1. Benson, T., Anand, A., Akella, A., Zhang, M.: Understanding data center traffic characteristics. ACM SIGCOMM Comput. Commun. Rev. **40**(1), 92–99 (2010)
2. Braun, L., Diekmann, C., Kammenhuber, N., Carle, G.: Adaptive load-aware sampling for network monitoring on multicore commodity hardware. In: 2013 IFIP Networking Conference, pp. 1–9. IEEE (2013)

3. Cao, L., Sharma, P., Fahmy, S., Saxena, V.: Nfv-vital: a framework for characterizing the performance of virtual network functions. In: 2015 IEEE Conference on Network Function Virtualization and Software Defined Network (NFV-SDN), pp. 93–99. IEEE (2015)
4. Eisenbud, D.E., Yi, C., Contavalli, C., Smith, C., Kononov, R., Mann-Hielscher, E., Cilingiroglu, A., Cheyney, B., Shang, W., Hosein, J.D.: Maglev: a fast and reliable software network load balancer. In: 13th USENIX Symposium on Networked Systems Design and Implementation (NSDI 2016), pp. 523–535. USENIX Association (2016)
5. Forconesi, M., Sutter, G., López-Buedo, S., de Vergara, J.E.L., Aracil, J.: Bridging the gap between hardware and software open source network developments. IEEE Netw. **28**(5), 13–19 (2014)
6. Heller, B., Seetharaman, S., Mahadevan, P., Yiakoumis, Y., Sharma, P., Banerjee, S., McKeown, N.: Elastictree: saving energy in data center networks. In: 7th USENIX Symposium on Networked Systems Design and Implementation (NSDI 2010), pp. 249–264. USENIX Association (2010)
7. Jackson, E.J., Walls, M., Panda, A., Pettit, J., Pfaff, B., Rajahalme, J., Koponen, T., Shenker, S.: Softflow: a middlebox architecture for open vswitch. In: 2016 USENIX Annual Technical Conference (USENIX ATC 2016), pp. 15–28. USENIX Association (2016)
8. Kandula, S., Katabi, D., Davie, B., Charny, A.: Walking the tightrope: responsive yet stable traffic engineering. ACM SIGCOMM Comput. Commun. Rev. **35**(4), 253–264 (2005)
9. Kandula, S., Katabi, D., Sinha, S., Berger, A.: Dynamic load balancing without packet reordering. ACM SIGCOMM Comput. Commun. Rev. **37**(2), 51–62 (2007)
10. McKeown, N., Anderson, T., Balakrishnan, H., Parulkar, G., Peterson, L., Rexford, J., Shenker, S., Turner, J.: Openflow: enabling innovation in campus networks. ACM SIGCOMM Comput. Commun. Rev. **38**(2), 69–74 (2008)
11. Mijumbi, R., Serrat, J., Gorricho, J.L., Bouten, N., De Turck, F., Boutaba, R.: Network function virtualization: state-of-the-art and research challenges. IEEE Commun. Surv. Tutorials **18**(1), 236–262 (2015)
12. Patel, P., Bansal, D., Yuan, L., Murthy, A., Greenberg, A., Maltz, D.A., Kern, R., Kumar, H., Zikos, M., Wu, H., Kim, C., Naveen, K.: Ananta: cloud scale load balancing. ACM SIGCOMM Comput. Commun. Rev. **43**(4), 207–218 (2013)
13. Ramaswamy, R., Weng, N., Wolf, T.: Analysis of network processing workloads. J. Syst. Architect. **55**(10), 421–433 (2009)
14. Center for Applied Internet Data Analysis: The CAIDA UCSD Anonymized Internet Traces 2015–15/02/19, 15/05/21, 15/09/17, 15/12/17. http://www.caida.org/data/passive/passive_2015_dataset.xml
15. ETSI Industry Specification Group: ETSI GS NFV-REL 001 V1.1.1, Network Functions Virtualisation (NFV) Resiliency Requirements, January 2015
16. Varga, A.: The omnet++ discrete event simulation system. In: Proceedings of the 15th European simulation multiconference (ESM 2001), vol. 9, p. 65 (2001)
17. Wang, H., Xie, H., Qiu, L., Yang, Y.R., Zhang, Y., Greenberg, A.: Cope: traffic engineering in dynamic networks. ACM SIGCOMM Comput. Commun. Rev. **36**(4), 99–110 (2006)

Dynamic Power Management
in a Heterogeneous Processor Architecture

Frehiwot Melak Arega$^{(\boxtimes)}$, Markus Haehnel$^{(\boxtimes)}$, and Waltenegus Dargie$^{(\boxtimes)}$

Faculty of Computer Science, TU Dresden, 01062 Dresden, Germany
{frehiwot_melak.arega,markus.haehnel1,waltenegus.dargie}@tu-dresden.de

Abstract. Emerging mobile platforms integrate heterogeneous, multi-core processors to efficiently deal with the heterogeneity of data (in magnitude, type, and quality). The main goal is to achieve a high degree of energy-proportionality which corresponds with the nature and fluctuation of mobile workloads. Most existing power and energy consumption analyses of these architectures rely on simulation or static benchmarks neither of which truly reflects the type of workload the processors handle in reality. By contrast, we generate two types of stochastic workloads and employ four types of dynamic voltage and frequency scaling (DVFS) policies to investigate the energy proportionality and the dynamic power consumption characteristics of a heterogeneous processor architecture when operating in different configurations. The analysis illustrates, both qualitatively and quantitatively, that knowledge of the statistics of the incoming workload is critical to determine the appropriate processor configuration.

Keywords: Dynamic power management · DVFS · Multicore processor · Heterogeneous processor architecture · Workload

1 Introduction

The volume of data generated and processed by mobile platforms has shown a rapid and sustained increment in the recent years, and evidence suggests that the trend will continue so in the near future. The driving forces behind this development are the introduction of advanced processor architectures and an improving communication infrastructure. At the same time, however, the complexity of the applications which run on the mobile platforms, generating and consuming some of these data, and their corresponding power consumption are increasing with comparable proportion. The implication is that both to meet users' requirements and provide sustainable services, there is a need for efficient resource management strategies which take the peculiar aspects of emerging mobile platforms (specifically, processor architectures) into consideration. One of these resources which should be managed is the energy consumption associated with the computation and communication demand of mobile platforms. Indeed, the research community is endeavouring to improve energy efficiency in

© Springer International Publishing AG 2017
J. Knoop et al. (Eds.): ARCS 2017, LNCS 10172, pp. 248–260, 2017.
DOI: 10.1007/978-3-319-54999-6_19

different ways, including noble dynamic voltage and frequency scaling, dynamic thermal management, workload-aware task scheduling, efficient thread-to-core mapping, and seamless runtime task migration [1–5]. Complementary to the runtime adaptation strategies, effort is also being made both by the academia and the industry to develop energy-efficient and energy-proportional processor architectures including (1) the efficient integration of multicore and heterogeneous processors, (2) fast and efficient simultaneous multi-threading, (3) non-uniform cache architecture, and (4) advanced branch prediction strategies, among others. The energy-proportionality (the ratio of consumed energy to work done) of these architectures has in general been improving at each generation, as their power consumption can be managed at core, processor, socket, and platform levels. The purpose of this paper is to qualitatively and quantitatively analyse the energy proportionality of runtime or dynamic power management strategies in emerging heterogeneous processor architectures. Most existing approaches rely on either simulation or static benchmarks neither of which truly reflects the type of workload these architectures process in reality. In contrast, we make an extensive and experimental investigation using stochastic workload (video transcoding) and four types of dynamic voltage and frequency scaling policies. The rest of the paper is organised as follows: In Sect. 2, we summarise related work; in Sect. 3, we introduce our experiment setup; in Sect. 4, we present and discuss experiment results and share the insight we obtained from the experiment results. Finally, in Sect. 5, we give concluding remarks and outline future work.

2   Related Work

Improving the performance and energy consumption of emerging heterogeneous processor architectures is an active research area. Some of the proposed approaches target one of the following goals: (1) Determining the optimal task-to-processor assignment strategy, (2) identifying effective and workload sensitive dynamic voltage and frequency scaling strategy for a specific processor configuration, and (3) managing the heat dissipation of processors by adapting operation frequencies to workload. Julio et al. [6] propose a model for estimating the execution duration of individual tasks under a specific clock frequency in a heterogeneous processor architecture without the need for analysing any source code or hardware specification. The resource consumption characteristics of a task is analysed at runtime during the first "hyperperiod" of the execution of a task using performance monitoring counters, computation time, waiting for memory, and "overlapping time" between computation and memory access. An overlap time is defined as the time the processor is executing non-dependent instructions while a memory request is being served. Petrucci et al. [7] propose a mechanism for (a) the optimal mapping of threads to specific cores in a heterogeneous architecture during task allocation and (b) periodic reassignment of threads with the aim on improving the runtime energy consumption while meeting performance requirements of application threads. The resource consumption characteristic and the different execution phases of running threads are analysed using performance monitoring counters (Instructions Per Cycle (IPC) and Last Level Cache (LLC) miss rate). Similarly, Liu et al. [8] propose a generic approach to formulate the map of threads to cores in a heterogeneous architecture using Integer Linear Program (ILP) for any number of threads, cores, and types of cores. Their main goal is to maximise throughput while keeping total power under a given budget. The approach first assigns threads to cores such that the assignment can achieve the highest possible throughput and, then, it performs virtual swapping of threads between adjacent core types. Pricopi et al. [9] investigate the relationship between the performance and power consumption of a heterogeneous architecture by using a large number of performance monitoring counters. Their approach focuses on accounting the way this relationship is affected when executions are migrated from one type of cores to another within the same processor architecture. Hanumaiah [2] aims to minimise the effects of high thermal design power (TDP) by combining different approaches such as performance-per-watt efficiency as a trade-off between performance and power consumption, DVFS, thread migration, and active cooling. Maiti et al. [1] investigate the consequences of configuration mismatch between core frequencies and core states and propose a framework for core selection, thread-to-core mapping and DVFS. The aim is to select the best distribution of jobs and the appropriate DVFS. Unlike the approach in [2], here optimisation serves one of the two purposes: either the energy of a server is minimised under performance constraints or its performance is maximised under power constraints. Likewise, Singla et al. [10] and Prakash et al. [11] propose thermal management strategies as a mechanism to minimise the energy consumption and to maximise the performance of emerging processor architecture. In both cases, the temperature of a processor is determined as a function of its power consumption and maximum operation frequency. From this relationship it was possible to determine the maximum operation frequency which sets the temperature of a processor below a set limit.

Complementary to state-of-the-art, this paper presents a comprehensive investigation of the power and energy consumption characteristics of different processor configurations and dynamic voltage and frequency scaling possibilities in a heterogeneous processor architecture given that the incoming workload of the processor architecture is of stochastic nature.

3   Experiment Setup

Processor Architecture. We employ the Odroid-XU4[1] processor architecture with Ubuntu 14.04 operating system installed for our experiment which consists of eight "big.LITTLE" cores. Four of these are energy-efficient ARM Cortex-A7 cores which are suitable for executing non-time-critical workloads. So they are denoted as "LITTLE" cores. The other four, which are high performance ARM Cortex-A15 cores, are suitable for executing compute intensive and time critical workloads. They are denoted as "big". The performance difference between

---

[1] http://www.hardkernel.com/main/products/prdt_info.php?
  g_code=G143452239825.

the two types of cores is a result of their difference in peak operation frequency (which is 2.0 GHz for the Cortex-A15 whilst it is 1.4 GHz for the Cortex-A7) as well as in size. We supplied one and the same task (transcoding the same video) for the two types of cores and let them process the task at different frequencies. On the same Cortex the transcoding duration is more or less inversely proportional to the frequency. But when we compared the transcoding duration between processor types for comparable operation frequency, the difference is considerable. For example, a given transcoding took 33 s on a Cortex-A7 core when it was clocked at 1.4 GHz but it took 20 s with a smaller frequency (1.2 GHz) on the Cortex-A15. The additional performance improvement comes from a higher degree of out-of-order execution as well as a larger L2 cache (2 MB of Cortex-A15 vs. 512 kB of Cortex-A7). The little cores have only one in-order execution pipeline. In contrast, the big cores have an out-of-order three-way execution pipeline, so that they can reorder the necessary instructions to utilise the subsets of logic more efficiently.

Table 1. The transcoding time of a single test video file on different cores with different frequencies.

Cortex-A7	68 s @ 600 MHz	33 s @ 1.4 GHz
Cortex-A15	20 s @ 1.2 GHz	13 s @ 2.0 GHz

The performance gain of the Cortex-A15 cores comes at a price of high power consumption because of its more complex and larger circuit architecture (pipeline and caches, for instance). The big cores consume approximately four times more power than the LITTLE cores. On the other hand, the Cortex-A15 are not four times faster (as can be seen in Table 1); therefore, they should be used only when their performance is really needed. Since the Cortex-A7 and Cortex-A15 cores have a different clocking range and separate phase-locked-loops (PLLs), their bias voltage and clock frequency can be set independently. Nevertheless, as cores of the same type share one and the same PLL, they run at the same frequency. Because an idling core consumes a certain amount of energy, it may be reasonable to prolong the execution of tasks to minimise idle durations. Alternatively, the load of an underutilised core can be migrated somewhere in order to switch it off entirely. But the wake-up latency of a disabled core is significant in case of load balancing.

Workload. The power consumption characteristic of a processor depends on the workload characteristic. Most existing power consumption analysis techniques [9,10] rely on static benchmarks which, in reality, do not reflect the workload of typical mobile platforms. Since the magnitude of the workload of mobile platforms experiences fluctuation over time, we generated stochastic workloads in order to reflect this fluctuation.

The process can be described as follows: First of all, using the Python statistical tool, we generated random numbers of predetermined probability density functions, means, and variances. Then for each random number belonging to a given probability density function, we generated a video the size of which corresponds to the random number (hence, the distribution of the video size follows the distribution of the random numbers). Secondly, we picked up the longest video from each probability density function and transcoded it using FFMPEG[2] and registered the time a processor core requires to complete the task. A processor core is 100% utilised when it undertakes a transcoding task and becomes idle when it completes its task. Thirdly, we divided time into slots. The duration of a time slot equals the time the processor required to complete the longest video. Fourthly, at the beginning of each time slot we randomly picked up a video for each activated core from a known probability density function and transcoded it. Notice that now the time the processor requires to transcode this video is random, as the size of the video is random. As a result, the processor experiences a random idle duration in each slot. Furthermore, the interference of several tasks within a time slot as a result of the competition for L2 cache and memory bandwidth is included. The reason is that they run concurrently on different cores of the same type (L2 cache) as well as different types (memory bandwidth). An example is illustrated in Fig. 1 where the maximum transcoding time and, therefore, the slot duration is 30 s. Thus, we produced the following workload distributions:

- Exponential – $\mathbf{E}\,(\lambda = 15\,\mathrm{MB})$: 3.6% of the videos have the maximum video size, which is 50 MB for all the experiments.
- Uniform – $\mathbf{U}\,(0, 30)$: The size of the videos assigned to a core varies uniformly between 0 and 30 MB.

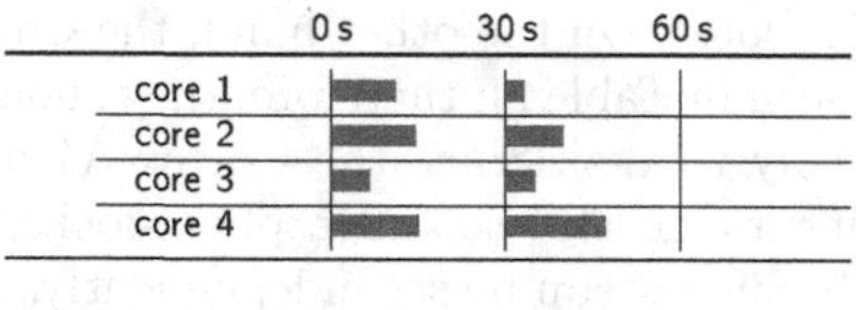

Fig. 1. An example of the workload distribution in a given time slot. A request to transcode videos of different size arrives in the beginning of each time slot; a time slot, for this example is 30 s.

Dynamic Voltage and Frequency Scaling. Most existing dynamic power management strategies aim to minimise the idle states of computing resources, because they consume a significant amount of power even when they are idle. In general, a computing system enters into an idle state due to two stochastically independent phenomena: (1) the interval between the arrival of any two compute tasks is a random process, and (2) there is a discrepancy between the time allocated by a scheduler to process a task (which is usually over-provisioned) and the time the processor requires to complete this task. The idle state can be

---

[2] https://www.ffmpeg.org/ (version 2.6.2).

minimised by either putting a computing resource into a deep sleep mode (or by turning it off altogether) whenever it is idle, by deliberately slowing down its processing speed so that the idle interval is minimised, or by adaptively varying its execution speed, so that execution speed and task completion deadline can overlap. Each approach has its own merits and demerits. One of the merits of the deep-sleep and the slow execution strategies is a significant reduction of idle time, but for both strategies this comes at a potential cost of increased execution latency. The adaptive execution frequency strategy foresees the potential change in the interval between the time a task is completed and the arrival of the next task and, therefore, is able to estimate the optimal execution frequency, but for that it requires sufficient task execution and task arrival statistics, as a result of which the gain in power consumption may not be appreciable. For our investigation we selected four types of DVFS policies, namely, *power-save*, *on-demand*, *conservative*, and *performance* policies [12,13]. The *power-save* policy operates cores at the lowest frequency while the *on-demand* and *conservative* policies adapt the clock frequency to the change in the workload of the servers. The last two policies estimate the utilisation of the processor using a moving average prediction technique, predict its future workload for the next time slot, and scale-down or scale-up the processor's speed accordingly. The essential difference between the two is that the *on-demand* policy scales up the CPU frequency to the maximum whenever an increment in the core's activity is predicted whereas this is done gradually in the *conservative* policy. But both strategies scale down the clock frequency gradually whenever they perceive the future workload as decreasing. The *performance* policy operates a core at its maximum clock frequency. The aim is to complete a task as fast as possible and to put the core into a deep sleep state. On the system side, the frequency of the LITTLE cores can be varied between 200 MHz and 1.4 GHz in step of 100 MHz whereas the frequency of the big cores can be varied between 200 MHz and 2 GHz in step of 100 MHz. Nevertheless, the frequency of an individual core in either group cannot be managed independently, as all the cores in the same group share the same phase-locked loop which generates the clock frequency of the group. Consequently, the frequency estimated by a DVFS policy for a particular core and the frequency assigned to the same core can be different.

Measurement. Our analysis involves three different configurations for the two groups of processors, four DVFS policies, and two types of stochastic workloads. Altogether we conducted 24 experiments. We run each experiment for 1 h and employed YOKOGAWA WT210 digital power analysers[3] to measure the power consumption of the Odroid-XU4 board at a rate of approximately 10 Hz. To get statistics pertaining to the CPU utilisation of each core, we used DSTAT[4].

---

[3] http://tmi.yokogawa.com/.

[4] http://dag.wiee.rs/home-made/dstat/.

4   Evaluation

In order to carry out reproducible experiments, we generated the workloads based on underlying probability density functions (uniform and exponential). These workloads are then processed in different configurations: LITTLE, big, and big.LITTLE configuration. In the LITTLE configuration we deactivated the A15 cores and transcoded videos only with the LITTLE cores. Likewise, in the big configuration, we deactivated the A7 cores. In the big.LITTLE configuration, all cores are activated. In each experiment, a specific DVFS policy determines at any given time a suitable operation frequency for all cores sharing a single PLL. For each experiment, we specify time intervals (the duration) which is determined by (1) the largest video which should be transcoded and (2) the speed of transcoding this video under the DVFS policy we selected for that particular experiment. Table 2 shows the time required to transcode the longest video for the three configurations under the different DVFS policies. This latency determines the task arrival interval during video transcoding. Except for the *power-save* policy, we discovered that the time required to transcode the longest video in a given processor configuration is almost the same for all the scaling policies. At the beginning of each interval, each active core is supplied with a video to transcode. The video is chosen randomly from a pool of videos; hence, a processor may not spend the entire time slot transcoding a video, in which case, it may spend some time idling. The idle time statistics is used by a DVFS policy to estimate the appropriate clock frequency of the core.

Table 2. Transcoding latency (in seconds) to determine task arrival interval.

Configuration	Conservative	On-demand	Performance	Power-save
LITTLE	45	45	45	105
big	30	30	30	90
big.LITTLE	45	45	45	-

Since the task arrival time is approximately equal for all the DVFS policies (excepting the *power-save* policy) in a specific processor configuration, the number of videos which should be transcoded within a fixed experiment duration is the same as well for all the policies. This enables to compare the power consumption characteristics of the different policies given the same workload statistics. In all our analysis we employ the cumulative (probability) distribution function which expresses the probability that the value of a given quantity ($\mathbf{x}$) is equal to or below a specified value (x): $F(x) = P\{\mathbf{x} \leq x\} = p$, where $F(x)$ is the cumulative distribution function(CDF), and p is the probability associated with $F(x)$.

CPU Utilisation vs. Power Consumption. The power vs. CPU utilisation of the three processor configurations exhibit distinct features. In order to plot the relationship between the two quantities, we normalised the CPU utilisation

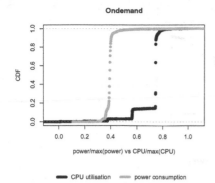

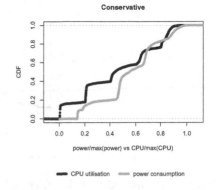

Fig. 2. Normalised CPU-Utilisation vs. Power for the LITTLE cores under *on-demand* DVFS policy for an exponential workload.

Fig. 3. Normalised CPU-Utilisation vs. Power for the big cores under *conservative* DVFS policy for an exponential workload.

by the maximum CPU utilisation. Likewise, the overall power consumption is normalised by the maximum power consumption. This way, both quantities have values ranging from 0 to 1. Figure 2 displays an example of the CDFs of the normalised power and the normalised CPU utilisation for the LITTLE cores under the *on-demand* DVFS policy. As can be seen, the CDF of the power consumption remains more or less unaffected by the change in the statistics of the CPU utilisation. In terms of the diversity of CPU utilisation (following the change in the statistics of the size of transcoding workload), the *conservative* and *performance* policies show responsiveness whereas the other two policies do not appear to be responsive, which indicates that the latter are slow to adapt to change. Figure 3 displays the CDFs of the normalised power and the normalised CPU utilisation under the *conservative* DVFS policy as an example for the big cores. Unlike the case with the LITTLE cores, here there is an almost ideal linear relationship between the two quantities. An exception is observed with the *power-save* policy which is not unexpected, as this policy operates the processors with the lowest frequency all the time. An interesting feature we observed is the pattern of the relationship. The CDF of the power consumption is always below or on the right-side of the CDF of the CPU utilisation which indicates that the probability of consuming more power is always slightly larger than the probability of utilising a corresponding amount of CPU (which we understand as an indication of energy disproportionality). The difference in pattern is bigger for the *performance* policy; since this policy operates the CPU with the maximum frequency, it is to be expected that it is not the most adaptive policy. Figure 4 displays an example of the CDFs of the normalised power and the normalised CPU utilisation under *conservative* DVFS policy for the big.LITTLE configuration. We excluded the *power-save* policy for this configuration because the completion time for the transcoding task becomes too big. The rest demonstrate the features that can be inherited from both types of cores when the system operates in a hybrid mode.

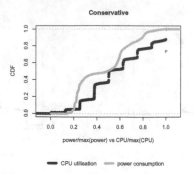

Fig. 4. Normalised CPU-Utilisation vs. Power for the big.LITTLE configuration under *conservative* DVFS policy for an exponential workload.

The almost linear relationship between the two quantities is visibly inherited from the big cores, but the pattern of the relationship is taken from the LIT-TLE cores, for the CDF of the normalised CPU utilisation is always below or on the right-side of the CDF of the normalised power (it is the other way round for the big cores). This indicates that power can be saved in this mode, but it must be recalled from Table 2 that the performance (in terms of transcoding latency) of this configuration is comparable to the performance of the LITTLE cores.

Power Consumption vs. Workload. Figures 5, 6 and 7 display the CDFs of the power consumption of the three configurations under the four DVFS policies for the two different types of workloads. In Fig. 5 the usefulness of DVFS is apparent, because the two graphs in the middle show the adaptiveness of the *conservative* and *on-demand* policies to a change in the workload statistics whereas the two extremes show the cost of operating the processors at fixed frequencies. While the reduced power consumption of *power-save* is a consequence of a lower throughput (more time is needed to complete transcoding all the

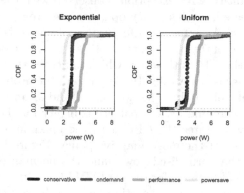

Fig. 5. Comparison of the power consumption of LITTLE cores under different DVFS policies.

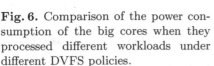

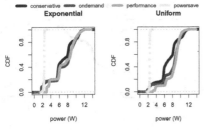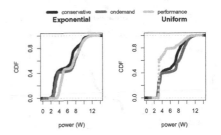

Fig. 6. Comparison of the power consumption of the big cores when they processed different workloads under different DVFS policies.

Fig. 7. Comparison of the power consumption of the big.LITTLE configuration when processing different workloads under different DVFS policies.

video files), the higher power consumption of the *performance* policy is unjustifiable, for there is no improved throughput. Both the *conservative* and *on-demand* policies completed transcoding all the video files within the same time period as the *performance* policy. For the big configuration, all except the *power-save* policy performed comparatively the same for both types of workloads, showing a broader range of values (from 1.8 W to 12 W) which suggests that they were comparatively adaptive to the fluctuation in the workloads. For both types of workloads the *conservative* policy was the most efficient policy (the gradual scaling up of clock frequencies in response to a perceived workload). The CDFs of the power consumption of the big.LITTLE configuration (as a trade-off between increased transcoding latency for reduced power consumption) can be seen in Fig. 7. For example, in Fig. 6 the probability that the overall power consumption of the A15 cores is equal to or below 6 W for all workload types and for all DVFS policies is approximately 0.2 whereas for the heterogeneous configuration the figure is approximately equal to or even greater than 0.4. Indeed, for the uniform workload, the *performance* policy in this configuration yields a probability of approximately 0.8.

Power Consumption vs. Processor Configuration. Figures 8 and 9 compare the CDFs of the power consumption of the three configurations for the two types of workloads using *on-demand* and *conservative* DVFS policies as example. Both figures consistently place the big.LITTLE configuration's power consumption between the LITTLE and the big configuration, regardless of the type of DVFS policy which manages the runtime power consumption of the processors. Moreover, both figures indicate that a wide range of dynamic power can be achieved in the big and big.LITTLE configurations by DVFS whereas this is not the case with the LITTLE configuration. This characteristic is more visible with the exponential workload.

Energy. Except for the *power-save* policy, the number of videos which can be transcoded in a specific amount of time for a specific processor configuration is fixed. Since the workload statistics are the same for all the DVFS policies for a

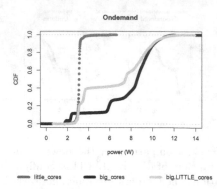

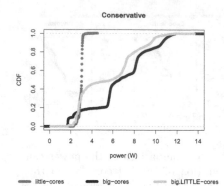

Fig. 8. An example of comparison of the power consumption characteristics of the three processor configurations (LITTLE, big, big.LITTLE) when they process a uniform workload under *on-demand* DVFS policy.

Fig. 9. An example of comparison of the power consumption characteristics of the three processor configurations (LITTLE, big, big.LITTLE) when they process an exponential workload under *conservative* DVFS policy.

Table 3. Cores energy consumption (in Watt-hour) under uniform workload with different DVFS

Configuration	Conservative	On-demand	Performance	Power-save
LITTLE	3.01	3.11	4.27	2.15
big	6.89	7.78	8.23	2.41
big.LITTLE	5.92	6.55	4.56	-

Table 4. Cores energy consumption (in Watt-hour) under exponential workload with different DVFS

Configuration	Conservative	On-demand	Performance	Power-save
LITTLE	2.95	3.05	4.21	2.07
big	6.69	7.17	7.31	2.40
big.LITTLE	5.54	6.23	6.63	-

specific configuration, it is possible to make an objective comparison between the energy consumption of the different policies for a given configuration. Tables 3 and 4 display the energy consumption (energy as the integration of power consumed with respect to time) of the different configurations. Interestingly, the *conservative* policy, which gradually scales the clock frequency of the processors as a function of the perceived change in the workload, performed best for all the configuration yielding the minimum amount of energy consumption. Exception to this is the big.LITTLE configuration where the *performance* policy produces the minimum energy consumption.

5   Conclusion

In this paper we experimentally investigated the energy-proportionality and the variation in the dynamic power of a heterogeneous processor architecture consisting of two quad-core CPUs. The CPUs are different in capacity as well as in the range of operation frequencies they support. We generated two stochastic video transcoding workloads (uniformly and exponentially distributed) and implemented four different types of dynamic voltage and frequency scaling policies. The processor architecture can be configured as LITTLE, big, and big.LITTLE. In the LITTLE configuration only the smaller and the slower of the two quad-core processors is active; in the big, only the bigger and the faster quad-core processor is active, and in the big.LITTLE all the processors can be active. The experiment results show that the three configurations have distinct energy-utility characteristics. The LITTLE configuration has the minimum average power consumption, but the range of its dynamic power is narrow and does not mirror the variation in the workload. The big configuration, on the other hand, exhibits a wide variation in its dynamic power and mirrors the variation in the workload. The dynamic power of the big.LITTLE configuration mirrors the dynamic power characteristic of the big configuration, but the magnitude of variation is smaller than the big configuration. When it comes to dynamic scaling of frequency and voltage, the *conservative* policy, which gradually increases and decreases the clock frequency of a processor in response to a perceived change in the workload, consistently produces the best performance in the big configuration, regardless of the workload type. The same scaling policy was the best policy for the exponential workload in the big.LITTLE configuration. For the LITTLE configuration, the *conservative* and the *on-demand* policies have comparable performance whereas in the other two no conspicuous saving or consumption of power can be observed without a corresponding sacrifice or gain in the job completion time. In general, it can be concluded that the implementation of a dynamic power management policy makes sense if the processor architecture has a wide range of dynamic power and the workload statistic is known. The latter can be estimated by taking samples at runtime. Hence, knowledge of this statistics can be used by a scheduler to determine both the configuration of the computing platform and the suitable DVFS policy.

References

1. Maiti, S., Kapadia, N., Pasricha, S.: Process variation aware dynamic power management in multicore systems with extended range voltage/frequency scaling. In: MWSCAS, pp. 1–4 (2015)
2. Hanumaiah, V., Vrudhula, S.: Energy-efficient operation of multicore processors by DVFS, task migration, and active cooling. IEEE Trans. Comput. **63**, 349–360 (2014)
3. Möbius, C., Dargie, W., Schill, A.: Power consumption estimation models for processors, virtual machines, and servers. IEEE Trans. Parallel Distrib. Syst. **25**(6), 1600–1614 (2014)

4. Dargie, W.: A stochastic model for estimating the power consumption of a processor. IEEE Trans. Comput. **64**(5), 1311–1322 (2015)
5. Dargie, W.: Analysis of the power consumption of a multimedia server under different DVFS policies. In: CLOUD, pp. 779–785. IEEE (2012)
6. Sahuquillo, J., Hassan, H., Petit, S., March, J.L., Duato, J.: A dynamic execution time estimation model to save energy in heterogeneous multicores running periodic tasks. Future Gener. Comput. Syst. **56**, 211–219 (2016)
7. Petrucci, V., Loques, O., Mossé, D., Melhem, R., Gazala, N.A., Gobriel, S.: Energy-efficient thread assignment optimization for heterogeneous multicore systems. ACM Trans. Embeded Comput. Syst. **14**(1), 15 (2015)
8. Liu, G., Park, J., Marculescu, D.: Dynamic thread mapping for high-performance, power-efficient heterogeneous many-core systems. In: ICCD, pp. 54–61. IEEE (2013)
9. Pricopi, M., Muthukaruppan, T.S., Venkataramani, V., Mitra, T., Vishin, S.: Power-performance modeling on asymmetric multi-cores. In: CASES, September 2013
10. Singla, G., Kaur, G., Unver, A.K., Ogras, U.Y.: Predictive dynamic thermal and power management for heterogeneous mobile platforms. In: DATE (2015)
11. Prakash, A., Amrouch, H., Shafique, M., Mitra, T., Henkel, J.: Improving mobile gaming performance through cooperative CPU-GPU thermal management. In: DAC (2016)
12. Pallipadi, V., Starikovisky, A.: The ondemand governer. In: Proceedings of the Linux Symposium, vol. 2 (2006)
13. Brihi, A., Dargie, W.: Dynamic voltage and frequency scaling in multimedia servers. In: AINA, pp. 374–380 (2013)

Author Index

Printed in the United States
By Bookmasters